Cupboard storage life

Item	Storage life
Dried fruits	*6 months*
Most canned fruits	*1–2 years*
Canned prunes and rhubarb	*9 months*
Dried or skimmed milk	*9–12 months*
Canned milk puddings	*1 year*
Jellies	*9–12 months*
Jams and marmalades	*1–2 years*
Cake mixes	*9 months*
Pastry mixes	*6 months*
Biscuits	*3–12 months*
Flour	*6 months*
Cornflour, custard powder	*1 year*
Sugar	*Up to 5 years*
Icing sugar	*1 year*
Instant coffee	*1 year*
Drinking chocolate, cocoa	*1 year*
Canned fruit juices	*1 year*
Packet soups	*1 year*
Canned soups	*2 years*
Dried peas, beans, lentils	*6–12 months*
Canned vegetables	*2 years*
Rice, pasta	*1 year*
Canned pasta foods in sauce	*2 years*
Canned meat	*Up to 5 years*
Canned meat meals	*2 years*
Canned fish in oil	*Up to 5 years*
Canned fish in sauce	*1 year*

A "bloom" on chocolate doesn't necessarily mean it is uneatable, it is merely the fat coming to the surface. Salted butter will keep better than unsalted when not refrigerated.

Cold storage life of the basics

	Freezer 0°F/−18°C	Refrigerator 35–45°F/2–7°C
Butter	*4–6 months*	*1 month*
Cheese	*4–5 months*	*1 month*
Cream cheese	*2–3 months*	*1 week*
Fruit and fruit juices	*8–12 months*	*2–3 days*
Vegetables	*6–12 months*	*3–5 days*
Bread, buns, rolls	*6 months*	—
Un-iced cakes	*3–4 months*	—
Baked pies	*6 months*	*1 day*
Unbaked pies	*1–2 months*	*1 day*
Cooked meat dishes	*1–2 months*	*3–4 days*
Pâté	*2 months*	*2–3 days*
Sauces	*2 months*	*2–3 days*
Mayonnaise	—	*3 months*
Egg whites or egg yolks	*8–12 months*	*2–3 days*
Cooked ham	*3–4 months*	*7–10 days*
Sandwiches	*4–6 weeks*	—
Steamed puddings	*1 year*	—
Fresh yeast	*1 month*	*3 weeks*

Conve

These are all approx
up or down, and occ
Use either metric *or* imperial.

Weight

Metric	Imperial
7 g	¼ oz
15 g	½ oz
25 g	1 oz
40 g	1½ oz
50 g	2 oz
75 g	3 oz
125 g	4 oz/¼ lb
225 g	8 oz/½ lb
325 g	12 oz/¾ lb
450 g	16 oz/1 lb
575 g	1¼ lb
675 g	1½ lb
800 g	1¾ lb
900 g	2 lb
1 kg	2¼ lb
1.1 kg	2½ lb
1.2 kg	2¾ lb
1.3 kg	3 lb
1.5 kg	3½ lb
1.8 kg	4 lb
2 kg	4½ lb

Measurements

Metric	Imperial
5 mm	¼ inch
1 cm	½ inch
2.5 cm	1 inch
5 cm	2 inches
7.5 cm	3 inches
10 cm	4 inches
13 cm	5 inches
15 cm	6 inches
18 cm	7 inches
20 cm	8 inches
23 cm	9 inches
25 cm	10 inches

Volume

Metric	Imperial
25 ml	1 fl oz
50 ml	2 fl oz
65 ml	2½ fl oz
75 ml	3 fl oz
100 ml	4 fl oz
150 ml	5 fl oz/¼ pint
300 ml	10 fl oz/½ pint
450 ml	15 fl oz/¾ pint
600 ml	20 fl oz/1 pint
750 ml	1¼ pints
900 ml	1½ pints
1 litre	1¾ pints
1.2 litres	2 pints
1.5 litres	2½ pints
1.75 litres	3 pints
2 litres	3¾ pints

Oven temperatures

	Gas	°F	°C
Very cool	¼	225	110
	½	250	120
Cool	1	275	140
	2	300	150
Moderate	3	325	160
	4	350	180
Moderately hot	5	375	190
	6	400	200
Hot	7	425	220
	8	450	230
Very hot	9	475	240

The FARMHOUSE KITCHEN Yearbook

A display of home baking from Yorkshire Television's Farmhouse Kitchen.

GRACE MULLIGAN

The FARMHOUSE KITCHEN

Yearbook

YORKSHIRE TELEVISION

WHSMITH
EXCLUSIVE
· BOOKS ·

Edited and designed by the Artists House Division of Mitchell Beazley International Ltd., Artists House, 14-15 Manette Street, London W1V 5LB

Editor Susan Fleming
Design Eljay Crompton
Production Peter Phillips, Stewart Bowling

This edition produced exclusively for W H Smith in consultation with Yorkshire Television Enterprises Limited

ISBN 0 86134 121 X

Typeset by Hourds Typographica, Stafford
Reproduction by La Cromolita s.n.c., Milan
Printed in Portugal by Printer Portuguesa Grafica Lda

CONTENTS

Grace Mulligan on the set at the Farmhouse Kitchen *studios.*

INTRODUCTION

There was a baker's shop opposite my childhood home, and early in May a sign would go up – "New Season's Rhubarb Tarts". I often think of this when I see the tender, pink, forced rhubarb for sale immediately after Christmas. And we have just about forgotten the exquisite pleasure of fresh strawberries on sale for those three or four precious weeks. It is hard to believe that there is still such a thing as seasonal availability when our supermarket shelves are groaning with every possible fruit and vegetable all year round. Much of this will be imported, but a careful shopper will look for signs like "home-grown" or "local" to get really good value for money. Luckier still if you grow your own fruit and vegetables, you win both ways.

The monthly structure of this book, therefore, in the tradition of my television series, *Farmhouse Kitchen*, aims to re-introduce and re-emphasize that feeling of seasonality, and has features on gooseberries and elderflowers in May, on new potatoes and strawberries in June, plums in August and game in October. There are marketplace listings of what is at its peak in the shops, whether from home or abroad, and in my tips and hints pages, I suggest a few "extras" concerning the month or season – whether it be using up the Christmas leftovers, cooking for the freezer to prepare for the influx of hungry children in the summer holidays, or cleaning the house just as the spring buds appear.

Food relating to the various festivals throughout the year is a great British tradition, and it is good to keep these alive. One custom is a Simnel cake for Easter, its rich fruitiness crowned with lightly toasted marzipan; round the edge go eleven small balls of marzipan to represent the faithful apostles – Judas being the one left out. Each month I have suggested a menu for a seasonal party, based on many of those annual festivals and using the recipes given throughout the book. These range from a buffet supper for the height of summer, perhaps for a wedding, to a children's (or indeed adults'!) Hallowe'en party.

In my TV series and in this book, we celebrate every possible occasion whether it be a national holiday or the first punnet of raspberries from your own garden. I hope you will find something in these pages to make you want to celebrate too.

Grace Mulligan

Grace Mulligan, February 1989

JANUARY

January, the start of the New Year, is the time to make resolutions. One I make every year is to keep the contents of my freezers in better order (I have three to cope with the demands of my series of cookery programmes, *Farmhouse Kitchen*). No matter how hard I try, I find unlabelled bags!

After the excesses of Christmas and the New Year, January can seem to stretch, cold and bleak, for ever. Fresh vegetables and fruit are available, however, and all the stored root vegetables can be used to make warming and nourishing soups and stews. Use the Seville oranges coming in towards the end of the month to make marmalade (see February), and top up your Vitamin C levels by eating citrus fruit – vital to keep colds at bay.

Market Place

Vegetables: avocados, beetroot, broccoli, Brussels sprouts, cabbages, carrots, chicory, celeriac, Chinese leaves, cranberries, fennel, garlic, greens, Jerusalem artichokes, kale, kohlrabi, leeks, marrows, onions, parsnips, potatoes, shallots, swedes, sweet potatoes, turnips.
Fruit and nuts: almonds, apples, Asian pears, Brazil nuts, Cape gooseberries, chestnuts, clementines, dates, kumquats, lychees, oranges, pears, pineapples, pomegranates, rhubarb (forced), satsumas, Seville oranges, sharon fruit, walnuts, waterchestnuts.
Fish: brill, carp, cod, coley, conger eel, Dover sole, grey mullet, haddock, halibut, herring, John Dory, lemon sole, mackerel, oysters, plaice, scallops, skate, sprats, turbot, whiting.
Meat: beef, chicken, goose, guinea fowl, hare, pigeon, pork, rabbit, turkey, venison.

Tips and Hints

Use any Christmas leftovers at once – the mincemeat, for instance, in a tart or tarts. If you are tired of the remainder of the cake, one way to use it up is to remove the icing and marzipan then break into crumbs into a roomy bowl. Moisten the crumbs with a little sherry diluted with water (2 tablespoons water to 1 of sherry); you want a damp but not wet mixture. Pack into small greased pudding basins, cover, and steam for about 25 minutes in the usual way for extra rich puddings, to be served with a rum sauce.

Sweep snow away from paths as soon as possible after it falls – it gets hard very quickly.

If you have a garden, now is the time to look through the catalogues and decide on seeds which have to be ordered and sown without delay.

Twelfth Night is also known as Old Christmas Eve and falls on the 6th January, and it is traditional all over Europe to "sweep out" all the Christmas decorations. When you pack away your cards, check them for addresses and messages that need answering. Carry the Christmas tree out as carefully as possible, and use a suction cleaner to gather up the inevitable carpet of pine needles. Pack the decorations away carefully, repairing the tree lights first – it is lovely if they light up first time the following year.

Look out for January sale bargains for the kitchen. There are often special offers on good quality casseroles, pans and dishes.

Clean out and re-organize the store cupboard and freezer. You will be using stores now, so relabel or throw out anything you cannot identify.

RECIPES

HOT DRINKS

A hot drink after a walk, or when the children return from school, is a warming necessity on icy, wind-blasted January days – and don't just think tea or coffee. A cup of liquidized soup will warm you down to your toes, and mulled wines and whisky drinks are traditional at this time – the latter most associated with the Scots and their New Year celebration of Hogmanay. Other drinks can be less alcoholic!

HOT TODDY

The 25th January in Scotland, and all over the world where her sons and daughters have settled, also means Burns' Night with haggis, bashed neeps (mashed turnips) and lots of whisky. A glass of hot toddy is often the final glory of such a feast.

"Sit roun' the table weel content,
An' steer about the toddy."
(Robert Burns)

Half fill a tumbler with very hot water and when the glass is warm, pour away the water. Put two or three cubes of sugar in the glass and pour over about 2.5cm /1 inch boiling water. Stir to dissolve the sugar. Stir in malt whisky and drink slowly. The strength of the drink is up to you: dilute with more hot water, or top up the whisky content!

MULLED WINE

Ingredients
a pinch of nutmeg
3 tablespoons brown sugar
juice and rind of 1 lemon or orange
1 stick cinnamon
3 cloves
300 ml/½ pint hot water
1 bottle dry red wine (elderberry, blackberry, or a cheap, dry red table wine)

Method
1 Simmer all the ingredients except wine for 20 minutes, then add wine. Reheat but do not boil.
2 Serve immediately in thick glasses.

PROPER COCOA

Mix ½–1 teaspoon cocoa powder with a little cold milk into a smooth paste. Add sugar to taste and whisk in boiling milk. Serve in heatproof glasses or beakers.

HOT CHOCOLATE MINT DRINK

Break a small bar of peppermint cream chocolate in pieces and liquidize with 300 ml/½ pint hot milk for 30 seconds. Serve at once.

CHAMOMILE TISANE

Infuse 1 teaspoon dried chamomile flowers in 1 cup boiling water for 3 minutes. Strain and drink hot. Sweeten with a little honey if you like. Good as a nightcap, and aids digestion.

CHILDREN IN THE KITCHEN

More accidents occur in the home than anywhere else. The kitchen is a particularly dangerous place, and all children's cooking should be supervised. It's not just the possibility of burns – there are breakable glasses and dishes, sharp knives, and a host of other potential hazards. The recipes here require minimum cooking – if any – and they will appeal to the tastes of junior cooks!

BANANA AND NUT FINGERS

Ingredients

225 g/8 oz porridge oats
225 g/8 oz sugar
225 g/8 oz wholewheat flour
½ teaspoon bicarbonate of soda
225 g/8 oz butter or margarine
2 eggs, beaten
4 bananas
a few chopped nuts (optional)

Method

1 Mix all dry ingredients together, then rub in butter or margarine.
2 Mix to a stiff dough with the beaten eggs, and divide in half.
3 Grease a shallow tin, 23 cm/9 inches square, and line with half the mixture.
4 Cover with finely sliced bananas and chopped nuts, then spread remainder of mixture over and press down firmly.
5 Bake in a moderately hot oven, Gas 5, 375°F, 190°C, for 20–25 minutes until golden brown. Cut into fingers while still warm and leave to cool in the tin.

DATE BARS

The tops of these could be iced with melted chocolate before cutting into bars, or the ends could be dipped into melted chocolate.

Makes 6–8

Ingredients

125 g/4 oz margarine
125 g/4 oz sugar
225 g/8 oz dates, chopped
225 g/8 oz sweet biscuits, broken

Method

1 Melt margarine and sugar in pan. Add chopped dates, mix well and cook for 2–3 minutes.
2 Remove from heat and add the well broken biscuits. Mix well.
3 Press into a shallow, greased Swiss roll tin. Leave to become cold, then cut into bars.

CHOCOLATE CLUSTERS

Makes 20

Ingredients

a 150 g/5.3 oz block plain cooking chocolate, broken into pieces
1 level tablespoon golden syrup
2 teaspoons water
75 g/3 oz raisins
75 g/3 oz salted peanuts
25 g/1 oz mixed peel, finely chopped

Method

1 Warm a bowl over a saucepan of boiling water without allowing the bowl to touch the water. Turn off heat.
2 Put the chocolate in the bowl with the syrup and water. Allow to melt and blend together, stirring occasionally.
3 Stir in raisins, peanuts and mixed peel, and put small teaspoons of the mixture on to a sheet of waxed paper (from a cornflakes packet).
4 Leave to set in a cool place before removing from paper.

SPICED APPLE AND YOGHURT DRINK

A pleasant creamy drink for one.

Ingredients

a 150 g/5 oz carton natural or home-made yoghurt
about 100 ml/4 fl oz unsweetened apple juice
a tiny pinch of ground cloves or nutmeg

Method

Whisk together chilled yoghurt and apple juice with spice, and drink while it is still frothy.

HOT SOUPS FOR COLD WEATHER

Nothing is as cheering as a bowl of good hot soup in cold weather. With the wealth of root vegetables available at this time of year, soup costs virtually nothing to make, and it's so easy. You need a good stock, though, for the best flavour (although, of course, a vegetable or chicken stock cube will do). Stock is easy to make as well (see below), and you should get into the habit of saving the water in which vegetables are cooked for a basic stock that will keep for 24 hours in the fridge. Serve soups with Melba toast or garlic bread.

TO MAKE STOCK

Poultry or Game

The carcasses of chickens, turkeys or game birds make good stocks. Put in a large saucepan with plenty of water, an onion, a piece of carrot, leek, celery, parsley stalks or any vegetable stalks or peelings (washed) that might otherwise get thrown out. Add 2–3 peppercorns and a bay leaf. Simmer gently for at least an hour. Strain off liquid, let it cool, and then refrigerate or freeze it. Giblet stock is made in the same way.

Beef

Put bones in a large saucepan with plenty of water and bring to the boil. Add pieces of onion, carrot, leek, celery tops, parsley stalks, washed vegetable peelings and hard outer leaves. Add peppercorns, bay leaf, herbs. Any of these will enrich the stock. Simmer for at least an hour, then strain and store as above.

Ham

Simmer a ham bone with peppercorns and 1 or 2 cloves. The flavour is rich, so use this stock with caution or add plenty of water.

Fish

Put an onion, large carrot, celery stick, all peeled and chopped small, into a large saucepan with 1.3 kg/3 lb white fish bones, heads and trimmings on top (ask your fishmonger for them; never use oily fish). Add 1.7 litres/3 pints water, bring to the boil and simmer for 15 minutes. Allow to go cold before straining. Use quickly.

CELERY SOUP

Serves 4

Ingredients

40 g/1½ oz butter or margarine
1 medium head celery, trimmed and chopped
1 small onion, peeled and chopped
40 g/1½ oz wholewheat or plain white flour
1 litre/1¾ pints vegetable or chicken stock
a bouquet garni, or sprig of parsley, thyme and marjoram or bay leaf, tied together
300 ml/½ pint milk
salt and freshly ground black pepper
2 tablespoons single cream

Method

1. Melt butter or margarine in a saucepan with a well fitting lid. Add the vegetables, saving a few of the chopped celery leaves for garnish.
2. Stir for 1 minute then put lid on the saucepan. Turn heat down very low and let the vegetables "sweat", without browning, for 10 minutes.
3. Stir in the flour and let it cook for 1 minute.
4. Add stock and bouquet garni. Bring to the boil and simmer, covered, until vegetables are tender but not mushy. Remove bouquet garni.
5. If you prefer a creamy soup, put it through liquidizer or a sieve. Return it to pan. Add milk, a little salt and pepper and reheat. Just before serving, stir in finely chopped celery leaves and cream.

PARSNIP SOUP

This is very sustaining, and keeps a day or two in the fridge. It freezes well too.

Serves 2–3

Ingredients

25 g/1 oz butter or margarine
1 large onion, peeled and finely chopped
$\frac{1}{2}$ level teaspoon curry powder
225 g/8 oz parsnips, scrubbed and diced
125 g/4 oz potato, peeled and diced
600 ml/1 pint hot light stock (a chicken or vegetable stock cube will do)
salt and freshly ground black pepper
single cream (optional)

Method

1 Melt the butter or margarine in a saucepan and fry onion gently until just softening.
2 Stir in the curry powder, and cook gently for 2–3 minutes.
3 Toss the parsnip and potato with the onion over gentle heat for 2–3 minutes more.
4 Add stock, bring to the boil and simmer, covered, for about 20 minutes or until vegetables are tender.
5 The soup is nice to have in its chunky state, but for a soft, creamy soup, liquidize and reheat, adding pepper and a little salt if necessary. Add a swirl of cream to each bowlful if you like.

CARROT AND CORIANDER SOUP

Serves 4–6

Ingredients

2 onions, peeled and sliced
40 g/$1\frac{1}{2}$ oz butter
1 clove garlic, crushed with a pinch of salt
450 g/1 lb carrots, scrubbed and thinly sliced
freshly ground black pepper
1 dessertspoon coriander seeds
1 sherry glass sherry
600 ml/1 pint chicken stock
600 ml/1 pint milk
chopped parsley

Method

1 Cook onions carefully in butter in a large pan until transparent.
2 Add the garlic, salt and carrots, and season with pepper. Add coriander seeds and sherry. Cover and cook gently until vegetables are soft, about 10–15 minutes.
3 Add stock and cook for a further 15–20 minutes. Allow to cool.
4 Liquidize or sieve the soup, then strain into a clean pan.
5 Add milk when ready to serve. Reheat carefully, and adjust seasoning. Sprinkle parsley in each bowl of soup.

CREAM OF TOMATO SOUP

Freezes well, but do so before milk or cream is added.

Serves 4

Ingredients

1 medium carrot, scrubbed and thinly sliced
1 onion, peeled and thinly sliced
2 sticks celery, washed and thinly sliced
75 g/3 oz butter or margarine
a 400 g/14 oz can tomatoes
1 teaspoon sugar
600 ml/1 pint light stock
salt and freshly ground black pepper
25 g/1 oz plain flour
1 tablespoon tomato paste or purée
150 ml/$\frac{1}{4}$ pint top of milk or single cream
chopped parsley

Method

1 Put the vegetables into half the melted butter in a large saucepan. Cover and cook gently until soft, shaking pan occasionally.
2 Add tomatoes with their juice, sugar, half the stock, and salt and pepper to taste. Simmer for 10 minutes, or until the vegetables are soft.
3 Sieve contents of pan into a bowl, then rinse out the pan.
4 Melt remaining butter or margarine in pan. Stir in flour and cook for 1 minute. Stir in rest of stock and tomato paste, and cook for 1 minute. Stir until boiling and simmer for 1 minute.
5 Add tomato mixture from bowl, and the milk or cream. Check seasoning. Heat to nearly boiling point, but do not actually boil or the soup may curdle. Serve sprinkled with chopped parsley.

HOT BEETROOT SOUP

This soup freezes well, but do so before yoghurt or soured cream is added.

Serves 6

Ingredients

450 g/1 lb raw beetroot, peeled and diced
450 g/1 lb potatoes, peeled and diced
2 onions, peeled and chopped
50 g/2 oz butter or margarine
1.5–1.75 litres/2½–3 pints strong chicken stock
salt and freshly ground black pepper
natural yoghurt or soured cream

Method

1. Cook vegetables gently in the melted butter in a large saucepan, covered, for about 5 minutes.
2. Stir in the stock, bring to the boil, and simmer until beetroot is cooked.
3. Cool the soup and reduce it to a purée in the liquidizer. Return to pan, and adjust seasoning.
4. Just before serving, bring soup to boiling point and serve with a swirl of yoghurt or soured cream in each bowl.

FISHERMAN'S CHOWDER

This substantial fish soup makes a filling main meal served with hot, crusty French bread.

Serves 2–3

Ingredients

15 g/½ oz butter or margarine
1 small onion, peeled and thinly sliced
25 g/1 oz rindless bacon, chopped
2 sticks celery, trimmed and chopped
½ small red pepper, cored and diced
125 g/4 oz potatoes, peeled and diced
300 ml/½ pint fish or chicken stock
325 g/12 oz smoked and white haddock (or whiting), skinned and cubed
150 ml/¼ pint semi-skimmed milk
1 tablespoon cornflour
salt and freshly ground black pepper
chopped parsley

Method

1. Melt the butter or margarine in a large saucepan and fry the onion, bacon, celery, red pepper and potato for 5 minutes.
2. Pour in the stock, lower the heat, and simmer until potatoes are just tender, then add the fish.
3. Mix together the milk and cornflour and stir it into the soup. Bring to the boil, stirring continuously, then simmer for 5 minutes.
4. Season to taste and serve, sprinkled with the parsley.

MELBA TOAST

This goes well with hot or cold soup.

Method

1. Cut slices of bread for toast – not too thick – and toast lightly brown on both sides.
2. Cut in half diagonally to make triangles. Then slice the bread through the centre between the toasted sides to make two pieces from one.
3. Place in a large roasting tin and dry off at the bottom of the oven until crisp. Store in an airtight tin.

GARLIC BREAD

Eat hot with soups or cold meat and salad, or omelettes. You could also, when they're available, use fresh chopped herbs with the butter to make herb bread.

Ingredients

½–1 clove garlic
a little salt
1 tablespoon chopped parsley
50 g/2 oz butter
a crusty loaf, French bread or rolls

Method

1. Crush garlic to a cream with a little salt.
2. Mix garlic and parsley into butter.
3. Slice loaf into thick pieces without quite cutting through the bottom crust, and spread one side of each slice with garlic butter.
4. Wrap loaf in greaseproof paper and foil and put in a moderate oven – Gas 3, 325°F, 160°C – for 15–20 minutes until butter has melted.

ORIGINAL DISHES WITH TRADITIONAL VEGETABLES

The vegetables available at this time of year can be made into soups (see pages 13–14), snacks, main courses and main-course accompaniments. Vegetables need never be simply boiled, as there is a multitude of ways in which their textures and flavours can be varied or enhanced, and I think some of the recipes below will open your eyes to the possibilities.

POTATO AND BEAN CASSEROLE

This is best eaten hot as a main course, and it reheats easily. Serve with a green salad.

Serves 2

Ingredients

15 g/½ oz butter, or a little oil
225 g/8 oz potatoes, peeled and thinly sliced
salt and freshly ground black pepper
50 g/2 oz mature Cheddar cheese, grated
a 213 g/7½ oz can red kidney beans, drained and rinsed
1 egg
300 ml/½ pint milk, hot but not boiling

Topping

15 g/½ oz butter
1 tablespoon sesame seeds
1 tablespoon sunflower seeds
1 tablespoon soy sauce

Method

1 Preheat oven to moderate, Gas 4, 350°F, 180°C, and use the butter or oil to grease a 900 ml/1½ pint ovenproof dish lightly.
2 Arrange half of the potatoes in the dish, and season with salt and pepper. Spread half of the cheese over the potatoes and cover with the beans. Season again and cover with remaining potatoes.
3 Beat egg into hot milk and pour this over the potatoes and beans. Top with the remaining cheese.
4 Bake in the preheated oven for about 1 hour, or until potatoes are tender.
5 Meanwhile prepare the topping. Melt butter in a saucepan and fry sesame and sunflower seeds for 2 minutes, or until golden. Add soy sauce and cook for 1 minute more. Leave to cool.
6 About 15 minutes before the casserole is cooked, sprinkle with the topping.

EGG AND LEEK NESTS

A snack or main course for two.

Ingredients

225 g/8 oz young leeks
a knob of butter
salt and freshly ground black pepper
2 eggs, beaten
2 tablespoons milk
a shake of paprika

Method

1 Top and tail the leeks and remove any very coarse green tops. Cut in half lengthways and wash under a running tap to remove any grit. Then slice them.
2 Cook the leeks gently in the butter over a medium heat, stirring all the time. Season lightly and keep hot.
3 Scramble the beaten eggs with the milk and take off the heat when just set. Season with salt and pepper.
4 Arrange the shredded leeks on two hot plates, making a nest. Spoon the eggs into the nests, dust lightly with paprika and serve at once.

ONIONS BAKED IN CIDER

Good with meat dishes, especially pork.

Serves 4

Ingredients

450 g/1 lb onions, peeled and sliced
25 g/1 oz butter
1 level teaspoon sugar
½ teaspoon salt
freshly ground black pepper
150 ml/¼ pint cider

Method

1 Place onions in a casserole and dot with the butter. Sprinkle on sugar, salt and pepper.
2 Pour the cider over and cover casserole tightly. Greaseproof paper and foil will do.
3 Cook in moderate oven, Gas 4, 350°F, 180°C, for 1¼ hours. Then remove lid and cook a further 15 minutes.

BRAISED RED CABBAGE

This heats very well the following day, losing none of its flavour.

Serves 4

Ingredients

1 small red cabbage, 675–900 g/ 1½–2 lb
50 g/2 oz butter or good bacon dripping
1 medium onion, peeled and sliced
1 large cooking apple, peeled, cored and thinly sliced
150 ml/¼ pint cheap red wine or stock
2 teaspoons salt
1 tablespoon vinegar
½ level teaspoon powdered cloves
½ teaspoon grated nutmeg
plenty of black pepper, to taste
1 level tablespoon soft brown sugar

Method

1. Cut the cabbage into quarters removing outer leaves, white root and any large pieces of white pith. Shred the cabbage finely and place in a large bowl. Pour over sufficient boiling water to cover, leave for 1 minute, then drain.
2. Melt butter in a large heavy pan. Add onion and cook gently to soften but not brown, about 5 minutes.
3. Add apple, the wine or stock, salt, vinegar, cloves, nutmeg and a good grating of black pepper. Add cabbage and turn over to mix into liquid. Cover tightly.
4. Cook gently until tender, turning over from time to time, about 1 hour.
5. Stir in sugar and serve – especially good with a hot joint, such as pork or bacon, or with goose.

SPICY CABBAGE WITH COCONUT

Serves 4

Ingredients

225 g/8 oz greens, cabbage or Chinese leaves, finely shredded
½ medium onion, peeled and chopped
2 cloves garlic, crushed
½ teaspoon each of ground cumin and coriander
¼ teaspoon turmeric
1 teaspoon salt
2 tablespoons unsweetened desiccated coconut
2 green chillies, deseeded, topped, tailed, and finely chopped
1 tablespoon water

Method

1. In a bowl mix all the ingredients thoroughly.
2. Using a heavy-bottomed frying pan, stir-fry the cabbage on a low heat for about 5 minutes.

GLAZED PARSNIPS WITH WALNUTS AND ROSEMARY

Carrots could be butter-glazed in the same way.

Serves 3–4

Ingredients

450 g/1 lb parsnips, scrubbed and sliced into even rings
salt
50 g/2 oz butter
75 g/3 oz broken walnuts
½ teaspoon dried rosemary
freshly ground black pepper
chopped parsley (optional)

Method

1. Steam the parsnips with a little salt or simmer with a good lid on pan in as little water as possible until just tender. Drain.
2. Melt most of butter in saucepan and toss parsnips and walnuts in it until both are lightly browned.
3. Mix in rosemary and black pepper, and serve with an extra dot of butter or parsley to garnish.

January Menu

A Day in Bed

Victorian invalid cookery was very strong on poached fish and beef tea: the first was easily digested, and the second was to build the patient up. I think we can be a bit more creative, though the emphasis should be on fresh goodness. So serve a healthy soup, plenty of fruit, and a protein dish that is easy to eat. Most importantly, present the food attractively and in small helpings.

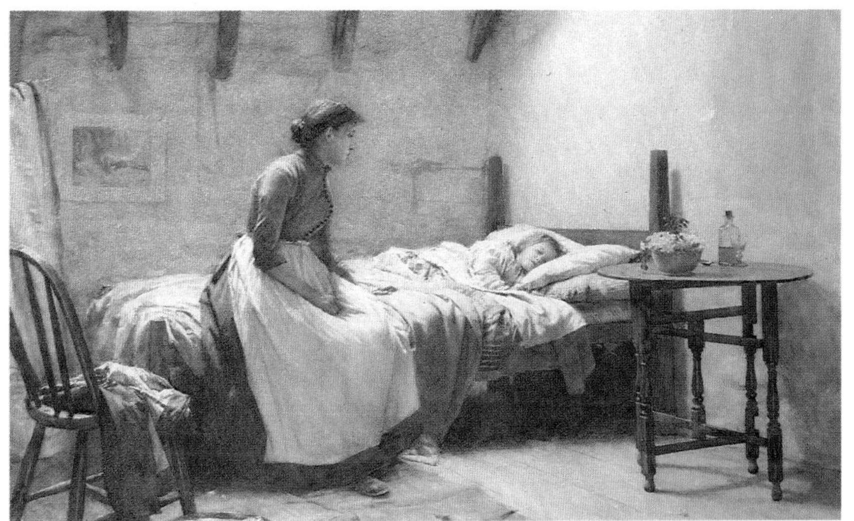

BREAKFAST

Home-made muesli

LUNCH

Parsnip soup
Melba toast

DINNER

Tasty fish pie
Lightly cooked vegetables
Compôte of fresh oranges
Chamomile tisane

Home Notes

FEBRUARY

30 days hath September
April, June and November.
All the rest have 31
Excepting February alone,
Which has 28 days clear
And 29 in each leap year.

The phrase "February Fill-Dyke" exactly describes this hard wet month, when dykes and ditches overflow with rain, and often with melted snow. Delicate snowdrops and yellow aconites help to brighten the short days of a month that calls for foods that will warm and satisfy – delicious warm stews and filling hot puds.

Market Place

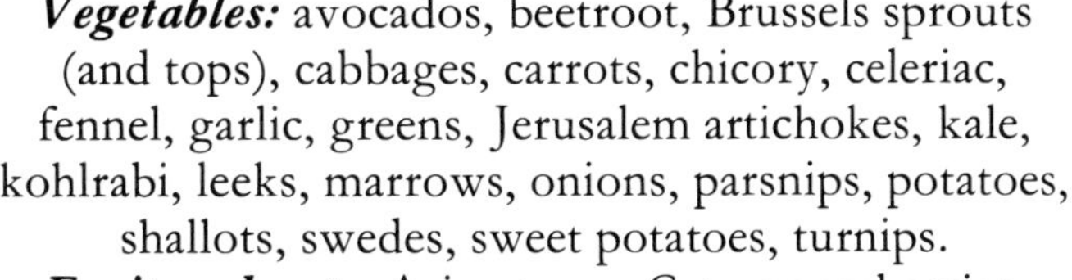

Vegetables: avocados, beetroot, Brussels sprouts (and tops), cabbages, carrots, chicory, celeriac, fennel, garlic, greens, Jerusalem artichokes, kale, kohlrabi, leeks, marrows, onions, parsnips, potatoes, shallots, swedes, sweet potatoes, turnips.
Fruit and nuts: Asian pears, Cape gooseberries, clementines, dates, kumquats, lychees, oranges, pears, pineapples, rhubarb (forced), Seville oranges, sharon fruit.
Fish: Brill, cod, coley, conger eel, Dover sole, flounder, grey mullet, haddock, hake, halibut, herring, John Dory, lemon sole, mackerel, oysters, scallops, skate, sprats, turbot, whitebait, whiting.
Meat: Beef, chicken, hare, lamb, pigeon, pork, rabbit.

Tips and Hints

During a Leap Year, when there are 29 days in the month (and the numerals of the year are divisible by four) girls may propose marriage to anyone they choose!

Because business is slow after the great buying spree at Christmas, look out for special offers in supermarkets – two items for the price of one, or labels offering so much off your next purchase.

If your Christmas present plants are beginning to look a little sad, perhaps they need feeding. Stick closely to the instructions on the plant food packet or bottle.

Citrus fruit is plentiful this month so why not make your own lemon and orange rind to store in airtight containers to flavour puddings, cakes and stuffing. Grate the peel finely and dry in a low oven on foil, or in a microwave on kitchen paper – about 1–1½ minutes on full power is enough. You can also store the shells in the freezer. If you can bear to hold a frozen one, you can grate a citrus shell straight into your dish if in a hurry.

To help the winter on, now is the time to look to the spring and decide on how much decorating you would like to get done. Look out for special offers of paint, emulsion, wallpaper, etc. Soft furnishing departments have sale tickets out on many items. Get several estimates, too, for any outside repairs you cannot tackle yourself.

With the ground frozen, February is a bad month for the birds. Give them a dish of warm water every day, and hang up pieces of coconut. You could also melt down fat and put bread, chopped nuts or various seeds in it. Place in a bowl, and on setting push a stick through the middle. This makes a hole for a knotted string from which to suspend the fat "cake". Children enjoy doing this – and watching the birds' responses!

RECIPES

SEVILLE ORANGES AND MARMALADE

Seville oranges start coming into the shops at the end of January, and they are available throughout February. Their season is very short so if you intend to make marmalade or freeze a few for adding to an orange sauce for duck (far sharper and better), now is the time to look out for them. Buy fruit with fairly unblemished skins – I say "fairly", because Seville oranges are very variable. They freeze well for future use: just scrub them well, dry, then freeze in usable quantities in strong plastic freeze bags.

TESTING FOR A SET

Seville oranges have a good pectin content, but if frozen, they tend to lose some, which is why a little extra fruit is added to the quantity. Start testing for set after 10 minutes of boiling. There are several ways of doing this.

1 **Volume test.** If you know the expected yield of your fruit – e.g. the recipe says you will get, say, 2.25 g/5 lb marmalade – then, before you start the recipe, measure out in water that amount. Take a 450 g/1 lb jam jar (not a 325 g/12 oz jar), fill it five times and pour this into your pan. Use a wooden spoon handle, stand it upright in the water, and mark this level with a pencil. Keep the spoon handy. Then, when you are testing for a set, draw pan off heat. Wait until bubbling subsides and stand spoon in the marmalade. When the volume has returned to the level of the pencil mark, it's ready.

2 **Cold plate test.** Have some small plates cooling in the refrigerator, and take a teaspoon of marmalade and drop it on the cold plate. Wait a minute and, if it wrinkles when pushed, the marmalade is ready. If not, go on boiling a little longer.

3 **Flake test.** Dip a clean wooden spoon in boiling marmalade. Allow the cooling marmalade to drop from the spoon. If the drops run together and form a flake or curtain, it is ready to pot.

4 **Temperature test.** Use a sugar thermometer. It is important to dip the thermometer in hot water immediately before using it in the marmalade. Submerge the bulb fully in the boiling marmalade but do not let it touch the bottom of the pan. When the thermometer registers 220°F or 106°C, it's ready.

ORANGE AND CIDER MARMALADE

Yields about 2.25 kg/5 lb

Ingredients
*675 g/1½ lb Seville oranges**
juice of 2 lemons
1.2 litres/2 pints dry cider
600 ml/1 pint water
1.3 kg/3 lb sugar
**If using frozen fruit, add 1-2 extra fruit to total weight*

Method

1 Wash oranges and cut them in half. Squeeze out juice and pips and retain, and cut peel into thin strips.
2 Put orange peel, orange and lemon juice into a large pan with the cider and water. Tie the pips in a muslin bag and add to pan.
3 Cook gently for 1½ hours or until the peel is soft.
4 Meanwhile, put the sugar in a bowl to warm in a very cool oven, Gas ¼, 225°F, 110°C. Prepare clean jars and put them to dry and warm in the coolest part of the oven.
5 Lift out the bag of pips and squeeze juice out by pressing the bag against the side of the pan with a wooden spoon.
6 Add the warmed sugar to the pan and stir over heat, without boiling, until completely dissolved, then bring to the boil and boil rapidly until setting point is reached (see below).
7 Remove the scum with a metal spoon, then allow the marmalade to cool for half an hour. This will prevent the peel rising in the jars.
8 Fill warmed jars to the brim. Immediately put on well-fitting waxed discs, waxed side down. This seals the marmalade and protects it from the atmosphere. Wipe jars and put on outer covers, either while marmalade is hot or cold, but *never* in between.
9 Label with name and date, and store in a cool, dark, dry place.

PANCAKES

One of the most celebrated festivals this month is Pancake or Shrove Tuesday, the day before the Lenten fast begins. This is when Christians confessed their sins and, to use up the luxuries of butter, flour and milk, they would make pancakes.

When I first came to live in England from my native Scotland, I found that what I called pancakes were called drop scones and sometimes Scotch pancakes. The other kind of pancakes made on Shrove Tuesday – the thin ones, served with lemon juice and sugar – we just called thin pancakes.

BASIC PANCAKES

Pancakes can be eaten, as traditional, with lemon juice and sugar, or with a sweet sauce, or sweet or savoury fillings. They're best served immediately, but can stay fresh for up to 48 hours if stacked on top of one another, interleaved with greaseproof paper, wrapped in a teacloth and put in the refrigerator. They also freeze successfully. When cool, stack in the same way and seal in a bag.

This quantity of batter will make about 14 pancakes 15 cm/6 inches in diameter. If you would like to use wholewheat flour to make 6–8 larger pancakes, simply substitute wholewheat flour for the plain. For light lager pancakes, use 125 g/4 oz plain flour, 2 eggs instead of one, 2 teaspoons olive oil in the mixture (and extra oil for the pan or lard), and lager instead of milk.

Ingredients
125 g/4 oz plain flour
½ teaspoon salt
1 large egg
300 ml/½ pint milk
lard

Method
1 Place flour and salt in a basin, and make a well in the centre. Drop in the egg and begin to mix, gradually adding 150 ml/¼ pint of the milk as the flour is drawn in.
2 Beat well until bubbles are visible, then gradually beat in the remaining milk.
3 Put into a jug for easier pouring into a small frying pan.
4 Heat pan and add a piece of lard the size of a hazel nut. Allow to spread over pan and become fairly hot.
4 Pour in a little batter, tilting pan to cover. When nicely golden, toss or turn over to cook the other side. Repeat to use up batter.

WINTER STEWS AND HOT-POTS

Careful housewives found out long ago the admirable qualities of a good stew, whether called a casserole, hot-pot or daube. It is the best way of all to make a little expensive protein go a long way. The meat, vegetables and gravy are all in the one dish, and it's warming and nourishing, especially in cold weather. Best of all, it usually lasts for more than one meal, freezes well, and accompaniments can be many – creamed potatoes, rice, noodles, or maybe just hunks of bread to mop up that good rich gravy.

CASSEROLED SHIN OF BEEF

This casserole may be made with varying quantities of meat and vegetables according to what you have and how many are to eat it. It is just as good reheated as when it is freshly made, so it is worth making enough for two meals.

Serves 6–8

Ingredients

900 g/2 lb shin of beef or stewing steak
40 g/1½ oz wholemeal or plain flour
½ teaspoon dried marjoram
½ teaspoon salt
freshly ground black pepper
40 g/1½ oz dripping
2 large onions, peeled and roughly chopped
75 ml/3 fl oz red wine or cider, or 2 tablespoons vinegar
2 large carrots, scrubbed and cut into large chunks
1 stick celery, trimmed and finely chopped
1 small parsnip or turnip, peeled and finely chopped
1 clove garlic, peeled and crushed
a 400 g/14 oz tin of tomatoes
water
lots of fresh parsley

Method

1. Trim off excess fat and hard gristle from the meat and cut it into easy pieces, about 5 cm/2 inches long, 1 cm/½ inch thick. Mix together flour, marjoram, salt and pepper on a plate or in a clean paper or polythene bag. Toss the meat in seasoned flour to coat.
2. Heat half the dripping in a heavy saucepan or flameproof casserole. Add onion and fry till it begins to brown. Then lift it out with a draining spoon on to a plate.
3. Now add remaining dripping and heat till it begins to smoke. Then add the meat, turning it over quickly to brown.
4. Turn down heat and add wine or cider, but not the vinegar. Let it bubble for a minute.
5. Now, if using a saucepan, turn the contents into a large casserole.
6. Add the onion, carrot, celery, parsnip or turnip and garlic, plus the vinegar (if used instead of wine or cider).
7. Now empty the tin of tomatoes on top, refill the tin with cold water, and pour in just enough to cover the meat and vegetables.
8. Tie a bunch of parsley together with cotton, and lay it on top.
9. Cover the casserole and put it in a moderate oven, Gas 4, 350°F, 180°C, for half an hour. By this time the pot will be bubbling nicely, so reduce heat to very cool, Gas ½, 250°F, 120°C, and let it go on cooking for another 2–2½ hours. If you are using shin of beef, a total of 3½ hours is not too long.
10. Remove the bunch of parsley and add freshly chopped parsley, if you can spare it, just before serving.

OXTAIL STEW

Serves 4

Ingredients

1 oxtail
salt and freshly ground black pepper
225 g/8 oz carrots, scrubbed and diced
225 g/8 oz turnips, peeled and diced
225 g/8 oz onions, peeled and chopped
2 tablespoons plain flour
chopped fresh parsley

Method

1 Trim any surplus fat from the oxtail and cut it into its separate joints. Put into a bowl, cover with water and leave for 1 hour.
2 Drain and put the pieces in a stewpan. Add seasoning and cover with fresh water. Bring to the boil and simmer for 1½ hours.
3 At this point, leave overnight. The next day, skim off fat which has risen to the top.
4 Add the chopped vegetables, and simmer for 1½ hours until tender.
5 Thicken just before serving. Mix flour to a smooth paste with a little cold water. Add to the stew, stir well and simmer again for a further 10 minutes. Sprinkle generously with freshly chopped parsley if you have it.

LAMB HOT-POT WITH PARSLEY DUMPLINGS

Serves 4

Ingredients

8 best end or middle neck lamb chops
1 tablespoon plain flour
40 g/1½ oz lard or dripping
1 medium onion, peeled and sliced
2 carrots, scrubbed and sliced
2 sticks celery, washed and sliced
a 400 g/14 oz tin of tomatoes
150 ml/¼ pint water
1 level teaspoon dried rosemary or mixed dried herbs
1 teaspoon salt
freshly ground black pepper

Parsley dumplings

125 g/4 oz self-raising flour
½ level teaspoon salt
40 g/1½ oz shredded suet
1 level tablespoon chopped parsley
a little water

Method

1 Coat the chops in the plain flour.
2 Melt half the lard in a frying pan. Add onion, carrot and celery and fry for 2–3 minutes. Lift out into a 1.5 litre/2½ pint shallow casserole.
3 Add the remaining lard to the pan, then brown the chops quickly on both sides. Arrange on top of the vegetables in the casserole.
4 Pour excess fat out of the pan, and put in the tomatoes, water, rosemary, salt and pepper. Bring to the boil, stirring, and pour over the lamb.
5 Cover the casserole and cook in the centre of a moderate oven, Gas 4, 350°F, 180°C, for 1–1½ hours until the meat is tender.
6 For the dumplings, sift the flour and salt into a bowl, then mix in the suet and parsley. Mix to a soft but not sticky dough with water. Form into eight small balls.
7 Place dumplings on top of hot-pot and cook, uncovered, for a further 15–20 minutes, until dumplings are risen and cooked. Serve immediately.

CASSEROLE OF PORK

Serves 4

Ingredients

450–675 g/1–1½ lb lean pork slices about 1 cm/½ inch thick, from the shoulder
1 heaped tablespoon flour seasoned with salt and pepper
dripping for frying
450 g/1 lb onions, peeled and sliced
3–4 cooking apples, cored
300–450 ml/½–¾ pint stock or water
2 tablespoons brown sugar

Method

1 Dip the pork slices in seasoned flour and fry them gently in some of the dripping until browned on both sides. Put into a casserole.
2 Fry the sliced onion in more dripping (if necessary) until softened but not brown, and add as a layer on top of the pork.
3 Slice the unpeeled apple into thick rings, and fry for a few minutes on each side. Put into the casserole on top of the onions.
4 Make a gravy with the residue from the frying pan, leftover seasoned flour and the stock. Strain into the casserole – it should just cover the *meat* only.
5 Sprinkle the apples with the brown sugar.
6 Cover the casserole tightly and cook in a moderate oven, Gas 3, 325°F, 160°C, for about 45–60 minutes, depending on maturity of meat, testing to see if pork is tender. Serve with vegetables.

SMOTHERED LIVER HOT-POT

Serves 4 or 5

Ingredients

3 rashers rindless streaky bacon
450 g/1 lb liver
1 level tablespoon plain flour, seasoned with salt and pepper
2 onions, peeled and sliced
1 apple, cored and sliced
1 teaspoon sugar
150 ml/¼ pint light stock
150 ml/¼ pint cider
25 g/1 oz bacon fat, if necessary
125 g/4 oz fresh wholemeal or white breadcrumbs

Method

1 Cut bacon into 2.5 cm/1 inch pieces, and fry lightly to extract a little fat.
2 Wash and slice liver, coat well in seasoned flour, and place in a shallow casserole.
3 Drain bacon and scatter on top of the liver. Add onions and apple and sprinkle on sugar.
4 Pour over the stock and cider.
5 Add a little fat to the bacon-frying pan to make up to a good tablespoon, tip in crumbs, and stir to combine. Spread crumbs over casserole, then cover (foil will do).
6 Cook in a moderately hot oven, Gas 5, 375°F, 190°C, for 45 minutes. Test with a skewer to ensure liver is cooked – pig's and ox liver take longer than lamb's.
7 Uncover and cook for a further 10–12 minutes to crisp the top.

GAUDY RABBIT

Serves 4

Ingredients

2 tablespoons oil, preferably olive
1 clove garlic, peeled and finely chopped
450 g/1 lb rabbit joints
75 ml/3 fl oz dry white wine or dry cider
1 tablespoon tomato paste
250 ml/8 fl oz light stock (a chicken stock cube will do)
125 g/4 oz button mushrooms
½ red pepper or a green one which is beginning to colour
15 g/½ oz butter

Method

1 Heat oil, add garlic and rabbit and cook over medium heat until rabbit is browned all over.
2 Add half the wine or cider, turn up the heat, and let it bubble to evaporate a little.
3 Stir in half the tomato paste with half the stock. Cover and cook over medium heat for 15 minutes.
4 Now turn the rabbit pieces over. Replace the lid and cook over low heat for 20–25 minutes – the sauce will be very much reduced.
5 Take pan off heat, lift out the rabbit pieces and, when cool enough to handle, strip flesh from bones.
6 Meanwhile, cut mushrooms into thin slices and de-seed and chop the pepper. Cook together very gently in the butter in another pan for 3–4 minutes, then add remaining wine or cider and simmer until pepper is tender.
7 Stir rabbit carefully back into sauce in pan in which it cooked. Mix in remaining tomato paste and stock.
8 Stir in mushroom mixture. Reheat gently and serve.

HOT PUDDINGS

A hot pudding is always welcome in this month when we seem to need more bulk to satisfy us. There is a huge variety to choose from.

We once had a lovely Danish girl on an exchange visit with one of my daughters. She had never heard of apple pie as we had it – hot with custard. I introduced her to that and lots more hot puds: baked rice done slowly in the oven to get a good skin; bread and butter pudding with a crunchy top and tender inside bursting with fat raisins or sultanas. I gave her a bundle of recipes to take back home to Denmark. I wonder if she ever uses them.

BAKED RICE PUDDING

You can use any type of milk for this recipe but the richer the milk the creamier the pudding. Gold Top milk (from Channel Islands' breeds of cow) is the best one, but a good substitute is Silver Top (ordinary pasteurized) or homogenized milk with a heaped tablespoon of dried milk mixed into it. Stir well to ensure the powder dissolves.

Serves 4

Ingredients

40 g/1½ oz round pudding rice, well washed
600 ml/1 pint milk
40 g/1½ oz granulated sugar
15 g/½ oz butter

Method

1 Put all the ingredients in a buttered pie dish and leave overnight.
2 Bake the pudding uncovered in a cool oven, Gas 2, 300°F, 150°C, for about 2 hours. Stir often during the first hour until the rice begins to thicken and the skin forms. When it begins to turn golden, gently slide a knife in at the edge of the dish to stir the pudding without disturbing the lovely brown skin – the part that many people like the best.

BREAD AND BUTTER PUDDING

This is delicious made from stale hot cross buns or from stale fruit loaves. If fruit is already incorporated in the stale bread, extra sultanas and candied peel are not needed, nor is it necessary to remove the crusts.

Serves 3–4

Ingredients

150 g/5 oz stale bread (without crusts)
butter
50 g/2 oz sultanas
a little candied peel
2 tablespoons demerara or plain white sugar
1 large egg
300 ml/½ pint milk
freshly grated nutmeg

Method

1 Butter a pie dish of approximately 1 litre/1½ pint capacity.
2 Slice the bread, butter it and cut into small pieces.
3 Place half the bread in the pie dish, sprinkle on the fruit, peel, and half the sugar. Cover with the remaining bread.
4 Beat the egg and milk together, pour over the bread, and leave for 30 minutes to soak.
5 Sprinkle top with remaining sugar and grate on a little nutmeg.
6 Bake in a moderate oven, Gas 4, 350°F, 180°C, for about 1 hour.

POURING CUSTARD

Serve hot or cold with pies, puddings etc.

Makes 300 ml/½ pint

Ingredients

300 ml/½ pint milk
1 dessertspoon vanilla sugar (sugar which has been stored with a broken vanilla pod)
2 eggs, lightly beaten

Method

1 Heat the milk and vanilla sugar together, but do not boil.
2 Pour on to the lightly beaten eggs, then strain into a heatproof basin.
3 Stand this over a pan of simmering water, not touching the water. Stir from time to time with a wooden spoon. It is cooked when there is a thin coating of custard on the spoon – about 10 minutes.

APPLE DAPPY

More than enough for 6

Ingredients
225 g/8 oz self-raising flour
1 teaspoon baking powder
a pinch of salt
50 g/ 2 oz margarine
150 ml/¼ pint milk
450 g/1 lb cooking apples, peeled, cored and chopped
1 tablespoon demerara sugar
½ level teaspoon cinnamon, nutmeg, ground cloves or mixed spice

Syrup

1 lemon or a little lemon essence
1 tablespoon golden syrup
15 g/½ oz margarine
125 g/4 oz sugar
200 ml/7 fl oz water

Method

1 Make the syrup first. Peel a fine strip of lemon rind and squeeze the lemon. Put rind, juice and all other ingredients in a pan and stir over a gentle heat until sugar is dissolved. Remove from heat and leave in the pan until needed.
2 To make the pastry, sift flour, baking powder and salt into a bowl. Rub in margarine, then mix to a dough with the milk.
3 Roll out on a floured board to a rectangle about 20 × 13 cm/8 × 5 inches, and 5 mm/¼ inch thick.
4 Spread the chopped apples over the pastry.
5 Mix sugar and spice together and sprinkle over the apple.
6 Roll up the pastry and apple like a Swiss roll. Then cut into slices about 2.5 cm/1 inch thick. Lay these slices flat in a greased ovenproof dish.
7 Remove lemon rind from syrup and pour over the apple slices.
8 Bake in a moderately hot oven, Gas 5, 375°F, 190°C, for about 30 minutes. Serve with cream or custard.

STEAMED PUDDINGS

This recipe is the basic one for a steamed pudding, but there are many variations, a few of which are given below.

Serves 4

Ingredients
125 g/4 oz margarine
125 g/4 oz caster sugar
175 g/6 oz self-raising flour
a pinch of salt
2 eggs, beaten
2 tablespoons milk

Method

1 Grease a 1.2 litre/2 pint heatproof basin.
2 Beat margarine until soft and creamy and then beat in sugar. Mix flour and salt and add to the margarine a little a time, alternately with the beaten eggs. Fold in milk.
3 Spoon into the greased basin and smooth the top. Cover with greased, greaseproof paper and foil, tucking edges securely round rim.
4 Steam the pudding in a steamer. *Or*, stand basin on a trivet or upturned, heatproof saucer in a saucepan with enough boiling water to come halfway up the basin. Steam for 1½ hours. Keep the water boiling, replenishing with boiling water as necessary. If you have a pressure cooker, cook at pressure for 30 minutes. Reduce pressure quickly.
5 Serve with custard or with warmed golden syrup.

Sultana Pudding
Follow the basic recipe adding 75–125 g/3–4 oz sultanas to the flour (paragraph 2).
Chocolate Pudding
Omit 25 g/1 oz flour from the basic recipe and replace it with 25 g/1 oz cocoa powder. Sieve this with the flour and add as instructed (paragraph 2).
Coffee Pudding
Dissolve 2 level teaspoons instant coffee in 2 teaspoons boiling water. Mix this with the milk and fold in as instructed (paragraph 2).
Orange or Lemon Pudding
Omit the milk from the basic recipe and add the rind and juice of 1 orange or 1 lemon.

February Menu

St Valentine's Day Dinner

The secret of a successful romantic dinner for two is food that is not too complicated, a beautifully laid table, candle-light and perhaps a lovely wine. The element of surprise is also worth thinking about. Our neighbours Peter and Elsa had six children, and I remember well how Peter, arriving home first one Valentine's Day, managed to get all the children to bed, cooked the meal, and lit the house with candles ready to surprise his wife. I can't think of a nicer compliment.

Pears with Stilton sauce
Stroganoff, served with heart-shaped, butter-fried croutons
Boiled rice
Green salad
Rhubarb and orange meringue
Coffee and Rich rum truffles

Home Notes

March

March is full of days to celebrate. St David's Day, the patron saint of Wales, is on the first and St Patrick's Day is celebrated on the 17th in Ireland and in New York, where there is a long connection with Irish immigrants (all the police in early films used to speak with Irish accents, and it was years before it dawned on me why). Mothering Sunday comes on the fourth Sunday in Lent and I much prefer that old name to the modern "Mother's Day". Easter, of course, is the most important of all the Christian festivals and since it is a moveable feast, can be in March or April. Although spring officially starts in March, it can still be rather cold. We rely to a great extent on imported foods, but there are still home-produced vegetables and fruit available.

Market Place

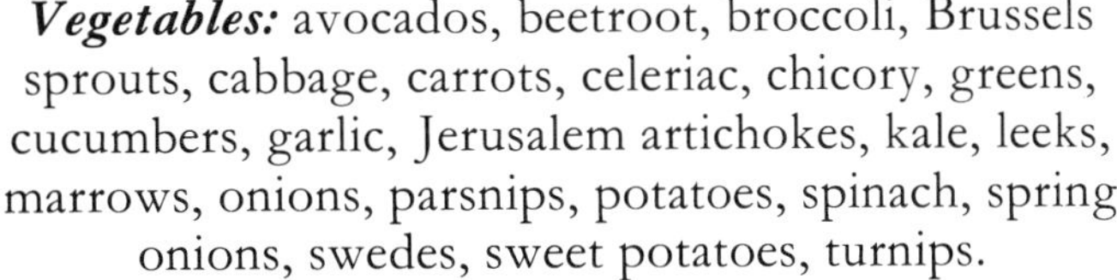

Vegetables: avocados, beetroot, broccoli, Brussels sprouts, cabbage, carrots, celeriac, chicory, greens, cucumbers, garlic, Jerusalem artichokes, kale, leeks, marrows, onions, parsnips, potatoes, spinach, spring onions, swedes, sweet potatoes, turnips.
Fruit and nuts: Cape gooseberries, dates, kumquats, pears, pineapples, rhubarb (forced and maincrop).
Fish: brill, cod, conger eel, flounder, halibut, John Dory, lemon sole, mackerel, oysters, scallops, sea trout, shrimps, sprats, whitebait.
Meat: beef, chicken, hare, pork.

Tips and Hints

This could be a good time to look over your garden tools. Even good metal can rust, and many garden chemicals have a caustic effect too. Tools should be brought indoors after use, cleaned and rubbed down with an oily rag kept for the purpose. Wooden handles need a little linseed oil on now and again.

A resolve I made last summer was to put moth repellant of some kind in with my winter woollies. Some little fellow had a field day on a new white cardigan so this year I shall shop early for something to repel their advances!

Early rhubarb – or indeed the maincrop variety coming in now – is so easy to cook in the oven (see page 34) with a tiny amount of water, and just enough sugar to taste. Stir it once or twice. Serve with hot custard (see page 25), or purée it and fold into whipped double cream for a fabulous fool. Don't forget, though, to use a stainless steel knife to cut it, as the acid juices will discolour carbon steel.

Jerusalem artichokes are good in March. Use them in soups, or thinly sliced, raw, in salads (they are pleasantly crunchy and remind me of waterchestnuts). To deal easily with their knobbly exteriors, wash, cook whole, and *then* peel them; done this way they do not discolour so easily.

To prepare a cake or loaf tin, grease it well all over the inside with butter or lard, and then cut out a piece of good greaseproof paper to fit the bottom. Simply lay the tin – round *or* square – on the paper, pencil round the outside, then cut slightly inside the pencil line.

This is the time when you can be starting to think about spring-cleaning. I always start with curtains – heavy ones cleaned or lighter ones washed. Next I brush walls down and wash woodwork with hot soapy water. An old toothbrush is handy for corners. Lights come next: shades and bulbs are sponged, and fittings rubbed clean. Then upholstery: a soft brush and soapy warm water for grubby arms; when dry I vacuum the cushions and into the corners. Lastly the carpets and rugs, which get an extra special vacuum, with carpet cleaner for the dirtiest bits. Finish up with a good polish for all furniture, then stand back and admire!

RECIPES

FISH

Meat was forbidden on a Friday in some Christian traditions. This was a penance in honour of Christ's crucifixion on Good Friday. In our small town this tradition dies hard and on Good Friday itself, the last Friday of Holy Week, there are queues outside the wet fish shops. Although March can be quite bleak as far as many fresh foods are concerned, there are some delicious varieties of fish available. Mackerel are particularly good now, for instance. Try also smoked fish, which is very adaptable.

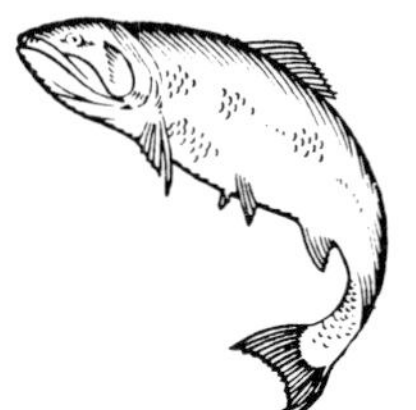

HADDOCK AND TOMATOES

Serves 4

Ingredients
450 g/1 lb haddock fillets
salt and freshly ground black pepper
2 teaspoons lemon juice
1 small onion, peeled and finely chopped
4 tomatoes, skinned and sliced
2 tablespoons finely grated cheese
4 tablespoons fresh breadcrumbs

Method

1. Wipe and trim fillets, cutting into portions if too large, and arrange them in a shallow oven dish. Sprinkle with salt, pepper and lemon juice.
2. Scatter onion on top and then make a layer of sliced tomatoes. Mix together the cheese and breadcrumbs, and sprinkle over the tomatoes.
3. Cook at the top of a moderate oven, Gas 4, 350°F, 180°C, for 30 minutes.

SMOKED HADDOCK PANCAKES

Serves 4

Ingredients
4 thin pancakes (see page 21)
225 g/8 oz smoked haddock
a little water
1 tablespoon finely grated cheese

Sauce
25 g/1 oz butter
25 g/1 oz wholewheat flour
300 ml/ $\frac{1}{2}$ pint warm milk
2 tablespoons cream or top of milk
freshly ground black pepper

Method

1. Prepare pancakes and keep them warm.
2. Wash the fish well and poach it gently in a little water, about 5–10 minutes. Then remove skin and break fish into small flakes. Keep it warm.
3. For the sauce, melt the butter in a pan, add flour and let it sizzle for a minute. Add warm milk gradually and bring to the boil. Let it simmer for 2–3 minutes then stir in cream and pepper to taste.
4. Pour half of this sauce into a jug to use later. Mix fish into rest of the sauce and fill the four pancakes.
5. Roll up the pancakes and lay them in a warmed ovenproof dish. Pour the remaining sauce over, sprinkle on the cheese, and put dish under a hot grill for 2–3 minutes to colour the top.

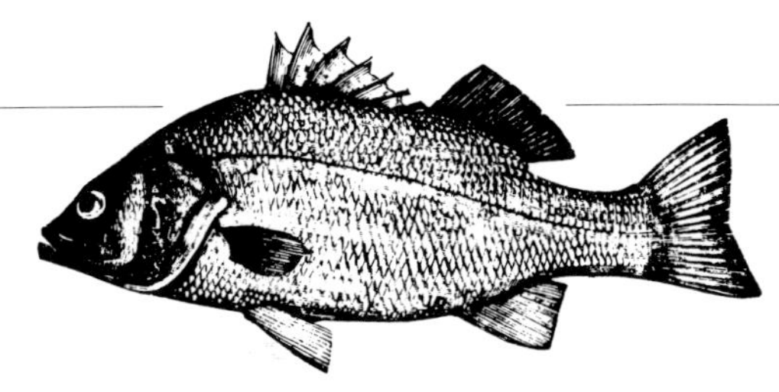

TASTY FISH PIE

A good recipe and very tasty, especially if you use new potatoes later on in the year. Cod, coley, haddock and whiting are all suitable.

Serves 2

Ingredients

3 medium potatoes, peeled
2 teaspoons flour
salt and freshly ground black pepper
225 g/8 oz cod fillet, skinned and cut into 2 portions
a little butter or margarine
150 ml/¼ pint milk
125 g/4 oz Cheddar cheese, grated
50 g/2 oz shrimps (optional)
4 medium mushrooms, chopped
25 g/1 oz red pepper, diced

Method

1 Slice potatoes thickly and parboil them for 6 minutes, then drain.
2 Season the flour with salt and pepper and toss the fish in it to coat.
3 Grease an ovenproof dish quite liberally with butter or margarine and put in the fish.
4 Pour in the milk and sprinkle fish with half the grated cheese. Add shrimps, mushrooms and red pepper, and season again.
5 Arrange the slices of potato on top and cover with the remaining cheese.
6 Cook near the top of a moderately hot oven, Gas 6, 400°F, 200°C, for 30 minutes.

CITRUS MACKEREL

Try them served hot with a green salad.

Serves 2

Ingredients

½ small red apple, cored and chopped
½ small orange, peeled and chopped
1 teaspoon chopped fresh tarragon, or ½ teaspoon dried tarragon
1 tablespoon lemon juice
15 g/½ oz butter or margarine
50 g/2 oz porridge oats
salt and freshly ground black pepper
2 mackerel fillets, 225 g/8 oz each

Method

1 Put the apple, orange, tarragon, lemon juice and butter or margarine in a saucepan and gently heat through until the apple has softened.
2 Stir in the oats and seasoning and divide the filling in two.
3 Place the mackerel on a board, skin side down, spread the filling over the mackerel and roll up each fish from the head end. Secure with cocktail sticks and place in a shallow dish.
4 Cover the dish and cook the mackerel in a moderately hot oven, Gas 6, 400°F, 200°C, for 10–15 minutes.

SEA FISH CAKES

The fish here is used raw, but you could use lightly cooked or leftover fish.

Enough for 2

Ingredients

225 g/8 oz white fish fillets, skinned
225 g/8 oz potatoes, peeled
1 egg yolk
salt and freshly ground black pepper
milk
2 tablespoons wholemeal flour
1 egg, beaten
4 tablespoons fresh wholemeal breadcrumbs

Method

1 Put the fish through a liquidizer or processor, or very finely dice.
2 Put the potatoes in a saucepan with a little lightly salted water and cook until tender. Drain and mash with the egg yolk and seasoning.
3 Allow potatoes to cool, then mix into the fish. Form into two large or four small fish cakes. If the mixture is too stiff add a few drops of milk.
4 Coat the fish cakes in flour, then beaten egg and breadcrumbs. Chill for 30 minutes.
5 Grill the fish cakes for 5 minutes on each side.

EASTER

Fish is traditional on Good Friday, and a main course for Easter Sunday or Monday is often spring lamb or chicken. You can make your own hot cross buns, Simnel cake, Easter biscuits and a rhubarb tart or meringue.

Easter eggs were associated with Eostre, the Saxon goddess of spring, and have come to symbolize the Resurrection. In Scotland, as children, we took a picnic to the hills to roll Easter eggs – a custom symbolizing the rolling of the stone from Christ's tomb.

SIMNEL CAKE

This semi-rich cake is made by the melting method. It should be decorated in the traditional way with eleven marzipan balls to represent the faithful apostles, or you can make a pretend pond with blue icing and toy chicks for a children's version. This cake keeps well in a tin for 2 weeks or in the freezer for 2 months.

Makes an 18 cm/7 inch round cake

Ingredients
75 g/3 oz butter
75 g/3 oz soft brown sugar
65 ml/2½ fl oz water
75 g/3 oz sultanas, washed and dried
50 g/ 2 oz raisins, washed and dried
125 g/4 oz currants, washed and dried
25 g/1 oz mixed peel, chopped small
140 g/4½ oz plain wholemeal flour
½ teaspoon bicarbonate of soda
½ teaspoon mixed spice
1 teaspoon ground cinnamon
1 teaspoon ground ginger
1 large egg, beaten

Marzipan
225 g/8 oz ground almonds
125 g/4 oz caster sugar
125 g/4 oz icing sugar, sifted
2–3 drops almond essence
½ beaten egg

To glaze
1 tablespoon apricot jam, sieved

Method

1 Make the marzipan first. Mix all the ingredients together, adding just enough beaten egg to get a firm texture. Knead lightly, then divide into three. Wrap each piece tightly in cling film.
2 For the cake, melt the butter in a roomy pan. Add the sugar and water and bring to the boil. Add the dried fruit and peel. Simmer for only 1 minute, then remove the pan from the heat. Allow to cool down to just warm.
3 Sift the flour, bicarbonate of soda, mixed spice, cinnamon and ginger into the fruit and mix in along with the beaten egg. Mix well but do not beat.
4 Have ready an 18 cm/7 inch round tin lined and greased (see page 29). Put half the cake mixture into this, and level the surface.
5 Roll one of the pieces of marzipan on a sugared board, and cut out a circle measuring 18 cm/7 inches in diameter. Position this circle on top of the cake mixture in the tin and press down gently. Spoon in the rest of the cake mixture, and level the surface again.
6 Put the cake tin on a baking sheet on top of a piece of thick cardboard. Position a thick collar of folded brown paper round the outside of the tin so that it rises about 5 cm/2 inches above the rim of the tin. This will keep the fruit from scorching.
7 Bake in a moderate oven at Gas 3, 325°F, 160°C, for about 1½ hours or until the risen cake is firm and shrinking from the sides of the tin. Leave in the tin for 20 minutes before lifting out to cool.
8 Level the top then turn the cake over and use the bottom as the top. Paint the cake with a thin film of warmed apricot jam.
9 Roll out the second piece of marzipan and cut a second 18 cm/7 inch circle. Add the trimmings to the third piece of marzipan and roll this into eleven even balls about the size of a big marble (set aside).

Position the second ring of marzipan on top of the cake, and press it down gently. Score the surface lightly in a criss-cross pattern and put the cake under a hot grill to toast the top. Do not go away and leave it as it burns easily. Now put the eleven balls of marzipan on a baking sheet and slip them under the grill as well to toast very slightly. Finish the cake by placing the marzipan balls evenly round the edges of the cake. If the balls won't stick a spot of beaten egg should do the trick.

EASTER BISCUITS

You can make these with currants *or* with chocolate chips!
If the latter, omit the spice.

Makes about 30

Ingredients

325 g/12 oz plain white flour
a pinch of salt
1 teaspoon mixed spice
175 g/6 oz butter
125 g/4 oz caster sugar
75 g/3 oz currants, washed and dried
finely grated rind of 1 lemon
1 medium egg, beaten
1 tablespoon milk

Method

1 Sift flour, salt and spice into a bowl, then rub in the butter. Add the sugar, currants and lemon rind.
2 Beat the egg into the milk, add to the mixture, and mix to make a pliable dough.
3 Roll out on a lightly floured board to just under 5 mm/¼ inch thick. Cut out biscuits using a 7.5 cm/3 inch fluted or plain cutter. Transfer the biscuits to baking sheets covered with non-stick paper. Make up the scraps into more biscuits.
4 Bake at Gas 5, 375°F, 190°C, for 10–12 minutes. Allow biscuits to crisp up on the trays then transfer them to a wire rack. Keep in an airtight tin for up to 3 weeks.

WHOLEWHEAT BUN LOAF AND HOT CROSS BUNS

The sign of the cross on hot cross buns is a relic of the time when all bread was cut with a cross on top to help the dough rise. Other explanations are that the bread was marked into quadrants to symbolize the four seasons, or that the cross kept evil spirits away.

Makes one 450 g/1 lb bun loaf and 8 hot cross buns

Ingredients

25 g/1 oz fresh yeast or 15 g/½ oz dried yeast
40 g/1½ oz dark brown Barbados sugar
150 ml/¼ pint tepid water
450 g/1 lb plain wholewheat flour
1 level teaspoon sea salt
1 teaspoon mixed spice
½ teaspoon ground cinnamon
a grating of nutmeg
50 g/2 oz margarine
125 g/4 oz mixed currants, sultanas and peel
warm milk and 1 beaten egg to make barely 150 ml/¼ pint

Glaze

1 tablespoon demerara sugar dissolved over low heat in 2 tablespoons water and boiled until syrupy

Method

1 Mix fresh yeast with 1 teaspoon of the sugar and stir it into the tepid water. If using dried yeast, mix 1 teaspoon of sugar into the tepid water, sprinkle in yeast, whisking with a fork to disperse the grains. Let it stand in a warm place for 10–15 minutes when it should be frothing well and ready to use.
2 Mix the flour, salt and spices together in a large bowl, then rub in the margarine. Mix in the rest of the sugar and the fruit.
3 Mix to a pliable dough with yeast liquid and egg and milk mixture, then knead thoroughly.
4 Place to rise in a greased bowl away from draughts. Cover with polythene or a clean tea-towel. Let it rise for about 1 hour until doubled in size.
5 Turn on to a floured board and knead well.
6 For *bun loaf*, weigh off 450 g/1 lb dough, shape into a loaf and put into a greased 450 g/1 lb loaf tin, or a round tin of similar capacity. Cover and leave to rise in a warm place, away from draughts, for about a further hour.
7 For *hot cross buns*, divide remaining dough into eight even pieces. Shape into buns, round or oval, and roll lightly. Make a cross on top with a knife. Place on a greased baking tray, cover and allow to rise in a warm place until puffy.
8 Bake buns for approximately 15 minutes in a moderately hot oven, Gas 6, 400°F, 200°C, until nicely browned. Remove from oven and turn on to a cooling rack. Brush with glaze while hot.
9 Bake loaf in the same moderately hot oven for 15 minutes, then reduce the heat to moderate, Gas 4, 350°F, 180°C, for a further 25–30 minutes until firm. Turn out on to a wire rack to cool. Glaze as for buns as desired.

SIMPLE BARBECUED CHICKEN

This dish freezes well. If you want a more splendid chicken dish for your Easter eating, turn to page 41.

Serves 4

Ingredients

4 chicken joints
1 tablespoon oil
40 g/1½ oz butter
1 onion, peeled and chopped
2 dessertspoons tomato purée
2 level teaspoons Barbados sugar
1 teaspoon prepared mustard
1 teaspoon Worcestershire sauce
1 level teaspoon salt
freshly ground black pepper
juice of ½ lemon
150 ml/¼ pint water

Method

1. To joint a chicken, cut it in half lengthways with a pair of secateurs (or a sharp knife, and a weight to help knock the knife through), through breast bone and then the backbone. Cut each half diagonally between the leg and the wing upwards from the leg. (If six joints are required, divide drumstick from thigh.)
2. Dry the chicken joints and fry in oil and 25 g/1 oz of the butter until nicely browned. Lift out into a casserole.
3. Add remaining butter to pan and lightly fry onion until soft and golden.
4. Add all remaining ingredients and simmer for 5 minutes. Pour over chicken.
5. Cover casserole and cook in a moderate oven, Gas 4, 350°F, 180°C, for 1 hour.

HONEYED WELSH LAMB

(Oen Cymreig Melog)
Good Welsh lamb is appropriate in this month that celebrates St David (although there are no leeks . . .). This recipe gives a gloss to the joint and a delicious gravy.

Serves 6–8

Ingredients

a 1.3–1.8 kg/3–4 lb joint of lamb, leg or shoulder
salt and freshly ground black pepper
1 teaspoon ground ginger
1 dessertspoon dried rosemary, or 2 sprigs fresh rosemary
2 tablespoons runny honey
about 300 ml/½ pint cider

Method

1. Rub salt, pepper and ginger all over the joint and put it in a tin that will be a fairly snug fit.
2. Sprinkle rosemary over it and dribble on the honey. Pour cider around it.
3. Allowing 30 minutes per 450 g/1 lb, roast near the top of a moderately hot oven, Gas 6, 400°F, 200°C, for the first half hour. Then baste meat and reduce oven heat to moderate, Gas 4, 350°F, 180°C, for remaining cooking time. Baste every 20 minutes, and add a little extra cider if necessary.
4. Lift meat on to a warmed dish and make gravy using residue in the roasting tin.

RHUBARB PLATE TART

Other fruits may be used. This pastry is quite satisfactory with a moist filling.

Makes one 25 cm/10 inch round tart

Ingredients

575 g/1¼ lb cooked rhubarb (see page 29)

Pastry

250 g/9 oz plain flour
75 g/3 oz self-raising flour
a pinch of salt
2 level teaspoons caster sugar
125 g/4 oz hard margarine
50 g/2 oz hard vegetable fat
3 tablespoons milk

Method

1. Sieve together the dry ingredients for the pastry, and then rub in the fats until the texture is like fine breadcrumbs. Bind to a firm dough with milk.
2. Using a floured board, roll out half of the pastry thinly to line a 25 cm/10 inch pie-plate. Roll out the second half to make a lid.
3. Place a generous layer of very well drained rhubarb to within 1 cm/½ inch of the edge of the pastry. Damp edge with water and put on pastry lid. Seal firmly around the edge.
4. Brush the top with milk. Cut two slits in the top to let steam out during cooking and prevent pastry from becoming soggy.
5. Bake in a moderately hot oven, Gas 5, 375°F, 190°C, for 35–40 minutes.

RHUBARB AND ORANGE MERINGUE

The orange and rhubarb flavours are delicious together, and the crunchy meringue is a perfect foil. You could substitute other fruit throughout the year – stewed apples, gooseberries, plums, anything you have a lot of.

Serves 4

Ingredients
450 g/1 lb young rhubarb
juice and finely grated rind of 1 orange
50 g/2 oz demerara sugar
40 g/1½ oz cornflour
2 eggs, separated
75 g/3 oz caster sugar

Method

1. Wash and trim rhubarb and cut into short lengths. Place in a 1.2 litre/2 pint shallow ovenproof casserole or pie dish.
2. Place the orange rind and juice in a measuring jug and add water to make up to 450 ml/¾ pint.
3. Place demerara sugar and cornflour in a saucepan and gradually blend in liquid. Bring to the boil, stirring, and simmer for 3 minutes. Allow to cool slightly.
4. Stir egg yolks into the orange sauce and pour over the rhubarb. Cook in the centre of a moderate oven, Gas 3, 325°F, 160°C, for 20 minutes. Lower temperature to cool, Gas 2, 300°F, 150°C.
5. Meanwhile, whisk the egg whites until stiff and dry, whisk in half the caster sugar and whisk until stiff again. Fold in remaining sugar.
6. Spread meringue over mixture in dish and return to oven to cook for a further 20–25 minutes until the top is golden brown and the rhubarb is tender.

EASTER FOR THE CHILDREN

The children can, of course, help with the Simnel cake (see page 32), but there are plenty of other things they can do.

HARD-BOILED EGGS

Decorating hard-boiled eggs – one for everyone in the family – is easy, but needs to be supervised. Coloured food pens are a great help. Bits of coloured felt can be glued in position for waistcoats, hats or bow-ties. Another good idea is to boil the eggs in water which has been heavily tinted with food colouring, or which contains onion skins (for yellow), beetroot (for pink) or spinach (for green, of course). It helps to stand the eggs in egg cups, or in a box of sand when decorating them.

EASTER BISCUITS

My children always enjoyed making a very simple Easter biscuit using bought plain Marie biscuits, and tiny Easter egg sweets. We melted chocolate-flavoured cake covering in a bowl over a pan of simmering water, then we spread a small teaspoon of it on each biscuit. Then, before the chocolate set, we stuck three Easter eggs on each.

EASTER NESTS

Another favourite and much messier "recipe" was Easter nests. For this we crushed shredded wheat and stirred plenty of the broken pieces into melted chocolate. When the shredded wheat was well coated, we spooned out dessertspoonfuls on to greaseproof paper, and made nest shapes using the back of a teaspoon. Into these nests we dropped several egg sweets to set with the chocolate.

HOT CROSS "BUNS"

A different version can be made in the shape of fondant sweets. Buy a pack of fondant or ready-to-roll icing. Cut off a 1 cm/$\frac{1}{2}$ inch strip at one side and leave white. Colour the rest a pale shade of brown with some cocoa paste ($\frac{1}{2}$ teaspoon cocoa powder plus 1–2 drops water). Work the colouring through the icing then cut into pieces about the size of a walnut. Roll the fondant into ball shapes. Cut the white fondant into strips to make a cross over each sweet.

March Menu

Mothering Sunday Tea

Traditionally young people, working away from home, were given time off to visit their mothers, and the gift was often a fruit cake, which is how the Simnel cake evolved. Afternoon tea can be a very pleasurable event. Everything is made in advance except the tea and there is no rushing about at the last minute. The bread for the sandwiches should be thin and fresh. Spread first with softened butter and then with the generous filling. A good and tasty spread can be made with a can of tuna mixed with some chopped walnuts, salad cream and chutney; or butter, cream cheese and chopped watercress. If you want cucumber sandwiches, make them at the last minute or the cucumber will go flabby and very nasty.

Sandwiches
Cheese sausage rolls
Fatless chocolate sponge with whipped cream
Simnel cake
Hot cross buns
Mrs Oade's ginger crisps

Home Notes

April

The sound of the cuckoo is said to herald spring, and this is when you suddenly notice vivid green shoots pushing their way up through the chilly soil. The first celebratory day is April 1st – April Fool's Day – and children would enjoy a party then. (Remember, though, that April Fool tricks must be achieved before midday!) St George's Day is celebrated on the 23rd. England's patron saint, it has to be said, does not enjoy the same popularity as St David for Wales or St Patrick for Ireland. (Dandelion flowers, traditionally gathered on this day, will make wine for Christmas). To celebrate Anzac Day on the 25th, and to honour Austrialia and New Zealand, you could make Anzac biscuits or Australian cakes (see pages 45 and 46).

Market Place

Vegetables: asparagus, avocados, broccoli, cabbages, carrots, cauliflowers, courgettes, cucumber, greens, leeks, lettuce, marrow, morels, parsnips, potatoes, radishes, spinach, spring onions, swedes, tomatoes, watercress.

Fruit and nuts: Asian pears, bananas, pineapples, rhubarb.

Fish: conger eel, crab, crawfish, halibut, lemon sole, lobster, mackerel, oysters, prawns, salmon, sea trout, shrimps, whitebait.

Meat: beef, chicken, duckling, lamb, pork.

Tips and Hints

In April I always enjoy the first snippings from my patch of chives. They might go into a mayonnaise to be stirred into freshly boiled cubed potatoes for a hot salad (Jersey new potatoes start coming in towards the end of the month), or just beaten into lactic cream cheese for a lovely sandwich filling (add softened butter as well if you wish a milder flavour).

If you have been foresighted you could have your own home-grown spring onions by the end of this month. Germinate seed early under glass in February, then plant out in March. I use spring onions in salads and dressings, but most of all in Chinese cooking, along with soy sauce and ginger.

Home-produced watercress is at its peak now. It is not easy to store – the leaves soon go yellow – so use within two days. High on the healthy eater's list, it is full of vitamins, and has ten times more calcium than any other vegetable.

Lemons are cheap at this time of year, so make lemon curd (see page 101), if your supplies of jam are running out. Lemons also freeze well: just scrub, dry and then freeze whole in polythene bags.

Eggs are graded for sale by numbers. Number one is the largest, and number seven is the smallest. These tiny eggs are very good value at half the price of a larger egg. Try to use them in rotation; if there are one or two left in the bowl when I bring in some fresh, I mark the older eggs so that I know which they are and to use them first.

To test for freshness, put an egg in a tumbler of cold water. If it lies flat on the bottom it is fresh; if it tilts slightly, it's a little older; if it floats it's probably bad.

Look out for duck eggs too, which are tasty and very good value. One duck egg can substitute for two hen's eggs in baking.

TRADITIONAL ROASTS

There is no doubt that the application of dry heat to meat and poultry which finishes up as a traditional roast is universally popular. The perfect roast is crisp and crusty on the outside and moist within. There should be enough juices in the roasting tin after the fat has been poured away, to flavour the gravy well so that it matches the roast. I do dislike the practice in many restaurants of using the same brown gravy for everything. See, too, pages 102, 122 and 124 for other traditional roasts.

ROAST RIB OF BEEF

Serves 8–10

Ingredients
2.3–3.6 kg/5–8 lb rib of beef
1 tablespoon dry mustard powder
freshly ground black pepper
2 tablespoons plain flour
dripping or butter, softened
4–6 tablespoons red wine or water

Gravy

300 ml/½ pint beef stock (or made with a stock cube)
25 g/1 oz plain flour
gravy browning
salt

Method

1 Preheat the oven to fairly hot, Gas 7, 425°F, 220°C.
2 In a small bowl mix the mustard, pepper and flour.
3 Dry the meat with kitchen paper. (This is particularly important if the meat has been frozen.) Now rub the softened dripping or butter all over the meat and then roughly coat it with the dry flour mix.
4 When the oven is hot place the beef in it on a rack over a roasting tin, and allow it to brown all over for 20 minutes. Turn the heat down to Gas 3, 325°F, 160°C, and pour the wine or water in the roasting tin. Allow 15–18 minutes per 450 g/1 lb for rare; 20–24 minutes for medium; and 25–30 minutes for well done. Baste the joint frequently.
5 When cooked to taste, transfer the joint to a hot plate and place in a warm place, while you make the gravy. This allows the juices of the meat to settle and also makes it easier to carve.
6 Pour off excess fat from pan juices. Set the roasting tin over direct heat and pour in the beef stock. Bring to the boil, stirring well and scraping up any crusty bits sticking to the bottom. At this point I find it easier to pour this liquid into a pan through a sieve.
7 To thicken the gravy, work the plain flour into a little cold water. When this is smooth, pour a little hot liquid from the pan into the mixture, stir well and pour the lot back into the pan. Stirring all the time over a medium heat, if appropriate add just a spot of gravy browning to darken the mixture and season with salt. When the gravy is ready, pour it into a hot sauce boat along with any further juices from the meat.

YORKSHIRE PUDDING

Makes 12 small puddings

Ingredients
125 g/4 oz strong plain flour
¼ teaspoon salt
1 large egg
300 ml/½ pint skimmed milk (ie skim off creamy top)

Method

1 Beat all well together until bubbles appear. Can be left to stand until required, but this is not necessary.
2 Heat a little dripping in twelve deep patty tins, and half fill with batter. Cook near the top of a hot oven, Gas 7, 425°F, 220°C, for about 30 minutes, until puddings are golden and puffy.

TO BONE POULTRY

A sharp knife is essential.

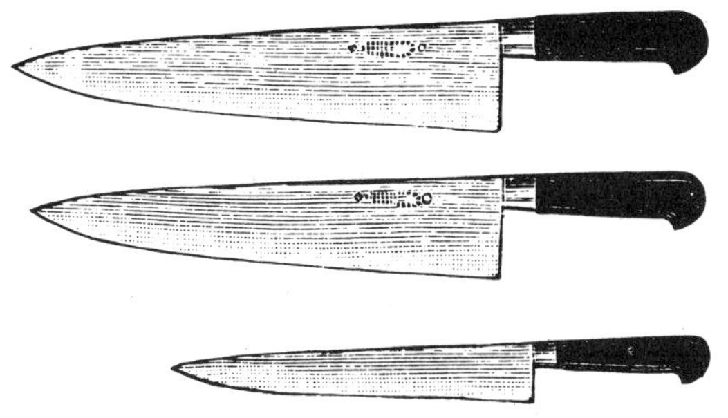

Method

1 Cut down the centre of the back of the bird from neck to tail.
2 Taking first one side of the bird, cut and work the flesh off the bones. Take care not to puncture the skin.
3 Work down the leg. To facilitate pulling the drumstick bone through, cut off at the joint any remaining lower limb.
4 Work down the shoulder in the same way as the leg.
5 Continue working flesh off until the centre breast bone is reached.
6 Now repeat the process on the other side of the bird from back bone round to breast bone.
7 When all the flesh is loose, it is ready to be lifted right off the carcass, take care not to cut through the skin at the edge of the breast bone where it is thin. Use the carcass to make stock (see page 12).

CHICKEN, BONED, STUFFED AND ROAST

This chicken could also be served cold, with a coating sauce and colourful decorations, see page 71.

Serves 4–6

Ingredients
a 1.3 kg/3 lb chicken, boned (see above)

Stuffing
450 g/1 lb pork sausagemeat
1 tablespoon finely chopped parsley
2 shallots (or 1 small onion), peeled and chopped
2 tablespoons stock, or wine

Garnish
4 hard-boiled eggs, ends trimmed

Method

1 Mix all the stuffing ingredients together.
2 Spread the boned bird out on a board, skin side down, and stuff the legs and shoulders with a little of the stuffing mixture.
3 Spread half the stuffing down the centre of the bird. Place the eggs down the centre, trimmed end to trimmed end. Cover with remaining stuffing.
4 Shape the bird again and stitch with fine string.
5 Wrap in tin foil with a little more stock and cook in a moderately hot oven, Gas 5, 375°F, 190°C, allowing 20 minutes to the 450 g/1 lb stuffed weight, plus a further 20 minutes. Open foil 30 minutes before end of cooking time to allow to brown.

ROAST LAMB WITH APRICOT STUFFING

Remember to start this dish the night before serving.

Serves 4–6

Ingredients
900 g/2 lb boned shoulder of lamb
salt and freshly ground black pepper
a little dripping

Stuffing
50–75 g/2–3 oz dried apricots
50 g/2 oz butter or margarine
1 medium onion, peeled and chopped
50 g/2 oz fresh wholemeal or white breadcrumbs
1 tablespoon chopped parsley
stock
1 egg yolk

Method

1 Put apricots to soak in water overnight. Then, the next day, drain and cut them up quite small.
2 Melt butter or margarine in a frying pan, then lightly fry the onion until transparent but not brown.
3 Mix in the apricots, breadcrumbs, parsley, salt and pepper. Moisten with 1–2 tablespoons stock.
4 Beat the egg yolk and add it to the stuffing with a little more stock if necessary, to make it moist but not sticky.
5 Open out lamb, season with pepper and a very little salt. Spread stuffing over it. Roll up and secure with string to keep in the filling.
6 Put in a roasting tin, dot with dripping, and roast in a hot oven, Gas 8, 450°F, 230°C, for 10 minutes. Reduce to moderate temperature, Gas 4, 350°F, 180°C, for a further 1–1½ hours.

ROAST HAND OF PORK WITH BRAISED ONIONS

It is more economical to buy a hand of pork at the weight given because there is a larger proportion of meat to bone and it is better value than buying a smaller joint. Cooking as suggested ensures that the skin is crisp.

Serves 8

Ingredients

1.8–2 kg/4–4½ lb hand of pork (ask the butcher to score skin finely)
15 g/½ oz pork dripping
1 small teaspoon salt
medium onions, 1 for each person
1–2 tablespoons wholewheat or plain flour

Method

1 Rub dripping over pork and sprinkle on the salt, then place on a small trivet or rack in a large roasting tin.
2 Roast in a moderately hot oven, Gas 6, 400°F, 200°C, for 30 minutes. Reduce heat to moderate, Gas 4, 350°F, 180°C, and cook for 2–2½ hours, depending on weight of meat.
3 Meanwhile, peel onions and put them whole into a saucepan with lightly salted water to cover. Boil for 20 minutes. Then drain, saving the water for the gravy.
4 Put onions in the fat around the meat for the last half hour of cooking time. Turn them over in fat once or twice to brown evenly.
5 When meat and onions are done, set on warmed dish and keep hot.
6 To make the gravy, pour nearly all fat off sediment in roasting tin into a basin. Stir flour into remaining fat in tin and let it sizzle for 1 minute. Pour in onion water and any other vegetable water, stir till gravy thickens, boil for 2–3 minutes, and season to taste.

ROAST POTATOES

Method

Peel, cut into even-sized pieces and boil for 10 minutes in salted water. Drain well and dry. Place around meat, in the fat, turning them to coat all sides. Allow 30–40 minutes cooking time in a moderately hot oven, Gas 6, 400°F, 200°C.

They can also be placed in a separate tin, allowing fat to become hot first, and roasted in a moderately hot oven, Gas 6, 400°F, 200°C, on top shelf of oven. If potatoes are not crisp enough when cooked through, place under medium grill for 5 minutes.

ROAST DUCKLING WITH WALNUT SAUCE

Serves 4

Ingredients

a 2 kg/4½ lb duckling

Sauce

2 tablespoons duckling dripping
1 medium onion, peeled and chopped
50 g/2 oz walnuts, chopped
1 level tablespoon plain flour
300 ml/½ pint duckling stock
grated rind and juice of 1 orange
2 tablespoons sherry
2 teaspoons chopped parsley
freshly ground black pepper

To serve and garnish

25 g/1 oz walnut halves
watercress
1 orange, cut into slices

Method

1 Wipe duckling dry inside and out. Place on a rack in a shallow roasting tin. Prick the skin all over with a fork. This allows the fat to flow out during cooking and bastes the bird without any attention. Sprinkle well with salt.
2 Place in a hot oven, Gas 7, 425°F, 220°C, and immediately reduce heat to moderate, Gas 4, 350°F, 180°C. Roast for 1½–1¾ hours, or until tender and well browned, and the juices run clear when the thickest part of the leg is pierced with a skewer.
3 To prepare the sauce, heat duckling dripping in a pan, add chopped onion and walnuts and cook gently until lightly browned.
4 Stir in flour and cook 1 minute, then gradually blend in stock, orange rind and juice. Simmer gently for 2 minutes, stirring throughout. Stir in sherry and chopped parsley and season to taste.
5 To serve, put duckling on a hot serving dish and garnish with the walnuts fried in 1 tablespoon duckling dripping, well drained, the watercress and orange slices. Serve the walnut sauce in a separate bowl.

TOPSY-TURVY APRIL FOOL PARTY FOR CHILDREN

In medieval England it was the custom to celebrate April Fool's Day with a "topsy-turvy" feast. In larger houses, it was the fool or court jester who presided at table, and the master of the house who did the serving; the lower tables were served before the top tables; even announcements were sometimes made backwards! Children do enjoy this! As the guests arrive, give each a small item of clothing to denote their temporary change of sex: each boy could have a tiny skirt on an elastic band to wear over his ordinary clothes and a bow to wear in his hair; each girl could have a bow tie and a stick-on moustache. Perhaps each child could have a new name for the afternoon. They might enjoy picking their own and writing it on a pin-on label badge. Games could also be topsy-turvy, with the last one declared the winner.

The food can be unusual as well. For the cake, buy or make a giant pizza, the one on page 92 – doubled in size – might be appropriate – and after it has been heated up, pick out the host or hostess's name in peas, and stick candles all round the outside. Serve sandwiches with sweet and sour fillings: try finely chopped dates and walnuts bound together with soft butter; crunchy peanut butter with chopped mandarin oranges; or, depending on the age of the children, fingers of buttered brown and white bread sprinkled with chocolate vermicelli or hundreds and thousands. And try tarts with savoury fillings: bought or home-made vol-au-vents, small flat pastry cases, or the following savoury cheesecake.

HOT SAVOURY CHEESECAKE

Cuts into 12 small wedges

Ingredients

75 g/3 oz butter
125 g/4 oz cream crackers, crushed in a bag with a rolling pin
3 fat pinches cayenne pepper
125 g/4 oz button mushrooms, sliced
450 g/1 lb curd cheese (or any soft cream cheese)
3 eggs, beaten
125 g/4 oz cold cooked ham, chopped
salt and freshly ground black pepper
3 firm tomatoes

Method

1. Melt 50 g/2 oz of the butter and stir in the crushed crackers and the cayenne pepper.
2. Press this into a 20 cm/8 inch flan ring set on a baking sheet, or into a flan tin with a removable base.
3. Melt the rest of the butter, stir in the mushrooms, and cook gently for 2–3 minutes.
4. In a roomy bowl beat the cheese to make it smooth. Gradually beat in the eggs. Add the cooked ham and mushrooms. Season and mix well.
5. Spoon the mixture into the flan ring. Smooth down.
6. Bake in a cool oven, Gas 3, 325°F, 160°C, for about 45 minutes until just set. Slice the tomatoes finely and arrange round the edge. Serve hot.

SAUSAGE CARTWHEEL FLAN

This pastry is delicious for savoury flans, meat pies, cheese straws, and sausage rolls. For the latter, simply roll out the pastry to a long strip, place a sausagemeat length along, then wrap up, sealing ends well. Glaze with milk, cut into individual sausage rolls, and bake in a moderately hot oven, Gas 6, 400°F, 200°C, for about 15 minutes.

Cuts into 12 small wedges

Cheese pastry

Ingredients

225 g/8 oz plain white or wholewheat flour
½ level teaspoon salt
½ level teaspoon dry mustard powder
a pinch of cayenne pepper
75 g/3 oz hard margarine or vegetable fat
75 g/3 oz well flavoured cheese, finely grated
1 egg yolk
2 tablespoons water (3 for wholewheat pastry)

Filling

15 g/½ oz margarine
1 medium onion, peeled and chopped
225 g/8 oz skinless sausages
1 large egg
150 ml/¼ pint milk
salt and freshly ground black pepper
50 g/2 oz cheese, grated

Method

1 For the pastry, sieve or mix flour, salt, mustard and cayenne together into a large bowl. Rub in margarine with fingertips until mixture is like breadcrumbs. Mix in cheese. Mix egg yolk with water and stir it in with a round-edged knife. Then knead lightly until smooth and a firm dough is formed.
2 Roll out pastry, use to line a 20 cm/8 inch flan ring, and bake blind as on page 89.
3 For the filling, melt margarine and fry onion gently until soft. Lift onion out of pan into flan case.
4 Lightly fry sausages in pan. Then cut six of them to fit in flan, like the spokes of a wheel. Put aside on a plate for a moment. Cut up remaining sausages and trimmed ends and put these on top of onion.
5 Beat egg, milk and seasonings together, and pour into flan.
6 Arrange the six sausages like a cartwheel in the flan, then sprinkle cheese between the spokes.
7 Bake in a moderately hot to hot oven, Gas 6–7, 400–425°F, 200–220°C, for about 35 minutes.

HOME-MADE BISCUITS

Home-made biscuits always taste better and can be served at any time of day – with morning coffee, for packed lunches, or at tea time. Some can accompany desserts, some can even serve as a major constituent of a dessert (see the shortbread biscuit recipe on page 63).

AUSTRALIAN CAKES

Makes about 20

Ingredients

75 g/3 oz margarine
75 g/3 oz caster sugar
1 egg
75 g/3 oz self-raising flour, sieved
½ teaspoon baking powder
cornflakes, crushed slightly

Method

1 Cream together the margarine and caster sugar, then stir in the egg. Fold in the flour and baking powder.
2 Take teaspoonfuls of the mixture and roll them in the crushed cornflakes.
3 Space them well apart on a greased baking sheet and bake in a moderately hot oven, Gas 6, 400°F, 200°C, for 15 minutes.
4 Transfer to a wire rack and allow to cool.

ANZACS

These large crisp biscuits are well-known all over Australia. They will keep very well in an airtight container.

Makes about 24 biscuits

Ingredients

150 g/5 oz butter or margarine
1 tablespoon golden syrup
2 tablespoons water
1 teaspoon bicarbonate of soda
125 g/4 oz plain flour
75 g/3 oz porridge oats
50 g/2 oz desiccated coconut
125 g/4 oz caster sugar

Method

1 Melt the butter gently with the syrup in a large saucepan. Remove from heat.
2 Stir in the water and bicarbonate of soda, then all the remaining ingredients.
3 Put teaspoonfuls of the mixture on to greased baking sheets. Leave plenty of room between the biscuits as they spread as they cook.
4 Bake in a cool oven, Gas 3, 325°F, 160°C, for about 20 minutes until just golden brown.
5 Leave the biscuits on the baking sheets for a few minutes to harden up slightly, then put them on a wire rack to cool.

MRS OADE'S GINGER CRISPS

Makes about 325 g/$\frac{3}{4}$ lb biscuits

Ingredients

225 g/8 oz plain flour
25 g/1 oz caster sugar
1 teaspoon ground ginger
1 level teaspoon bicarbonate of soda
125 g/4 oz golden syrup
50 g/2 oz butter or margarine

Method

1 Sift dry ingredients into a bowl.
2 To be precise with golden syrup, put a small pan on to scales, weigh it and then weigh syrup into it.
3 Melt fat and syrup together over low heat, then mix this very thoroughly into the dry ingredients.
4 Line a 450 g/1 lb loaf tin with greaseproof paper, and press the soft mixture into it. Make the top level and smooth. Leave for several hours, or overnight, in a cool place or refrigerator.
5 Turn biscuit loaf out of tin and use a sharp knife to cut very thin biscuits, about 6 mm/$\frac{1}{4}$ inch thick or less.
6 Put biscuits on greased baking trays (or use non-stick baking paper to line trays) and bake in middle of a warm oven, Gas 3, 325°F, 160°C, until golden – 3 mm/$\frac{1}{8}$ inch thick biscuits take about 12 minutes.
7 Leave on baking trays for 5 minutes to firm up, then put biscuits on to a wire rack to cool.

FLORENTINES

Makes 28 small bars

Ingredients

225 g/8 oz plain cooking chocolate
50 g/2 oz margarine
125 g/4 oz soft brown sugar
1 egg
5 heaped tablespoons desiccated coconut
3 heaped tablespoons chopped nuts
2 heaped tablespoons chopped glacé cherries
2 heaped tablespoons mixed peel
2 heaped tablespoons sultanas

Method

1 Melt chocolate in a small bowl over a pan of simmering water.
2 Spread melted chocolate in bottom of a Swiss roll tin 33 × 23 cm/13 × 9 inches. Leave to set.
3 Beat together margarine and sugar, then beat in the egg. Add all the other ingredients.
4 Spread mixture over the chocolate and then bake in a moderate oven, Gas 3, 325°F, 160°C, for 30–40 minutes.
5 Leave to cool, then cut into slices. Remove from tin when quite cold, and store in an airtight tin in a cool place.

April Menu

TRADITIONAL SUNDAY LUNCH

Our traditional Sunday lunch usually means roast beef and Yorkshire puddings with a hot pudding to follow if it is winter and a cold one in summer. The starter is often something simple like soup or again in summer a good wedge of cold ripe melon. We like the flavour of ginger with melon but not the ground ginger powder. Instead I give everyone a small liqueur glass of ginger wine to pour over the melon. A rib of beef on the bone gives by far the best flavour. However, it is rather more difficult to carve so a boned and rolled sirloin joint is the answer.

Carrot and coriander soup
Roast rib of beef
Roast potatoes
Turnips with orange
Glazed carrots
Gravy
Horseradish sauce
Fruit pie

May

"My wife away to Woolwich in order to get a little air, and to gather May dew" (Samuel Pepys' *Diary*). This tradition of washing your face in dew on the first day of May was carried on in my student days in Edinburgh. Whether any of us became more beautiful, I doubt, but we all ended up with rosy cheeks and wet feet! The maypole tradition, too, is a charming one, and children dance round the maypole on the village green to simple catchy tunes, weaving intricate patterns with their ribbons. Incidentally, it is on occasions such as this that you often find some treasures of home-grown produce, fruit and vegetables picked that morning, especially now, one of the best months for produce in the whole year.

Market Place

Vegetables: asparagus, avocados, broad beans, broccoli, cabbages, carrots, cauliflowers, Chinese leaves, courgettes, cucumbers, greens, lettuce, mangetout, morels, peas, potatoes, radishes, samphire, sorrel, spinach, spring onions, tomatoes, turnips, watercress.
Fruit and nuts: bananas, elderflowers, gooseberries, loquats, pineapples, rhubarb.
Fish: crab, crawfish, haddock, lobster, mackerel, prawns, salmon, sea trout, shrimps, squid, whitebait.
Meat: Beef, chicken, lamb.

Tips and Hints

I freeze a great quantity of fruit and vegetables; so, early in the year, in April and May, I check on what's left. I know it is good sense to keep a list of what's in your freezer and tick off as each item is used up, but it is a New Year resolution which nearly always goes by the board.

This "using up" process is a good excuse to try out new recipes and perhaps be rather more extravagant in everyday eating!

This month asparagus will make the easiest of starters – lightly cooked then served hot with hollandaise or melted salty butter or, cold, with vinaigrette. I like it sprinkled with grated Parmesan too, which sounds rather like heresy! Look out for the very thin stalks called sprue which are a good bargain. Always use asparagus cooking water as the basis for a soup or stock. Thin, crustless slices of bread with soft butter wrapped round a stick of cold cooked asparagus makes the most expensive – and delicious – sandwich I know!

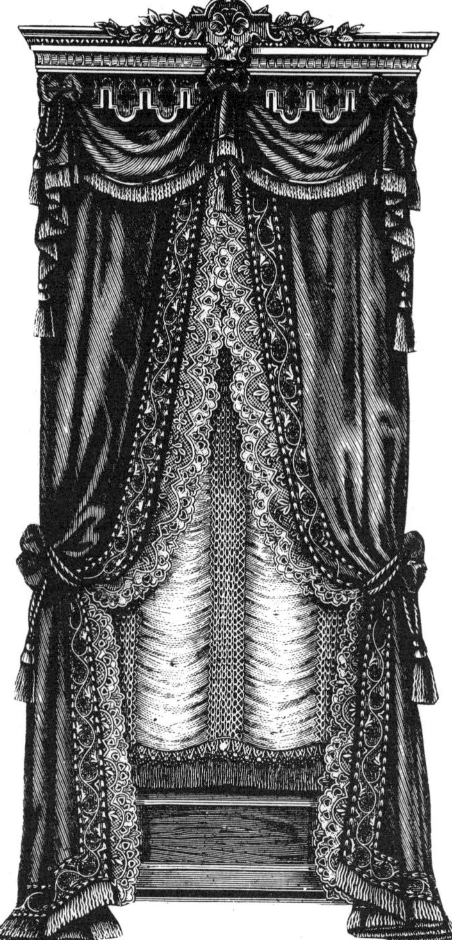

Look out for fresh herbs that will be ready now – dill, chervil, mint and parsley.

Long ago my mother had separate curtains for winter and summer. It was an easy job to get them cleaned and there was no great hurry to get the windows covered up again. Nowadays that luxury has almost gone. One tip, though, is to starch the linings. All my curtains have detachable linings so that as they get older and lose "body", I can wash and starch the linings very stiffly which helps to fill the curtains out again.

RECIPES

SPRING VEGETABLES

We all appreciate fresh young vegetables which need so little cooking and even less seasoning. Soup played a major part in my Scottish childhood and the first spring vegetable soup was looked on with great reverence. Raw vegetables are, of course, wonderfully good too in salads, and as crudités (see page 76). An unusual starter is just a few new potatoes about the size of marbles, boiled in their jackets and served with a good grating of black pepper and butter; new carrots too can be steamed and sprinkled with sesame seeds and some melted butter; tiny broad beans no bigger than a fingernail can be lightly and plainly cooked, tossed in butter and served on top of crunchy lettuce leaves.

PEA AND MINT SOUP

This soup makes a refreshing start to a meal. It may be served chilled, and it also freezes well.

Serves 4

Ingredients

15 g/½ oz butter
1 small onion, peeled and finely chopped
225 g/8 oz peas, fresh or frozen
2 potatoes, peeled and diced
600 ml/1 pint chicken stock
12 stems fresh mint (or 2 teaspoons dried mint)
salt and freshly ground black pepper
a pinch of sugar
whipped cream and sprigs of mint to garnish

Method

1. Melt the butter in a saucepan, add the onion and cook until soft.
2. Add the peas, potatoes, stock, mint and seasonings and bring up to the boil. Cover with a lid and simmer for 25 minutes.
3. Purée the soup in a blender or food processor, then sieve it to remove the mint stems and to ensure it is completely smooth.
4. Reheat the soup and decorate each bowl with a spoonful of whipped cream and a sprig of fresh mint.

STIR-FRY VEGETABLES WITH BEANSPROUTS

Serve as a light meal with brown rice or wholewheat pasta. You could use other spring vegetables such as mangetout, tiny broad beans, broccoli or cauliflower sprigs, courgettes or spring onions.

Serves 4–5

Ingredients

2 tablespoons oil, sesame is best
1 onion, peeled and cut into rings
1 clove garlic, crushed
½–1 teaspoon ground ginger
1 green pepper, thinly sliced
1 large carrot, thinly sliced
1 leek, sliced
125 g/4 oz small button mushrooms
150 ml/¼ pint water
1–2 tablespoons white wine (optional)
1–2 teaspoons soy sauce
225 g/8 oz beansprouts

Method

1. Heat oil in a large frying pan with a lid, then fry onion, garlic and ginger until soft but not brown.
2. Add green pepper and fry for 1 minute more.
3. Toss in carrot and fry 3–4 minutes more, stirring often.
4. Add leek and mushrooms and stir-fry for 3 or 4 minutes more.
5. Stir in water, wine and soy sauce and lay beansprouts on top.
6. Cover pan, bring to boil and simmer very gently for 1 minute before serving.

COURGETTES

A vegetable with a lovely appearance but so delicate a taste that it needs some other flavour with it. Takes only 5 minutes to prepare.

Serves 4

Ingredients

450 g/1 lb courgettes, unpeeled
25 g/1 oz butter
½ clove garlic, crushed
salt and freshly ground black pepper

Method

1 Wash courgettes, trim the ends and cut into even-sized, very fine rings. This can be done very quickly on the mandolin cutter of a grater.
2 Melt butter and fry garlic for 1 minute.
3 Add courgettes and stir over moderate heat so that garlic butter is well distributed. Season with a little salt and plenty of pepper.
4 Put on lid, lower heat and let courgettes just heat through for 3–4 minutes. Shake pan every now and then. Serve at once while the green slices are crisp and still brilliantly green, and not jaded with over-cooking.

GLAZED CARROTS

You could also sprinkle in some thyme leaves, which go well with carrots.

Serves 2

Ingredients

225 g/8 oz baby carrots
1 teaspoon sugar
100 ml/4 fl oz water
a knob of butter
chopped parsley to garnish

Method

1 Scrub the carrots and put them into a pan with the sugar and water. Bring to the boil, cover pan and simmer (making sure the pan does not boil dry) for about 6 minutes or until they are tender, slightly crisp, but not soft.
2 Drain, add butter and stir. Serve sprinkled with chopped parsley.

SPINACH WITH CREAM

Serves 4

Ingredients

1–1.3 kg/2–3 lb fresh spinach
25 g/1 oz butter or margarine
3–4 tablespoons fresh breadcrumbs
2–3 tablespoons single cream
a good grating of whole nutmeg
salt and freshly ground black pepper

Method

1 Trim and wash spinach. Put it in a large saucepan with no extra water. Boil for 4–5 minutes.
2 Meanwhile heat butter or margarine and fry breadcrumbs till golden, stirring often.
3 Drain spinach, chop, drain again and squeeze out moisture.
4 Mix cream, nutmeg, pepper and a little salt into spinach. Put in a warmed dish and sprinkle piping hot breadcrumbs on top. Serve at once.

TURNIPS WITH ORANGE

These are particularly good served with duck or pork.

Serves 4–6

Ingredients
2 oranges
12 young turnips, peeled
salt
50 g/2 oz butter
coarsely ground black pepper

Method

1 Grate rind finely from 1 orange and squeeze juice from them both.
2 Put whole turnips with orange juice in a saucepan. Just cover with water and add a little salt. Bring to the boil, cover pan and simmer until tender, about 20–25 minutes.
3 Drain turnips, saving liquid for soup or gravy, and put into a warmed, buttered, heatproof dish. Put a dab of butter on each and sprinkle all over with grated orange rind and coarse black pepper.
4 Put under a hot grill for 2 minutes to melt butter and crisp and dry the orange rind and tops of turnips.

WHOLE POD BROAD BEANS

If you grow your own beans you will be able to pick them when they are just 7.5–10 cm/3–4 inches long.

Serves 6

Ingredients
900 g/2 lb small broad beans in pod
300 ml/$\frac{1}{2}$ pint chicken stock
4 sprigs mint
25 g/1 oz butter
150 ml/$\frac{1}{4}$ pint double cream
2 tablespoons finely chopped parsley
salt and freshly ground black pepper

Method

1 Top and tail the bean pods and wash. Cook in the chicken stock with the mint sprigs until just tender – about 10 minutes. Drain the beans and return them to the pan.
2 Toss in the butter, and shake well. Pour on the double cream, parsley and seasonings. Serve at once.

GOOSEBERRIES

The gooseberry is much more respected in Britain than anywhere else, perhaps because the fruit is not over-fussy about soil conditions and will thrive practically anywhere. Even in food-conscious France they hardly ever use the fruit and indeed do not even have a special word for it: one name is *groseille à maquereau*, the mackerel currant, and certainly gooseberry sauce with any oily fish is excellent. I pick gooseberries from my three standard bushes when they are small and very hard. I freeze some just as they are, for later purées and jellies, and others I trim to use for jam, fruit tarts or ice cream. Dessert gooseberries which ripen later in the summer have a taste all of their own.

PORTLAND STYLE MACKEREL

To gut and bone a round fish like mackerel, cut off head below gill flaps and slice the belly open from head to tail. Remove the innards. Open the fish out and place on a board, skin up. Press down firmly all along the backbone. Turn over and the backbone should come away fairly easily if you start at the head end.

Serves 4

Ingredients

4 fresh mackerel, boned
wholewheat flour, seasoned with salt and pepper

Gooseberry sauce

225 g/8 oz gooseberries
2 tablespoons water
50 g/2 oz sugar
25 g/1 oz butter
a pinch of nutmeg

Method

1 Pat fish dry and dust with seasoned flour.
2 For the sauce, simmer the gooseberries in the water until tender, then put through a sieve.
3 Return purée to the pan, add sugar and stir over gentle heat till it is dissolved. Add butter and nutmeg and simmer for 5 minutes.
4 Grill the mackerel until golden brown, 4–5 minutes each side. Time varies according to size of fish. Serve immediately, with the sauce separately.

GOOSEBERRY PAVLOVA TART

The meringue on this tart has a crunchy outside and soft marshmallow-like centre. It goes perfectly with the sharp gooseberries. Other fruit could also be used – rhubarb, plums, apples etc.

Serves 6

Ingredients

1 baked 20 cm/8 inch sweet shortcrust pastry flan (see page 116)
50 g/2 oz butter
50 g/2 oz soft brown sugar
450 g/1 lb early gooseberries, topped and tailed
caster sugar
2 large egg whites
1 large egg yolk
25 g/1 oz plain flour, sifted

Method

1 Melt the butter in a heavy pan, then stir in the brown sugar and the gooseberries. Cook briefly, do not stew. Remove from heat and cool.
2 Strain the fruit if it is very juicy, and stir in some caster sugar to taste.
3 Strain again and put the fruit in the pastry case which you have set upon a flat heatproof serving plate.
4 Whisk the egg whites until they are stiff, then fold in the beaten egg yolk, 175 g/6 oz caster sugar and the flour.
5 Pile the mixture on top of the fruit, making sure that it covers and seals to the pastry rim. Bake in a cool oven, Gas 1, 275°F, 140°C, for about 40 minutes until the meringue is lightly coloured. Serve hot or cold and eat the same day.

GOOSEBERRY CRUMBLE

Other fruit can be used as well, adding sugar to taste. Try plums with Barbados sugar, and 125 g/4 oz flour and 65 g/2½ oz brown sugar instead of flour, oats and coconut. Try apples or apples and figs with this topping.

Serves 4

Ingredients

450 g/1 lb gooseberries, topped and tailed
175 g/6 oz caster sugar

Topping

50 g/2 oz wholewheat flour
40 g/1½ oz rolled porridge oats
15 g/½ oz coarse desiccated coconut
50 g/2 oz butter, melted
2–3 drops vanilla essence

Method

1 Rinse the berries and cook gently until the fruit is just cooked and no more. Strain off any juice and stir the sugar into the fruit. Put this mixture in the bottom of a heatproof casserole.
2 Mix all the topping ingredients together and spread this dry mixture over the top of the fruit.
3 Bake in a moderately hot oven, Gas 5, 375°F, 190°C, for 25–30 minutes.

GREEN GOOSEBERRY JAM

For a unique and delicate muscat flavour, you could add some elderflowers to this jam. Wrap about 1½ teacups of elderflowers in muslin and cook with fruit. Lift out before sugar is added, and squeeze out juice into pan.

Yields about 4.5 kg/10 lb

Ingredients

3 kg/6½ lb gooseberries, young and hard
1.2 litres/2 pints water
3 × 1 kg/2.2 lb bags granulated sugar
a knob of butter

Method

1 Top and tail the gooseberries, rinse and dry, and put with the water into a large heavy-based pan or preserving pan.
2 Cook gently until the fruit is pulpy and reduced by about half – 30–35 minutes.
3 Stir in the sugar and stir over a low heat until the sugar has dissolved. Add the butter.
4 Now bring up the heat to a full rolling boil. Boil for about 10 minutes. Test for setting point by dropping about a dessertspoon of jam on to a cold saucer. Allow to cool in the fridge, then push with your finger from one side. If the jam wrinkles, it's ready; if not, boil the jam for a further 5–10 minutes and repeat the test.
5 Remove the pan from the heat and pot the jam into warm clean jars. Cover closely with a waxed disc then allow to cool before covering finally (see page 99).

GOOSEBERRY CURD

Delicious as a filling for tartlets and sponges. Also in meringue baskets, but fill them, of course, at the very last minute. Can be eaten straightaway, but keeps for 6 weeks, preferably in the refrigerator.

Yields 900 g/2 lb

Ingredients

675 g/1½ lb young green gooseberries
300 ml/½ pint water
125 g/4 oz butter
325 g/12 oz sugar
3 eggs

Method

1 There is no need to top and tail the gooseberries. Put them in with the water in a pan, bring to the boil and simmer until pulpy.
2 Place jars to warm in a cool oven, Gas ¼, 225°F, 110°C.
3 Push gooseberries through a nylon sieve, taking care to scrape purée from underside of sieve.
4 Put butter and sugar into a double saucepan or into a basin standing in a pan of simmering water. Stir to dissolve sugar. Add purée.
5 In another bowl, beat eggs but do not whisk. Stir in hot gooseberry mixture, then return to double cooker.
6 Cook, stirring all the time until mixture thickens.
7 Pour into warmed jars. Put a waxed disc on top then, when quite cold, put on jam pot covers (see page 99).

ELDERFLOWERS

The white flowers of the elder, which appear towards the end of May, and the berries which form in autumn, are both highly prized – and they're free! Use the flowers from the green-leaved rather than the yellow-leaved elder, and search up country lanes for the flowers, not beside a busy road where petrol fumes abound. In the past elderberry wine and elderflower tea were said to be good for sore throats, flower lotions for the skin, and the berries were used for such diverse things as hair colourings and dyes for Scottish tartans!

ELDERFLOWER FRITTERS

Pick absolutely perfect flowers with a strong perfume. Strip off the thicker stems, leaving the flowers on short stems and in small bunches.

Serves 6

Ingredients

12 elderflower heads prepared as above
125 g/4 oz plain white flour
2 tablespoons caster sugar
1 large egg, separated
150 ml/¼ pint water
2–3 drops vanilla essence
oil for deep-frying
extra caster sugar

Method

1 Sift the flour into a bowl, and stir in the sugar. Now beat in the egg yolk, water and essence until the batter is smooth.
2 Whisk the egg white until it is very stiff. Fold it into the batter.
3 Heat the oil. Dip the bunches of elderflowers in the batter then shake off the excess. Fry about three bunches at once for 2–3 minutes until lightly browned. Drain, sprinkle with extra sugar and serve at once.

ELDERFLOWER ICE CREAM MILK SHAKE

For this recipe you have to pick each flower off its stem and rinse in a sieve. Reserve a few flowers for decoration.

Serves 4

Ingredients

300 ml/½ pint rich milk
225 g/8 oz plain vanilla ice cream
300 ml/½ pint elderflower "champagne" (see below)
2 heads elderflowers

Method

1 Put the milk, ice cream, elderflower "champagne" and flowers into a blender or processor for about 1 minute.
2 Pour out the foamy drink into four chilled glasses and serve at once with the reserved elderflowers sprinkled on top.

ELDERFLOWER LOTION

One of the best-known properties of elderflowers is their cleansing, softening and soothing action on the skin. The lotion will nourish as well as soften.

Ingredients

enough flowers to fill a breakfast cup
600 ml/1 pint boiling water
2 tablespoons glycerine (buy from the chemist)
1–2 drops pale pink food colour

Method

1 Put the sweetly scented flowers in a bowl. Pour over the boiling water. Stir, cover and leave to infuse overnight.
2 Next day, strain the liquid through a nylon strainer, and bottle into clean bottles. Label and store.
3 When you want to make the lotion, whisk 6 tablespoons of this elderflower water with the glycerine until well blended, then add the food colour. Pour into a small bottle, cover, label and use.

ELDERFLOWER "CHAMPAGNE"

This delicately flavoured and fizzy drink is very refreshing. Serve it chilled with a slice of lemon.

Yields about 4.5 litres/1 gallon

Ingredients

4 large heads elderflowers
4.5 litres/8 pints water
575 g/1¼ lb caster sugar
2 tablespoons white distilled vinegar
2 large lemons

Method

1 Cut off the main stalks of the elderflowers and put the rest in a large bowl (either china or plastic, but not metal). Pour over the water, and add the sugar and vinegar.
2 Squeeze the juice from the lemons, cut into small chunks, then stir into the bowl. Leave covered for at least 24 hours.
3 Strain and pour into airtight screw-capped bottles. Label and store, for about 3 weeks.

May Menu

Birthday Party Dinner

With the beginning of summer, now is the time to move over to a menu which reflects the season – and this birthday menu could be enjoyed by vegetarians and meat-eaters alike. Instead of the soup – which can be prepared in advance and frozen (very useful when you're entertaining) – you could of course serve some of the new asparagus. Instead of making a separate birthday cake, the birthday candles could be pushed into the outside ring of the pavlova. An alternative dessert could be home-made yoghurt with wild honey sprinkled with chopped almonds.

Pea and mint soup
Nut and mushroom loaf
Whole pod broad beans
New potatoes
Gooseberry pavlova tart

June

June is a month rich in home-grown produce, most famously and deliciously new potatoes, asparagus and the strawberries so beloved of sport enthusiasts at Royal Ascot, Wimbledon and the Henley Regatta. The 21st is the longest day of the year, the 24th is Midsummer's Day, and the third Sunday is Father's Day, all candidates for possible celebrations. June is also the month traditionally associated with weddings – "This is the best month to enter marriage state" (*Poor Robin's Almanac* 1683) – and, if numbers are not too large, it's very satisfying to cater for such an occasion. With very careful planning, most things can be done in advance as long as you have plenty of freezer and fridge space, and lots of willing and friendly helping hands!

Market Place

Vegetables: asparagus, aubergines, broad beans, broccoli, cabbages, carrots, cauliflower, Chinese leaves, courgettes, cucumber, fennel, globe artichokes, green beans, lettuce, mangetout, peas, potatoes, radishes, samphire, sorrel, spinach, spring onions, tomatoes, turnips, watercress.
Fruit and nuts: bananas, cherries, gooseberries, grapes, melons, raspberries, strawberries.
Fish: crab, crawfish, haddock, herring, lobster, mackerel, prawns, salmon, sardines, sea bream, sea trout, shrimps, squid, whitebait.
Meat: beef, chicken, lamb.

Tips and Hints

For the most delicious scent and flavour, you can't beat herbs freshly picked from the garden – among them at this time, basil, dill, fennel, mint, parsley, rosemary, tarragon and thyme. The plants will respond to regular picking – for use in salads and other seasonal dishes – by increasing their growth. You can also prepare and freeze some for use in winter when the plants have died down (see pages 139–140 for more details).

One interesting way of freezing herbs is as a savoury butter for making herb bread, or for using as a dressing for steaks, chops, fish or baked potatoes. Beat 25 g/1 oz chopped herb into 50 g/2 oz soft butter, shape into a small sausage, wrap in foil and freeze. Saw off rounds as needed.

Since my family lives in potato country, we only grow early potatoes, and we try to keep some for our Christmas dinner. To do this we fill an old biscuit tin kept specially for this job with the newly dug small potatoes along with the soil sticking to them. The lidded box is immediately put into a hole dug in the soil near our back door, buried, and the spot marked with a stick. The only thing which might defeat us is frozen ground at Christmas, but so far this has never happened.

BASIL

ORIGANUM (MARJORUM)

Make a wonderful "beef" tomato and basil salad by slicing the tomatoes thinly, and mixing with 3–4 fresh, chopped basil leaves, a good French dressing (see page 80), and a teaspoon of finely chopped onion. Leave to marinate for at least an hour.

Sorrel's acidic leaves look like spinach, and are delicious added sparingly to green salads, or made into a soup. Difficult to find in shops, but it's so easy to grow yourself.

Look out for samphire in May and June – from fishmongers or stalls in East Anglia. Known as *salade de mer* in France, it's delicious boiled or steamed until tender then served hot, rather like asparagus, with melted butter.

RECIPES

NEW POTATOES

British new potatoes usually come into the shops in late May and the season goes on until August. (Those that turn up about Christmas are often from Egypt, and are followed by the lovely Jersey potatoes in late April.) Avoid potatoes which look like "new", but are in fact last season's doctored with wet peat. There is absolutely nothing wrong with them, but you may well be paying "new" potato prices.

When buying, choose potatoes which can be scraped easily – test with your thumbnail. Turn out of polythene bags into paper bags; they will keep fresher longer away from the light, which turns skins green. I rarely scrape early potatoes but just wash and scrub in cold water and cut away any blemishes. Boil or steam for a perfect result.

NEW POTATOES

Served in a sweet glaze, these potatoes go well with cold meat like ham, and a crisp green salad.

Serves 4

Ingredients

450 g/1 lb new potatoes, scrubbed
25 g/1 oz butter
25 g/1 oz sugar
2 tablespoons lemon juice

Method

1 Boil potatoes in their jackets until tender.
2 In a clean pan melt butter and sugar and cook gently together until golden.
3 Put in potatoes with or without skins, along with the lemon juice. Turn them over in the glaze until they are coated and light brown.

SCALLOPED NEW POTATOES

Can be made with old potatoes, but choose really waxy ones like Desirée or Dr Mackintosh.

Serves 4

Ingredients

450 g/1 lb new potatoes, scrubbed
125 g/4 oz mushrooms, chopped
15 g/½ oz butter
125 g/4 oz cooked ham, cut in small pieces

Cheese sauce

50 g/2 oz butter
50 g/2 oz plain flour
1 teaspoon made mustard
a grating of nutmeg
600 ml/1 pint milk
50 g/2 oz cheese, grated

Method

1 Steam potatoes or cook them over low heat in a very little water. Then drain and slice.
2 Meanwhile, chop mushrooms and fry for 1 minute in the butter.
3 Make sauce. Melt butter, stir in flour and cook 1 minute. Stir in mustard and nutmeg. Then add milk gradually, stirring as sauce thickens, and simmer for 3 minutes. Stir in cheese and reheat but do not boil.
4 Arrange slices of potato overlapping in a buttered, shallow oven dish. Cover with mushrooms and ham, and pour over the cheese sauce.
5 Bake at top of a moderately hot oven, Gas 6, 400°F, 200°C, for 15 minutes.

POTATO OMELETTE

This is the Spanish Tortilla. You'll need a heavy frying pan about 23 cm/9 inches in diameter.

Serves 2–3

Ingredients
275 g/10 oz new potatoes, scraped
about 200 ml/7 fl oz olive oil
1 clove garlic (optional)
1 small onion, peeled and chopped
3 large eggs, lightly beaten
sea salt and freshly ground black pepper

Method

1 Chop potatoes into 1 cm/½ inch cubes. Rinse and dry.
2 Heat the oil and fry the peeled garlic clove for a minute, then remove.
3 Put potato cubes into hot oil and cook gently until soft, turning occasionally. Towards the end of the cooking add onion. Do not let oil get too hot.
4 Remove potatoes and onion and mix gently with eggs.
5 Pour off oil, leaving a light film in pan, and heat again. Put in the mixture of eggs, potato and onion and cook gently until the underside is cooked but not too brown and the top is still moist. Season well with salt and pepper.
6 Traditionally the tortilla is turned over at this point. It is inverted on to a large plate, then slid back into the pan, cooked-side uppermost. That is the correct way to do it but a satisfactory method is to put the frying pan and its contents under a hot grill for a couple of minutes. The aim is to serve the tortilla with the centre just a little moist.

NEW POTATO SALAD I

Can be made with leftover potatoes.

Serves 4

Ingredients
450 g/1 lb new potatoes, scrubbed
a little boiling water
1 very small onion, peeled
1 tablespoon mayonnaise (see page 76)
2 tablespoons milk or, if using a bland mayonnaise, 1 tablespoon milk and 1 tablespoon cider vinegar
½ teaspoon sugar (try dark cane)
sea salt and freshly ground black pepper
chopped mint
chopped parsley

Method

1 Put the potatoes in a pan with a good lid. Add a very little boiling water. Bring to the boil, then turn heat very low. Simmer and steam potatoes for 10–12 minutes until done but still firm. Drain and cool.
2 Meanwhile, chop onion very small and put in a serving bowl with the mayonnaise and milk (or milk and vinegar). Add sugar and a very little salt and pepper.
3 Stir in as much chopped mint as you can spare, and a little chopped parsley.
4 Cut potatoes into quarters or thick rings and then mix into the dressing until the pieces are nicely coated.

NEW POTATO SALAD II

For more substantial salads, you could add any of the following to the basic salad below: cubes of garlic sausage; strips of green pepper; some tuna fish, drained and chopped.

Serves 4

Ingredients
450 g/1 lb new potatoes, scrubbed
4 tablespoons French dressing (see page 80)
chopped chives or spring onion tops

Method

1 Steam potatoes or cook as above, then drain, skin and slice when they have cooled down a bit.
2 Meanwhile, mix dressing ingredients together, then toss the potato, while still hot, in the dressing, adding chives or spring onion tops.

STRAWBERRIES

Why do we love strawberries so much? Is it because they are a challenge to grow and to gather, or is it because of their wonderful colour and flavour? They're perfectly partnered by cream, and I like to serve them whole with the green calyx attached, each guest having a small pot of slightly sweetened whipped cream into which to dunk the fruit. You could also serve them fresh and whole as the filling for a flan case, pavlova or meringue, or the shortbread biscuits opposite. For not quite perfect fruit, cut each berry in two, cutting away any blemishes, and put into a glass bowl with a sprinkling of sugar on each layer. Tumble the fruit about gently, and a lovely syrup will form. I like to sprinkle Maraschino (a liqueur made from a bitter black cherry) over the fruit as well – but don't over-do it! Whole strawberries do not freeze well – their substance and flavour change too much. However, fresh strawberry purée will defrost very tastily.

STRAWBERRY SURPRISE

A surprise because the flavour usually baffles guests – a nice talking point!

Serves 4

Ingredients

675 g/$1\frac{1}{2}$ lb ripe strawberries

Sauce

175 g/6 oz raspberries
25 g/1 oz caster sugar
1 tablespoon fresh lemon juice
75 ml/3 fl oz Crème de Cassis (blackcurrant liqueur)
4 tiny sprigs fresh mint

Method

1 Hull and rinse the strawberries and dry them carefully. Divide between four large wine glasses.
2 To make the sauce, liquidize the raspberries with the sugar, lemon juice and Cassis. Pass through a very fine sieve to eliminate the seeds. If the sauce is very thick, just add 1–2 teaspoons cold water.
3 Just before serving, pour the sauce over the strawberries. Decorate with a tiny sprig of mint.

STRAWBERRY JAM

Yields 4.5 kg/10 lb

Ingredients

3.5 kg/$7\frac{1}{2}$ lb small, firm, almost under-ripe strawberries
6 tablespoons fresh lemon juice
3 × 1 kg/$2\frac{1}{4}$ lb bags preserving sugar
a knob of butter

Method

1 Hull and wipe the fruit if necessary and put in a preserving pan or a very large heavy-based saucepan.
2 Simmer gently in their own juices until soft and pulpy. Mash down the fruit to extract the pectin in order to get a good set. Go on simmering until the volume has diminished by half and you have a very thick pulp. Stirring is important to prevent the fruit sticking.
3 Stir in the lemon juice, sugar and the butter and stir to dissolve the sugar.
4 Turn up the heat and bring to a full rolling boil (the mixture will spit and you will understand the need for a large pan). Boil for 15–20 minutes then cold saucer test for a set (see page 20). If it is ready, and wrinkles on top, then give your jam a final 2 minutes' boiling and remove from the heat. Allow to stand until a thin skin forms on the surface. (This should prevent the fruit rising in the jars.) Stir the jam gently. Pot in warm jars and cover in the usual way (see page 99).

STRAWBERRY SHORTCAKES

These shortbread biscuits can be served as biscuits, or can be turned into individual strawberry puddings. I serve mine with a sauce made out of frozen or fresh strawberries, lightly sweetened and liquidized. Don't forget, though, that the sauce is made from fruit which is not cooked and will need to be eaten within 3 days. The biscuit mixing can be done by hand or with an electric mixer, and it freezes well.

Makes about 40 biscuits (or 18 pairs)

Ingredients

225 g/8 oz unsalted or slightly salted butter, softened
4 oz caster sugar
325 g/12 oz plain white flour, sifted

Filling

whipped double cream
fresh strawberries
icing sugar
sauce made from frozen or fresh strawberries (see above)

Method

1 Put softened butter in a warm bowl, and beat in 125 g/4 oz sugar and the flour. Work mixture together thoroughly. If using an electric mixer, warm the bowl, put all ingredients in together and beat until mixture looks like damp breadcrumbs.
2 Knead the crumbs together by hand and form into a very fat sausage about 7.5 cm/3 inches across. Wrap this in foil or cling film and put into the fridge to firm up.
3 Using a very sharp knife, cut thin slices from the roll not more than 6 mm/$\frac{1}{4}$ inch thick (or even less). From these slices and using *two* biscuit cutters (7.5 cm/3 inches and 5 cm/2 inches) cut out your biscuits. The trimmings just have to be gathered up and re-rolled. You should finish with an equal number of small and bigger biscuits.
4 Place the biscuits on greased baking trays, or trays lined with non-stick baking paper and bake above middle of a cool oven, Gas 2, 300°F, 150°C, for about 30 minutes until golden. Take care not to overbake or the biscuits will develop a bitter taste.
5 Remove from oven and dredge with some caster sugar while still hot (this is for the biscuits only). Leave on trays to firm up. Then slide on to a wire rack to cool. When cold, store in airtight tins and remove from tins just before serving.
6 To fill the shortcakes, set the small biscuits on a flat surface and sift icing sugar through a sieve to cover the surface thickly. Do not move the biscuits until needed.
7 Set the bigger biscuits on a flat serving dish and pipe or spoon a ring of whipped double cream on top of each.
8 Slice the strawberries in two or four depending on size. (Reserve some small ones with the green calyx still on and slice these in two so that each piece has a green bit for decoration.)
9 Set the sliced strawberries round the outside edge of the cream on the biscuits. Have the pointed bits towards the centre. Balance the icing-sugar-dredged smaller biscuits on top, and decorate with a strawberry half. Serve with a little sauce poured round each biscuit tower.

STRAWBERRY MILK SHAKE

Serves 2

Ingredients

300 ml/$\frac{1}{2}$ pint good milk
1 tablespoon home-made strawberry jam
2 tablespoons crushed ice
3–4 fresh strawberries, chopped

Method

1 Put all the ingredients into a blender and process until foamy.
2 Pour into two tall chilled glasses. Drink at once.

STRAWBERRY BOATS

Filled with confectioners' custard and topped with sliced glazed strawberries, these tartlets are superb. Serve two each as a glamorous dessert.

Makes 12 boats

Ingredients

75 g/3 oz sweet shortcrust pastry (see page 116)
225 g/8 oz perfect fresh strawberries
4 tablespoons redcurrant jelly

Confectioner's custard

300 ml/½ pint milk
1 vanilla pod, or ½ teaspoon vanilla essence
1 egg, plus 1 egg yolk
50 g/2 oz caster sugar
25 g/1 oz plain flour, sifted

Method

1. Roll out the pastry thinly and use to line twelve 10 cm/4 inch boat-shaped tartlet tins. I find the easiest way to do this is to cut pastry rectangles. Brush each tin with oil or melted fat and press in each piece of pastry, trying not to stretch it. Trim off the surplus and use to line more tins.
2. Chill the raw tartlet cases, then prick the pastry well and bake in a moderately hot oven, Gas 5, 375°F, 190°C, for about 10–12 minutes. Keep checking them and if any pastry starts to rise up in a bubble, prick it with a knife point. Allow to cool in the tins then move them to a wire tray. Store when cold in an airtight tin.
3. Now make the custard. Put the milk and vanilla pod in a pan and bring up to boiling point. Remove the pan from the heat and set aside to infuse for about 30 minutes.
4. In a small bowl beat together the egg, egg yolk and the sugar. Add the flour and mix until smooth.
5. Remove the vanilla pod from the milk, wash and set aside to dry. Reheat the milk until almost boiling. Pour some on to the egg mixture, stir well and return to the pan. Over a low heat continue to cook and stir for about 3 minutes or until the custard thickens. Leave aside to cool. (An old tip to prevent a skin forming on the surface was to sprinkle over a fine layer of sugar which can be stirred in when needed.)
6. Spoon a little custard into each tartlet. Slice the strawberries into three or four slices cutting from the top down. Lay them neatly in each tart in overlapping slices.
7. To glaze the fruit put the redcurrant jelly in a bowl and set it in a pan of simmering water. Allow it to melt then to cool down again to a sticky consistency. Brush the fruit with the melted jelly.

A SUMMER BUFFET

A buffet can be served as a lunch, a dinner or indeed as a meal to celebrate a wedding or similar festive occasion. It's one of the easier ways to entertain, as dishes can be prepared in advance and, if the weather is its seasonal best, served cold. Most recipes suitable for a buffet can be doubled or trebled without too much worry.

Good starters are chilled soups, little mousses as overleaf, or crudités (see page 76). At a buffet serve soups in tiny bowls, or medium coffee cups, which will stretch the recipes.

For a main course, nothing is simpler or more delicious than a whole poached or baked salmon. A 2.7–3 kg/6–7 lb fish will feed twelve easily. Poach it in court-bouillon (see below) for 8–10 minutes per 450 g/1 lb, or wrap loosely in buttered foil and bake in a cool oven, Gas 1–2, 275–300°F, 140–150°C, for 1 hour for the first 2.25 kg/5 lb, then a further 12 minutes per 450 g/1 lb for anything over. When cold, skin and decorate with aspic or with thin cucumber slices overlapping to look like scales. You could also offer main course salads of chicken or meat (see pages 70–71). Serve with new potatoes and lots of vegetable salads (see pages 60–61 and 81–82).

Any seasonal pudding would be appropriate – the meringue one here, one of the strawberry puddings on pages 62–64, or simply fresh fruit and cream.

TO DECORATE WITH ASPIC

Skin a whole cooked salmon first, and bone it carefully. Lay out on a huge platter or plastic tray. First, organize your decorations – usually "floral" – which can be all sorts of coloured things. Cut carrots into wafer-thin circles, then cut into petal shapes; cut the skin off peppers, shaving it as finely as you can, then cut into petal shapes with tiny biscuit cutters; cut small fans from thinly shaved lemon peel. Use herbs like tarragon for "flower leaves" and chives (snipped in half lengthwise) as "stems".

Using packets of aspic, make the jelly up as per the packet instructions, but using a proportion of dry white wine instead of water (about 120 ml/4 fl oz per packet). Allow the jelly to cool until thick but still liquid. Spoon some jelly over each steak or over a whole fish, trying to avoid too much going down the sides. Allow this first layer to set, then decorate each steak or the whole fish with "flowers". Dip each piece in the liquid jelly using eyebrow tweezers, and then arrange. Leave this to set before spooning on a second layer of aspic. (If the aspic starts to set, return it to a gentle heat, but do not stir: just *shake* the pan).

COURT-BOUILLON

Ingredients

900 ml/$1\frac{1}{2}$ pints cold water
300 ml/$\frac{1}{2}$ pint dry white wine
1 Spanish onion, peeled and sliced
2 sticks celery, chopped
1 bay leaf
2 sprigs thyme
salt and freshly ground black pepper

Method

1 Mix all the ingredients in an appropriate pan (a salmon poacher for a whole fish, a roasting tin or similar for steaks), and bring to the boil. Reduce heat and simmer for 15 minutes.
2 Place the whole fish or steaks carefully in the pan, cover and simmer for the recommended time. Lift out carefully and leave to get cold.

MINTED CUCUMBER MOUSSE

This is the recipe, doubled, which won Simon Dunn (14) third place in the 1987 Junior Cook of the Year, organized by the Young Cooks Club of Great Britain.

Serves 6

Ingredients

15 cm/6 inch piece firm crisp cucumber, peeled and very finely diced
salt
3 level teaspoons powdered gelatine
100 ml/4 fl oz chicken stock
225 g/8 oz soft cream cheese
2 pinches mace
2 tablespoons finely chopped fresh mint
4 teaspoons wine or cider vinegar
2 teaspoons caster sugar
100 ml/4 fl oz double cream
2 egg whites
a little oil
cucumber curls and mint to decorate

Method

1 Put cucumber in a nylon sieve over a bowl and sprinkle with salt. Leave to drain for 30 minutes, then rinse well in cold water and dry thoroughly on kitchen paper.
2 In a small saucepan, sprinkle the powdered gelatine over the chicken stock. Leave it for a few minutes, then gently warm it until the gelatine has dissolved. Set aside to cool a little.
3 Beat the cream cheese with the mace, mint, vinegar, sugar and gelatine mixture. Stir in the chopped cucumber and put the bowl aside until the mixture just begins to set.
4 Whip cream and fold into the cucumber mixture.
5 Whisk the egg whites until stiff and fold in as well.
6 Lightly oil a ring mould or six small ramekins. Pour in the cucumber mousse and chill until set.
7 Turn out and decorate with cucumber curls and sprigs of mint. Serve with fingers of hot buttered toast.

HAZELNUT MERINGUE GÂTEAU

Try your own fillings too, such as fresh raspberries or strawberries, or sliced pears. You could also use walnuts, ground and whole, instead of hazelnuts.

The gâteau bases keep well in an airtight tin before filling and decorating. Also, when filled and decorated, they may be frozen successfully, and will thaw quite quickly.

Serves 4

Ingredients

3 large egg whites
a pinch of salt
175 g/6 oz granulated sugar
75 g/3 oz ground hazelnuts
40 g/1½ oz fine semolina

To fill and decorate

150–200 ml/5–7 fl oz double or whipping cream
50 g/2 oz chopped hazelnuts
a few whole hazelnuts
15 g/½ oz plain cooking chocolate

Method

1 Line the base of two 18 cm/7 inch sandwich tins with rounds of Bakewell paper or greased, greaseproof paper (see page 29).
2 Beat egg whites with salt till firm, then add 75 g/3 oz of the sugar and beat again.
3 In another bowl, mix remaining sugar with ground hazelnuts and semolina. Fold this mixture into the egg whites.
4 Divide mixture between the tins, spread it evenly and smooth the tops, then bake in a moderate oven, Gas 4, 350°F, 180°C, for 25–30 minutes until crisp and golden.
5 Turn meringues out of tins to cool on a wire rack, then, when quite cold, sandwich with whipped cream.
6 Spread cream round the sides and roll in chopped nuts.
7 Pipe cream roses on top and decorate with whole hazelnuts. Finish with decorations of grated chocolate.

WATERCRESS AND GRAPEFRUIT SALAD

Serves 4, but can easily be expanded

Ingredients

25 g/1 oz shelled hazelnuts
1 large grapefruit
1 small lettuce, washed and dried
1 bunch watercress, washed and dried

Method

1 To roast hazelnuts, put them in a shallow tin in a moderate oven, Gas 4, 350°F, 180°C, for 10 minutes. Or put them under grill, turning often. Then rub the skins from them and chop coarsely.
2 Peel and segment grapefruit and chop flesh into bowl.
3 Break lettuce and watercress into small pieces. Toss with grapefruit and put in a salad bowl. Sprinkle hazelnuts over the top.

June Menu

BUFFET LUNCH

For numbers over ten, it's always easiest to prepare cold dishes, with the centrepiece something like a whole poached (or baked) salmon. Everything can be done in advance, covered and chilled, and all you have to do on the day itself is arrange things beautifully on your buffet table. Decorate this too, with a pretty cloth, and lots of fresh flowers around, particularly if for a wedding.

Salted almonds
Minted cucumber mousse
Whole poached or baked salmon
New potatoes
Green salad
Watercress and grapefruit salad
Hazelnut meringue gâteau
Strawberry surprise
Cheese and grapes
Coffee and Florentines

July

Excluding the annual holiday, with the children at home for the summer, the thing most often on Mum's mind (and theirs) seems to be food! With my children grown up and away I tend to forget just how much it takes to stoke up active teenagers. Luckily, however, there is a wealth of wonderful fresh foodstuffs available this month, which can be turned into filling and nourishing meals for everyone.

There are several anniversaries in July: the Americans celebrate Independence Day on the 4th, and the French, Bastille Day on the 14th. Both conjure up all sorts of food ideas which, if the weather is good enough, can be enjoyed outside.

Market Place

Vegetables: aubergines, beetroot, broad beans, broccoli, cabbage, carrots, cauliflowers, celery, Chinese leaves, courgettes, cucumbers, garlic, globe artichokes, green beans, lettuces, mangetout, peas, peppers, potatoes, radishes, spring onions, sweetcorn, tomatoes, watercress.
Fruit and nuts: apricots, bilberries, blackberries, blackcurrants, blueberries, cherries, gooseberries, grapes, loganberries, mangoes, melons, nectarines, peaches, raspberries, redcurrants, strawberries, whitecurrants.
Fish: Dover sole, grey mullet, haddock, halibut, herring, lobster, plaice, prawns, red mullet, salmon, sardines, sea bass, sea bream, sea trout, shrimps, squid, whitebait.
Meat: beef, chicken, guinea fowl, lamb.

Tips and Hints

Pasta, rice and noodles are great fillers for a hungry family. Whenever I cook any of them, I double or even treble the quantity so that I can freeze portions for future meals. (I simply turn the frozen bag out into a pan of boiling water, or use my microwave.)

July is *the* month for soft fruit, and if you grow your own, you should freeze some. All freeze well with the exception of strawberries (which defrost into a mush, and are better frozen as a purée). Always gather the fruit on a dry day as wet fruits become mouldy very quickly. (See pages 138–139 for further information on freezing fruit.)

If freezing soft fruit for jam-making later, remember that the pectin content – which makes the jam set well – diminishes with freezing, so always add 10 per cent more frozen fruit than the recipe states.

This is also a good time of year to pickle vegetables like cauliflower (see page 100.) I also like to pickle two or three tiny jars of nasturtium seeds, as they make a perfect substitute for capers, and can be used in a caper sauce for fish, or sprinkled over salads or pizzas. Gathering the seeds is a good job for the children!

B*uying* cold meats for salads is fraught with risk. Meat which has been cooked, pressed, and then sliced wafer-thin on a machine has lost something at each stage. Always try to prepare your own, or buy from a good shop where the meat is sliced by hand.

Ox tongue is easy. Buy it from your butcher already brined (it is against the law to sell otherwise), boil for 3–4 hours with vegetables, skin, press into a soufflé dish until set and slice cold – far superior to prepacked slices.

RECIPES

MAIN-COURSE SALADS

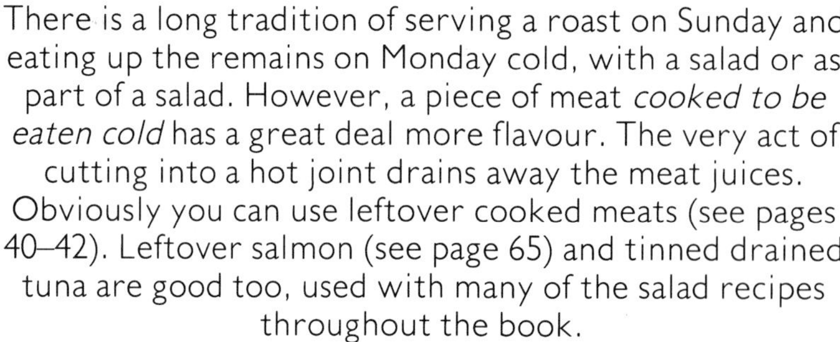

There is a long tradition of serving a roast on Sunday and eating up the remains on Monday cold, with a salad or as part of a salad. However, a piece of meat *cooked to be eaten cold* has a great deal more flavour. The very act of cutting into a hot joint drains away the meat juices. Obviously you can use leftover cooked meats (see pages 40–42). Leftover salmon (see page 65) and tinned drained tuna are good too, used with many of the salad recipes throughout the book.

The *Farmhouse Kitchen* cookery series has always tried to keep alive the old cookery traditions, but many butchers no longer brine meat for their customers (or pickle it, depending on which part of the country you come from). They tell me no one wants it. However you can always ask or have a go yourself – see the beef recipe following.

SALT BEEF

This is an excellent brine for silverside or brisket, and it can be used again. It is worth doing a large piece while you are about it: 1.8–2.7 kg/4–6 lb piece is ideal. This will serve 8–10 people. (A piece of frozen meat can be done straight from the freezer without thawing.) Salt beef can be eaten hot or cold. If to be eaten cold press it lightly after cooking in a tight-fitting dish, and keep the excess liquid for stock.

Ingredients

a piece of beef as above
2 onions, peeled, stuck with 2–3 cloves
2–3 carrots, sliced
a bouquet garni (see page 144)
5–6 peppercorns

Brine

4 litres/7 pints water
675 g/$1\frac{1}{2}$ lb coarse salt
450 g/1 lb dark brown sugar (Barbados or muscovado)
50 g/2 oz saltpetre (from chemist)
1 bay leaf
1 sprig thyme
10 juniper berries, crushed
10 black peppercorns, crushed

Method

1. Put all brine ingredients in a large saucepan, bring to the boil and boil hard for 5 minutes. Then leave to cool.
2. Strain the brine into a crock or a polythene bucket, and put it in a cool place. Immerse the meat and leave it for 7–10 days or longer.
3. To cook the salt beef, take meat out of brine and rinse in cold water. If it has been in brine over 10 days steep it in plenty of cold
4. Put meat in a large pan, cover with cold water and bring it to the boil. If water tastes salty throw it away and start again with fresh.
5. Add the onions, carrots, bouquet garni and peppercorns to the pan, bring slowly to the boil and cover. Just simmer, allowing 30 minutes per 450 g/1 lb and 30 minutes over.

FOREHOCK OF BACON

A big joint for a special occasion, to be served cold. Remember to start the night before. Boil up the bones separately for more stock, which makes excellent soup.

Serves 10–12

Ingredients

1 forehock of bacon, weighing about 3.25 kg/7 lb before cooking
3 level tablespoons demerara sugar
2 sprigs rosemary, or 1 teaspoon dried
whole cloves

Method

1 The forehock should be soaked first, then boned. Soak it overnight in cold water then, working on the underside of the joint, take a small sharp knife and cut off rib bones. Slit meat down to the inner bones and work round them to expose completely. Remove them.
2 To prepare and cook, sprinkle inside of meat with 2 tablespoons of the demerara sugar. Tie up joint with string at 5 cm/2 inch intervals.
3 Weigh joint and calculate boiling time at 25 minutes per 450 g/1 lb.
4 Put joint in a pan, cover with water, and add rosemary. Bring slowly to the boil. Simmer gently for the calculated time. Leave in the cooking water until cool enough to handle.
5 Skin carefully and score fat in a lattice pattern. Press a clove in each "box" and sprinkle on the last tablespoon of sugar.
6 Set under a pre-heated grill until brown and bubbly. Leave to get cold, then slice and serve with assorted salads.

COLD BONED, STUFFED ROAST CHICKEN

Serves 4–6

Ingredients

1 cold stuffed chicken (see page 41)

Coating sauce

50 g/2 oz butter
50 g/2 oz plain flour
450 ml/¾ pint milk
25 g/1 oz powdered gelatine
150 ml/¼ pint water
2 tablespoons top of the milk, or cream
salt and freshly ground black pepper

Method

1 Melt the butter, add flour and allow to sizzle without browning for 1–2 minutes. Pour on milk, and stir until boiling, then simmer 1–2 minutes, stirring continuously.
2 Dissolve gelatine in the water. Reserve 1 tablespoon of it in a cup and add the rest to the sauce with cream and seasoning.
3 Put through a fine sieve, or even a clean, damp tea cloth, to be sure sauce is completely smooth. Stir frequently whilst cooling to keep the sauce smooth and velvety. When the consistency of thick cream, it is ready for coating.
4 Place the cold bird on a wire tray over a dish, and remove strings and skin. Pour over the coating sauce. Allow to set. Give another coating if necessary (the sauce may need rewarming for this).
5 Decorate with the small cuttings of colourful vegetables, peels etc., first dipping the pieces in the reserved dissolved gelatine which will stop them slipping off.

HONOLULU CHICKEN

Easy to expand to serve more. A rice salad and a tomato and cucumber salad make excellent partners.

Serves 2

Ingredients

20 g/¾ oz butter
50 g/2 oz whole blanched almonds
salt and freshly ground black pepper
150 ml/¼ pint mayonnaise (page 76)
1 teaspoon lemon juice
225 g/8 oz cooked chicken, chopped
2 sticks celery, chopped
2 rings canned pineapple, chopped
a pinch of sugar

Method

1 Melt the butter in a pan, add the nuts and cook until golden brown. Drain on kitchen paper, then sprinkle with a little salt and leave to cool.
2 Put the mayonnaise and lemon juice in a bowl and add the bite-sized chicken pieces, celery, pineapple, nuts and seasonings.
3 Toss all the ingredients together and serve in a bowl lined with some lettuce leaves.

PEAS AND BEANS

Frozen peas have just about knocked out the market for fresh peas, and unless you grow or pick your own, that distinct flavour of freshly podded and lightly cooked peas will be unknown to you. Peas always look good mixed with other vegetables as in a macedoine of chopped vegetables like carrot, turnip etc. Tomatoes look good when stuffed with peas and sweetcorn mixed. Cooked peas often go into the middle layer of my cottage pies, and they also go into a starter I do in scallop shells, with mussels, haddock, parsley in a fish sauce and piped round with creamed potatoes. Beans can be either broad beans (see also page 52), French beans or the bigger runner or snap beans (because that is what they should do if they are really fresh and crisp). Wonderful vegetables!

SAVOURY JELLY RING

This always looks very nice on a buffet table.

Serves 6 as a starter

Ingredients

125 g/4 oz Quark or any low-fat cream cheese
175 g/6 oz soft cream cheese
4 tablespoons garlic mayonnaise (see page 76)
125 g/4 oz cucumber, grated or finely chopped
75 g/3 oz cooked peas
4 spring onions, cleaned and chopped small
2 large celery stalks, stringed and chopped finely
salt and freshly ground black pepper
1 tablespoon lemon juice
2 tablespoons water
15 g/½ oz powdered gelatine (1 envelope)

Method

1 Put the Quark, cream cheese and mayonnaise in a blender and make smooth. Turn this out into a bowl.
2 Stir the cucumber, peas, onions and celery into the cream cheese mixture. Now season well with salt and pepper.
3 Put the lemon juice and water in a small bowl and sprinkle the gelatine over the surface. Set the bowl in a pan of simmering water and stir. When the gelatine has dissolved, fold into the vegetable mixture.
4 Spoon into a 600 ml/1 pint ring mould and chill until set.

PEA POD SOUP

Serves 4

Ingredients

50 g/2 oz butter
1 large onion, peeled and chopped
575 g/1¼ lb empty young pea pods, roughly chopped
1 litre/1¾ pints chicken stock
2 sprigs fresh mint
1 bay leaf
150 ml/¼ pint single cream
salt and freshly ground black pepper
2 tablespoons chopped fresh mint

Method

1 Melt the butter in a roomy pan, add the onion and cook gently for about 3 minutes.
2 Add the pea pods, stock, mint sprigs and bay leaf. Bring to a boil and simmer for about 1 hour.
3 Remove the bay leaf and mint, and liquidize everything else in a blender or processor. Now put the soup through a sieve to strain out all the pea pod strings and tough bits.
4 Reheat the purée and stir in the cream and seasonings. Serve hot with a generous sprinkling of mint over each bowl.

PEAS, BACON AND ONION

Cooked broad beans and other varieties of green beans can be cooked as in this recipe.

Serves 4

Ingredients
15 g/$\frac{1}{2}$ oz butter
4 rashers streaky smoked bacon, rinded and chopped
450 g/1 lb onions, peeled and chopped
225 g/8 oz cooked peas
salt and freshly ground black pepper

Method

1 In a frying pan melt the butter and fry the bacon for 2 minutes, before adding the onion. Continue cooking until the onion is soft, about 6–8 minutes.
2 Stir in the peas, and season. Heat up again and serve.

SPICED PEAS AND CABBAGE

Serves 4

Ingredients
3 tablespoons vegetable oil
2 tablespoons cumin seeds
2 dried bay leaves, broken up
225 g/8 oz cooked peas
1 level teaspoon curry powder
$\frac{1}{2}$ teaspoon turmeric
75 ml/3 fl oz chicken stock
450 g/1 lb cabbage, shredded
2 tablespoons natural yoghurt
salt and freshly ground black pepper

Method

1 In a roomy pan heat the oil and gently fry the cumin seeds and bay leaves. Add the peas, curry powder, turmeric and stock. Stir well and cook for 5–6 minutes.
2 Steam or boil the cabbage until tender. Drain, season with salt and pepper, then add the yoghurt.
3 Mix everything together and reheat. Pick out the bay leaves and serve.

BROAD BEAN PURÉE

This is a recipe for huge beans which have really tough skins. You can shell them before or after cooking.

Serves 4

Ingredients
900 g/2 lb large broad beans, podded
25 g/1 oz butter
$\frac{1}{2}$ clove garlic, crushed
65 ml/2$\frac{1}{2}$ fl oz single cream (or more)
salt, black pepper, a fat pinch of mace

Method

1 Cook the beans in lightly salted water until very soft. Drain and cool.
2 Put the beans (after removing the shells) into a liquidizer along with the butter, garlic, cream, salt, pepper and mace. Process until smooth. Add more cream so that the purée is soft. Reheat carefully in a double saucepan.

FRENCH BEAN SALAD

Serves 4

Ingredients
450 g/1 lb French beans

Dressing
4 tablespoons tomato juice
2 tablespoons salad oil
1 tablespoon fresh lemon juice
$\frac{1}{2}$ teaspoon caster sugar
1 small clove garlic, crushed
1 tablespoon finely chopped onion
salt and freshly ground black pepper

Method

1 Top, tail and chop the beans, then cook in salted water until just done, and drain.
2 Mix the dressing ingredients and pour over the beans. Allow to marinate for at least 2 hours, and serve cold.

SOFT FRUIT PUDDINGS

No country can compete with the variety of puddings which are traditional to us. Soft fruit time gives us the chance to show off some of the best – especially the summer pudding below. You can eat most soft fruit on its own, raw, with yoghurt, custard or ice cream, but often it is a good idea just to warm it through to start the juices running, and then allow it to cool again. All, apart from strawberries, just need a little water added and some sugar.

SUMMER PUDDING

Serves 6–8

Ingredients
225 g/8 oz redcurrants
125 g/4 oz blackcurrants
450 g/1 lb raspberries
150 g/5 oz caster sugar, or to taste
a little butter
8 slices medium-cut white bread, crusts removed

Method

1 First of all prepare the fruit. Take the currants, separately, off the stalks with a fork, pulling downwards so that the berries drop into a bowl beneath. Check over the raspberries. Cook the blackcurrants over a gentle heat first then add the sugar and the rest of the fruit. Cook only until the sugar is melted and the fruit soft but not mushy. Set aside to cool.
2 Now grease a 900 ml/1½ pint traditional pudding basin well with soft butter, then line it with the bread. Overlap the edges and make sure the bottom is well covered too. Press the edges together.
3 Strain off some of the juice and put the cold fruit into the "bread" bowl. Cover the top with another slice of bread and trim so that it is a good fit. Find a saucer which will fit inside the bowl and on top of the pudding. Put a weight on the saucer – a tin of beans, for instance – and put the whole lot into the fridge overnight.
4 Immediately before serving turn the pudding out on to a large dish which will not overflow with all the juice. Pour over the reserved juice. Serve with thick whipped and sweetened cream.

FRUIT BRÛLÉE

This really is not a proper brûlée, but it does taste wonderfully rich. Other fruits can be used instead of strawberries – try peaches with a little peach brandy, or raspberries with some Framboise.

Serves 4

Ingredients
325 g/12 oz fresh firm strawberries, hulled and sliced
4 teaspoons orange liqueur
50 g/2 oz flaked almonds
250 ml/8 fl oz soured cream
4–5 tablespoons demerara sugar

Method

1 First divide the sliced strawberries between four small heatproof ramekins. Pour 1 teaspoon of liqueur in each ramekin, and sprinkle the almonds over the top in a neat layer.
2 Whip the soured cream until stiff, then spoon on top of the fruit and nuts. Set the pots in the fridge to firm up.
3 Heat the grill. Sprinkle each pot with a thick layer of demerara sugar. Put the pots on a baking tray and slip under the grill until sugar starts to melt. Set aside to cool down. Serve chilled.

ICE CREAM

Fresh fruit may be used to flavour this ice cream instead of vanilla essence. First make a purée of the fruit. A cupful is enough for the quantity of ice cream made in this recipe.

Serves 3–4

Ingredients
2 eggs, separated
a few drops of vanilla essence
150 ml/¼ pint double cream
50 g/2 oz icing sugar

Method

1 Beat egg yolks and vanilla together. (If using fruit purée it is added later; leave out vanilla.)
2 Whip the cream, and beat egg whites and icing sugar together.
3 Combine all three mixtures and beat again. (If using fruit purée fold it in now.)
4 Pour mixture into a freezer tray with lid and freeze.

HOME-MADE YOGHURT

The easiest way to make yoghurt is to buy a kit. However, by trial and error you can make it without special equipment, especially if you have a warm place in which to set or thicken it such as an airing cupboard or gas oven with pilot light. So many factors affect yoghurt in the making that everybody has to experiment.

You can use pasteurised milk, homogenised or UHT, and sterilised milk. However, the flavour and thickness will vary – e.g. UHT and sterilised milk give a thinner yoghurt.

For an instant and delicious summer dessert, mix some soft fruit into your own yoghurt.

Ingredients
600 ml/1 pint milk
1 tablespoon dried skimmed milk (optional, but makes yoghurt thicker and creamier)
1 tablespoon natural yoghurt, bought or home-made

Method

1 Bring milk to boiling point, then allow to cool to 120°F/48°C. If using UHT milk heat it only to blood temperature and proceed straight to paragraph 2.
2 Stir in dried skimmed milk, if used, and add yoghurt. Whisk well.
3 Pour mixture into a clean, warm bowl, or small bowls, wide-necked jars or cartons. Cover with a plate, saucers or lids. If you have a wide-necked Thermos flask, preheat it by rinsing out with boiling water, and pour in the mixture. Put on lid.
4 Containers must be put at once into a slightly warmer place, preferably 110°F/43°C, and where temperature will remain constant for 4–6 hours. During this time (if you are lucky) it will turn to curd.
5 As soon as it is set, place it in the fridge. If you leave it in the warmth it will go on working and the acid flavour will become stronger, although it will also become thicker.
6 Save a tablespoon of your yoghurt to make the next batch (spoon it from the middle of the container where the activity of the yoghurt-making bacteria is greater). After three batches of yoghurt have been made from your own culture it is advisable to buy another carton of commercially-made yoghurt to use as the next starter. Choose a brand which has as few additives as possible as this will more easily make a good new yoghurt.

RASPBERRY MOUSSE

Blackberries can be used as an alternative.

Serves 4–5
Ingredients
450 g/1 lb raspberries
3 level tablespoons sifted icing sugar
2 tablespoons water
15 g/$\frac{1}{2}$ oz powdered gelatine
150 ml/$\frac{1}{4}$ pint whipping cream
2 egg whites

Method

1 Cook raspberries until soft. This is best done without water in a casserole with a lid in a slow oven (certainly no higher than moderate, Gas 4, 350°F, 180°C). If cooked in a saucepan, 2–3 teaspoons water may be required if fruit is dry, but liquid should be kept to a minimum.
2 Sieve the fruit and add icing sugar. Measure purée, there should be 300 ml/$\frac{1}{2}$ pint. Pour into a bowl.
3 Measure water into a small basin, and trickle in the gelatine. Stand this in hot water to dissolve gelatine, stirring once to combine.
4 Pour this very gently into fruit, stirring continuously. Allow to become quite cold, and slightly thick.
5 Whip cream until holding its shape. Fold in, then whisk egg whites until firm, but not dry and fold in.
6 Spoon into a large bowl, or 4–5 sundae glasses.

CRUDITÉS AND DIPS

Crudités and dips are good as a starter, or just as a light lunch with fruit to follow. The vegetables must be in tip-top condition though, and must be prepared at the last minute. Use young thin carrots with green tops or older carrots peeled and cut into chunks; small florets of raw cauliflower; small sticks of raw celery; red, yellow and green peppers, de-seeded and cut in strips; baby mushrooms wiped clean; small crisp radishes; firm cucumber chunks; spring onions, strips of raw fennel heart; or fingers of crisp toast or warm pitta.

Dips must be thick enough to cling to the vegetables or bread. My daughters love dips, but my generation is rather more inhibited about dunking into a communal bowl, so the solution is to give each guest a small ramekin of dip to themselves!

BASIC MAYONNAISE

Made in liquidizer. Keeps in refrigerator for 3–4 weeks. Can be thinned down when required with milk, single cream or natural yoghurt, or more lemon or orange juice or vinegar. Try different flavours too – tomato or anchovy purée, crushed garlic, chopped chives, onions, capers, cucumber or celery – but add after it's made.

Makes 425 ml/¾ pint

Ingredients

2–4 egg yolks (according to how extravagant you feel!)
2 dessertspoons lemon or orange juice or wine or cider vinegar
300 ml/½ pint good salad oil (olive or sunflower are best)
1 rounded teaspoon French mustard (try Dijon)
½ level teaspoon cooking or sea salt
¼ teaspoon freshly ground black pepper

Method

1 Put egg yolks in liquidizer and switch on for 2 minutes, or until thick and creamy.
2 With machine running, add juice or vinegar. Then add oil gradually until 150 ml/¼ pint has been absorbed.
3 Now add all the seasonings, switch on again and gradually add the last of the oil.

SOURED CREAM AND CHIVE DIP

This is also delicious as a dressing with a crunchy salad such as chopped white cabbage, carrots and onion.

Ingredients

150 ml/¼ pint soured cream
2 level tablespoons chopped fresh chives
1 tablespoon wine vinegar
1 level teaspoon made mustard
salt and freshly ground black pepper
a little milk (optional)

Method

1 Combine all the ingredients, adding milk to thin it down if necessary.

YOGHURT AND TAHINI DIP

This also makes a lovely dressing for salads.

Ingredients

3 tablespoons natural yoghurt
1 tablespoon tahini (from a deli)
1 clove garlic, crushed (optional)
lemon juice
salt and freshly ground black pepper

Method

1 Simply mix yoghurt, tahini and garlic, then beat in lemon juice, salt and pepper to taste. Will keep in fridge for a few days. Stir before serving.

July Menu

High Summer High Tea

This is an early-evening meal which seems to be dying out over the country, except perhaps in the north. It's a wonderful welcome home from work or school in the winter, when home-made breads and scones might be hot from the oven; it's a relaxing meal for the cook in the summer when cold food can be made well in advance. Have breads, cheeses and other pickles on offer too, and a hot pot of good tea.

Salt beef
Horseradish sauce
Pickled cauliflower
New potato salad
French bean salad
Fruit brûlée with Shortbread biscuits

Home Notes

August

This is a holiday month, and it's usually warm – a good excuse for eating out of doors, either just moving out to a table in the back garden, or barbecuing or picnicking. There are many recipes throughout the book suitable for taking on picnics – the salads here will be useful too (pack in rigid boxes, dressings separate). Barbecue meats don't need special recipes, although some – chicken legs or pieces, or lamb or pork for kebabs – could benefit from a prior marination. Don't forget about prawns and some fish which are wonderful when briefly charcoal-grilled. Crudités (see page 76) would make a good open-air starter, and a fruit salad made from the many varieties available now would be a delicious and healthy dessert.

Market Place

Vegetables: aubergines, beetroot, broccoli, cabbages, carrots, cauliflowers, celery, chanterelles, Chinese leaves, courgettes, cucumbers, fennel, garlic, globe artichokes, green beans, kohlrabi, leeks, lettuces, mangetout, marrows, okra, onions, parsnips, peppers, potatoes, radishes, sweetcorn, tomatoes.
Fruit and nuts: apricots, Asian pears, bilberries, blackberries, blackcurrants, blueberries, cherries, gooseberries, grapes, loganberries, mangoes, melons, nectarines, peaches, plums, raspberries, redcurrants, strawberries, whitecurrants.
Fish: Dover sole, grey mullet, haddock, halibut, herring, lobster, pilchards, plaice, prawns, red mullet, salmon, sardines, sea bass, sea bream, shrimps, squid, turbot.
Meat: beef, chicken, duck, grouse, guinea fowl, lamb, quail, rabbit.

Tips and Hints

Leaves for salads should be as dry as possible after washing. Use a collapsible chain mesh basket, a revolving drum dryer, or, easiest of all, lay on a clean tea towel, bundle up and give a few vigorous shakes outside!

To ensure a dressing only goes on a salad at the last moment, I usually make up the dressing in the bottom of the salad bowl. I lay my wooden salad servers in a cross over this, then pile the leaves on top. Mix at the table just before serving.

Store lettuces in the salad drawer of the fridge or, in the old way, wrapped in damp newspaper in a covered saucepan in the coolest part of the house.

Now is a good time to freeze fruit like plums, peaches, nectarines and apricots (see pages 138–139). To keep the fruit submerged in the freezing syrup – which keeps it a good colour – I use those long, narrow, plastic bacon boxes, and closely pack the fruit in in one layer. I lay two stainless steel knives on the fruit and pour in syrup to just cover the knives. When the fruit is frozen, I dig out the knives (used again when I'm defrosting).

Whole plums freeze well – just wipe and bag in useable quantities. But, it is *very* important to discard any that are not perfect.

To make the basis of horseradish sauce that will keep 12 months or more, dig root from late summer onwards and wash and peel (under water to avoid severe eye watering). Cut up and mince finely. Make a syrup by beating and dissolving 225 g/8 oz white sugar and a little salt in 300 ml/$\frac{1}{2}$ pint white vinegar. Allow to go cold then pack horseradish and syrup in a wide-necked jar with vinegar-proof lid. To serve, add 1 tablespoon double cream to 1 tablespoon horseradish, with extra vinegar to taste.

RECIPES

LEAFY SALADS, AND DRESSINGS

Garden lettuces are grown by the million, and they range from the thin-leaved cabbage type to the crisply crunchy Webb's Wonderful and iceberg type. Cos lettuces have tougher leaves, as do Chinese leaves. Radicchio is the red lettuce with a slightly bitter taste, and other salad leaves include lamb's lettuce, oak-leaf and curly endive or frisée. All are good in leafy salads (see also JUNE and JULY). Dressings or vinaigrettes for thin-leaved lettuces should be very light; the crunchy, juicier type of leaf can take a heavier dressing (and see page 76 for mayonnaise).

SIMPLE DRESSING WITHOUT OIL

A mild dressing especially if young children are to eat the salad.

Ingredients

3 tablespoons tarragon vinegar (wine or cider vinegar can be used)
2 tablespoons water
½ teaspoon sugar
salt and freshly ground black pepper
1 large teaspoon chopped fresh mint, parsley, chives, tarragon, fennel or onion

Method

1 Mix all the dressing ingredients thoroughly in a salad bowl, and at last minute toss in your chosen salad ingredients.

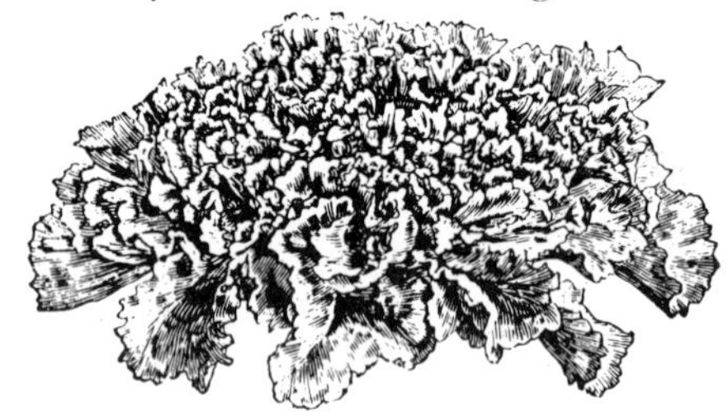

FRENCH DRESSING

Made in a jar in quite a large quantity, will keep in a cool place for several weeks, to be used a little at a time as required. You can add different flavourings if you like, but only to the small amount of dressing required when salad is made, as they go stale if kept in the dressing for long. Try crushed garlic, chopped onion or herbs.

Ingredients

1 rounded teaspoon French mustard
1 rounded teaspoon cooking or sea salt
½ teaspoon ground black pepper
½ level teaspoon sugar (optional)
juice of 1 lemon (optional)
300 ml/½ pint olive or good salad oil
4 tablespoons wine or cider vinegar

Method

1 Put all ingredients in a jar with a well-fitting screw top. Shake vigorously to combine.

DRESSING WITHOUT VINEGAR

Ingredients

4 tablespoons good salad oil, such as olive or sunflower
1 tablespoon lemon juice
1 teaspoon dark cane sugar or 1 teaspoon honey
a pinch of salt
freshly ground black pepper

Method

1 Simply mix all ingredients in a salad bowl, and toss salad in it thoroughly just before it is to be eaten.

LETTUCE AND BEANSPROUT SALAD

Serves 6

Ingredients

1 small crunchy lettuce, broken into pieces and washed
225 g/8 oz fresh beansprouts, chopped
1 very small red pepper, de-seeded and chopped
½ small cucumber, wiped and cubed
1 small onion, peeled and sliced into wafer-thin rings

Dressing

1 teaspoon grated fresh ginger
½ small onion, peeled
175 ml/6 fl oz good salad oil
50 ml/2 fl oz each white wine vinegar and water
2 tablespoons light soy sauce
1 small stick celery, chopped
2 teaspoons tomato purée
2 teaspoons fresh lemon juice
salt, pepper and sugar to taste

Method

1 Put the lettuce, beansprouts, pepper, cucumber and onion rings in a large bowl and mix well.
2 Combine all the dressing ingredients (except the salt, pepper and sugar) in a blender and process until smooth. Taste and adjust the seasoning.
3 Serve the dressing separately.

CRUNCHY SALAD WITH NUTTY DRESSING

Serves 4–6

Ingredients

1 small head iceberg lettuce, torn into small pieces
1 crisp red-skinned apple, cored and finely sliced
2 tablespoons lemon juice
50 g/2 oz hazelnuts, roughly chopped
1 orange, peeled, finely sliced and chopped

Dressing

1 tablespoon sunflower oil
2 tablespoons natural yoghurt
25 g/1 oz hazelnuts
1–2 teaspoons lemon juice
1 teaspoon chopped chives
2 fat pinches sugar
salt and freshly ground black pepper

Method

1 After preparing the lettuce, lay the cored and finely sliced apple in a flat dish with the lemon juice, coating the slices on all sides.
2 Put the lettuce pieces, apple, hazelnuts and orange pieces in a roomy bowl.
3 Liquidize the dressing ingredients together. Taste and adjust the seasoning. Pour over the salad at the last minute and toss well.

ENDIVE SALAD

This dressing could be used as the basis for a dip for crudités (see page 76).

Serves 6

Ingredients

1 head curly endive, washed and chopped
125 g/4 oz beansprouts, chopped
½ medium yellow pepper, de-seeded and cut into thin strips
125 g/4 oz salted peanuts, roughly chopped

Dressing

50 g/2 oz blue cheese, crumbled
single cream
6 tablespoons low-fat soft cheese
2 tablespoons white wine vinegar

Method

1 Put the endive leaves in the serving bowl, and stir in the beansprouts, pepper and nuts.
2 In another bowl mash down the blue cheese with a little single cream, then add the soft cheese and vinegar. Add enough extra single cream to get a thick pouring consistency.
3 Pour the dressing over the salad just before serving.

TOMATOES

This is the month when "Tomatoes for Sale" signs are everywhere. We are lucky now to have different varieties of tomatoes to choose from – the ordinary medium sized ones, both green and ripe red; those tiny, crisp ones not much bigger than marbles; the huge beef or Marmande tomatoes which are often uneven in shape but full of flavour (Big Boy is a variety I can recommend); and plum tomatoes, oval in shape and better known to us from a tin. Tomatoes can be eaten raw in salads and sandwiches, cooked with other vegetables (delicious with cauliflower and with aubergine), and they can be stuffed with savoury fillings and baked or served cold. They also make wonderful preserves.

TO SKIN TOMATOES

Either: Put tomatoes in a bowl, pour boiling water over them and leave for 1 minute. Plunge them into cold water and skin when required.
Or: If only one is needed, spear it on a fork and turn it in the hot air just above a gas flame. Skin will contract and burst and tomato can be easily peeled.
For green tomatoes: Prick them in several places with a fork. Then pour on boiling water. Leave for a few minutes. Skins will be easily removed.

INDONESIAN TOMATO SALAD

Remove the chilli seeds if you are nervous!

Serves 4

Ingredients

4 ripe tomatoes
salt to taste
2 fresh green chillies
3 tablespoons sugar
juice of 2 lemons

Method

1 Slice the tomatoes and arrange in a serving platter. Sprinkle with a little salt.
2 Slice the green chillies slantwise into elongated rings and arrange over the tomato slices.
3 Sprinkle with sugar and lemon juice and allow to stand for an hour or two before serving.

CHILLED TOMATO AND APPLE SOUP

Always serve a chilled soup in smaller bowls than your usual everyday ones. Make this when fresh tomatoes are plentiful and taste the flavour of *real* tomato soup. It freezes well.

Serves 4

Ingredients

450 g/1 lb fresh ripe tomatoes, chopped
225 g/8 oz onion, peeled and chopped
450 g/1 lb cooking apples, peeled, cored and chopped
600 ml/1 pint chicken stock
salt and freshly ground black pepper
finely chopped basil or chives to garnish

Method

1 Put all the ingredients, except the basil or chives, into a saucepan. Bring to the boil, then lower the heat and simmer together for 20 minutes, or until the onions are soft.
2 Purée the soup in a liquidizer or processor, then sieve to remove the tomato skins and pips and to ensure the soup is completely smooth.
3 Leave to cool, then garnish the soup with the basil or chives.

TANGY TOMATO SAUCE

Good eaten hot with grills, or as a pizza topping, with added cheese, mushrooms and chopped peppers. Keeps well in the refrigerator for 2 weeks. A liquidizer or food processor is useful.

Makes about 450 ml/$\frac{3}{4}$ pint

Ingredients

1 tablespoon oil
1 large onion, peeled and finely chopped
675 g/1$\frac{1}{2}$ lb fresh tomatoes, skinned (see left) and chopped, or a 400 g/14 oz can tomatoes
3 tablespoons brown sugar
1 tablespoon Worcestershire sauce
2 teaspoons lemon juice
1 teaspoon dry mustard powder
4 tablespoons malt vinegar
2 tablespoons water
salt and freshly ground black pepper

Method

1 Heat the oil and fry the onion for a few minutes until soft.
2 Liquidize the tomatoes and add them, with all the other ingredients, to the onions.
3 Bring to the boil and cook gently for 3 minutes, seasoning to taste.

TOMATO RELISH

Yields about 1.8 kg/4 lb

Ingredients

1.5 kg/3$\frac{1}{2}$ lb firm ripe tomatoes, skinned (see left), or use 2 × 675 g/1$\frac{1}{2}$ lb tins tomatoes
900 g/2 lb onions, peeled and finely chopped
1 teaspoon salt
900 g/2 lb sugar
90 g/3$\frac{1}{2}$ oz demerara sugar
25 g/1 oz fresh ginger, peeled and finely chopped
7 g/$\frac{1}{4}$ oz chilli powder
600 ml/1 pint malt vinegar

Method

1 Chop tomatoes and place all ingredients, except vinegar, in a pan. Stir over low heat until sugar is dissolved. Cook gently for about 1 hour to a thick consistency, stirring occasionally.
2 Add vinegar and cook for another 10 minutes.
3 Pour the mixture while hot into warmed, clean, dry jars with vinegar-proof lids.
4 Put on the lids when relish is cold. Label and store in a cool, dry place.

PLUMS

With the soft fruit over, August sees the start of the plum harvest. It's a short season, so we ought to make the most of it – and the plum's relations, too, damsons and gages, which follow in September. Plums used to be very much more popular, a staple fruit virtually, until World War Two, and since then many orchards have disappeared. My two plum trees are a source of many good homely meals ranging from plum pies to stewed plums with custard, and there is a brown plum sauce that I have made every year since we came to our house.

PLUM PIE

You could also use gooseberries, rhubarb, apples, or half-and-half apples and blackberries for this pie. You'll need a pie plate, 18 cm/7 inches diameter and about 3 cm/1¼ inches deep, or a pie dish, 750 ml–1 litre/ 1¼–1¾ pint size.

Serves 4

Ingredients

½ quantity sweet shortcrust pastry (see page 116)

a little caster sugar

Filling

675 g/1½ lb plums, stoned

2 tablespoons sugar

1 tablespoon cornflour

Method

1. Make the pastry as described on page 116, and use half only. Allow to rest for 15 minutes. This will prevent shrinkage during cooking.
2. Arrange half the fruit in the pie dish or plate. Mix sugar and cornflour, sprinkle over the fruit, and cover with rest of fruit.
3. Using a floured board, roll out pastry 1 cm/½ inch larger than top of pie dish.
4. Cut a circular 1 cm/½ inch strip from the pastry, damp edges of pie dish with water and press this pastry strip on firmly. Damp the strip, place pastry lid on top, press to seal and trim level.
5. Flute edges, make four small slits on top, brush lightly with water, and sprinkle with caster sugar.
6. Bake in a moderately hot oven, Gas 6, 400°F, 200°C, for 30 minutes, then reduce heat to moderate, Gas 4, 350°F, 180°C, and bake a little longer until fruit is cooked. To test fruit, put a skewer through slit in pastry.

PLUM CARAMEL PUDDING

A delicious bread pudding which can be made in any quantity to suit your household.

Ingredients

plums

butter or margarine

brown sugar

slices of stale bread (wholewheat, brown or white)

Method

1. Wash plums and cut in halves, removing stones.
2. Thickly butter sides and bottom of a pie dish and sprinkle all over with sugar. Line with pieces of stale bread.
3. Place a layer of plums over bread, cut side uppermost. Sprinkle with sugar. Cover with another layer of bread, and a second layer of plums and sugar. Finish top with slices of buttered bread, butter-side upmost.
4. Cover with greaseproof paper and bake in middle of a moderate oven. Gas 3–4, 325–350°F, 160–180°C. Remove paper after 30 minutes, and cook for a further 10 minutes to crisp up the bread on top.
5. Turn pudding out on to a warmed dish and serve with cream or custard.

BROWN PLUM SAUCE

A simple recipe, which keeps very well. I served it with sausages and mash when the children were small. It's also nice to use like mustard in cold meat sandwiches.

Yields about 1.75 litres/3 pints

Ingredients

1.1 kg/2½ lb red plums, wiped
3 medium onions, peeled and sliced
125 g/4 oz sultanas
15 g/½ oz root ginger
25 g/1 oz pickling spice
1.2 litres/2 pints malt or white vinegar
225 g/8 oz granulated sugar
50 g/2 oz salt
25 g/1 oz dry mustard powder
1 teaspoon grated nutmeg
1 level teaspoon turmeric

Method

1 Stone plums and put in a large pan. Don't worry if stones are firmly anchored – pick them out later. Add onions and sultanas.
2 Bruise the ginger by hitting it with a hammer. Tie it with pickling spice in a piece of muslin. Put in pan.
3 Add half of the vinegar and boil for 30 minutes.
4 Meanwhile put sugar to warm in a very cool oven, Gas ¼, 225°C, 110°C. Put clean bottles into oven to warm at same time. (Choose bottles with vinegar-proof lids.)
5 Remove spice bag and stir in all the other ingredients. Stir to dissolve sugar and bring to boiling point.
6 Simmer for 40–60 minutes, stirring occasionally, then leave to cool.
7 When cool, push contents of pan through a nylon sieve. Remember to scrape all the purée off underside of sieve. (If the sauce is too thin, simmer and reduce the volume by evaporation until it is thicker but still of pouring consistency.)
8 Pour into warmed bottles, right to the brim and put on clean lids immediately. Label and store, leaving for at least 4 weeks to mature.

PLUM CHUTNEY

Dark-skinned varieties give the best colour.

Yields 1.8 kg/4 lb

Ingredients

1.1 kg/2½ lb plums
450 g/1 lb onions, peeled and finely chopped
900 g/2 lb cooking apples
600 ml/1 pint cider vinegar
a piece of root ginger
1 dessertspoon each of whole cloves, whole allspice berries and black peppercorns
450 g/1 lb soft brown sugar
3 level teaspoons salt

Method

1 Wipe, halve and stone the plums.
2 Put onions in a saucepan, cover with water and boil for 5 minutes to soften them. Drain (saving liquid for soup etc.).
3 Peel, core and chop apples. Put these in a large pan with half of the vinegar. Bring to the boil and cook for 20 minutes to a soft pulp.
4 Meanwhile, bruise the ginger by hitting it with a hammer. Then tie it with the other spices in a piece of muslin.
5 Put spice bag with remaining vinegar and the sugar into another pan. Bring to the boil and simmer for 5 minutes, stirring all the time. Draw pan off heat and infuse for 30 minutes. Remove bag.
6 Add spiced vinegar, onions, plums and salt to apples. Bring to the boil and simmer for about 2 hours until chutney is thick and pulpy. Stir frequently to avoid burning.
7 Pot, and store as usual. Allow to mature for 4 weeks before using.

GREEN EGG PLUM JAM

A variety of plum with high pectin.

Yields about 2.25 kg/5 lb

Ingredients

1.3 kg/3 lb plums
300 ml/½ pint water
1.3 kg/3 lb granulated sugar

Method

1 Wash plums, remove stalks and simmer them in the water in a large pan until skins are really tender. Skim off stones as they surface.
2 Meanwhile put sugar and clean jars in a very cool oven, Gas ¼, 225°F, 110° C, for about 20 minutes to warm.
3 Add warmed sugar to pan of fruit, and stir until dissolved.
4 Then boil rapidly, stirring occasionally, until setting point is reached (see page 20). Begin testing after 6 minutes.
5 Pot, seal, cover and store as usual.

PASTA AND RICE

Pasta and rice are marvellous store-cupboard stand-bys, and come in very handy when trying to think of quick, nourishing and filling meals for the family.

Rice comes in many varieties, and is available brown or white. Serve it as below; cook it with stock; mix it with separately fried vegetables; cover with a sauce; or serve cold with finely chopped vegetables, pieces of cold meat or shellfish and a good dressing as a salad.

Pasta comes in differing shapes, forms, flavours and colours. It can be used as the basis for a meat, fish (see page 106) or cream sauce, for chopped vegetables and leftovers, and can also be served cold as a salad. Allow 50–75 g/2–3 oz dried pasta, 75–125 g/3–4 oz fresh pasta per person. Cook in plenty of boiling water, with salt and a few drops of oil (to help prevent sticking). Do not cover, and keep boiling vigorously. Stir occasionally. Test by taking a piece out, and biting. It should be neither too hard nor too soft – *al dente.*

BOILED RICE

This is the best way of making fluffy white rice to serve with curries and other savoury dishes. This method is suitable for all good rice – Basmati, Patna, Chinese, Japanese and Italian. For part-cooked rice follow manufacturer's instructions on packet.

Serves 4

Ingredients

1 × 175 ml/6 fl oz cup white or brown rice (washed in a sieve under running cold water until the water runs clear)
2 × 175 ml/6 fl oz cups water
salt and freshly ground black pepper

Method

1 Put rice and water in a saucepan and bring to the boil.
2 Stir, cover pan, put on a well-fitting lid, reduce heat and simmer for 15 minutes (25 minutes for brown rice). At the end of that time the rice will have absorbed all the water and be perfectly cooked, but *it is vital* that the lid be kept on for the full time.
3 Fluff with a fork, season to taste and serve.

A RICH MEAT SAUCE FOR SPAGHETTI

This sauce freezes well. It is enough to serve six portions.

Ingredients

2 tablespoons oil
2 rashers streaky bacon, rinded and finely chopped
1 onion, peeled and finely chopped
1 clove garlic, crushed
225 g/8 oz beef mince
1 small pig's kidney, cleaned and diced
1 carrot
1 tablespoon tomato purée
150–300 ml/$\frac{1}{4}$-$\frac{1}{2}$ pint stock
a pinch of mixed herbs
salt and freshly ground black pepper
2 teaspoons wholewheat flour or cornflour
1 tablespoon water

Method

1 Heat oil and fry bacon gently, then add onion, garlic, mince and kidney. Cook gently for 5 minutes, stirring occasionally.
2 Grate the carrot and add it with tomato purée, 150 ml/$\frac{1}{4}$ pint stock, herbs, salt and pepper. Bring to the boil.
3 Lower heat, cover pan and simmer for 20 minutes. Stir occasionally to prevent sticking, and add more stock if necessary.
4 Meanwhile, cook spaghetti in plenty of boiling salted water (see above).
5 Thicken meat sauce at last minute, if necessary, by mixing flour and water, stirring in and bringing back to the boil.
6 To serve, mix the sauce with cooked spaghetti, and sprinkle grated Parmesan cheese on top.

August Menu

A Picnic Feast

Apparently the 1st August is officially Picnic Day in the Northern Territories of Australia (although I wonder why, since eating out of doors is an everyday thing for them with all that wonderful sunshine!). While I like spur-of-the-moment picnics, there is something very special about a planned picnic. For many years we made an annual pilgrimage to the first day of the Headingley Test Match in Leeds. A friend always got us the best seats, and at lunchtime we moved to a grassy area, spread out our rugs and enjoyed our food – traditionally, a Yorkshire cricket combination of pork pie and pickled onions – as well as the inevitable discussion about the game.

Crudités and Dips
Pork pie
Pickled onions
Crunchy salad with nutty dressing
Fresh fruit

SEPTEMBER

September marks the beginning of autumn in the northern hemisphere, and it is also the month of harvest home, rich in home-grown produce. There are two harvest festivals in our very small village, one at St Mary's, and the other at the Wesleyan chapel. Both are well supported by each others' members and a traditional harvest supper is enjoyed by all. It is the Wesleyan chapel which has the old tradition of sending a large marrow round the village for donations. The money is pressed into the flesh of the marrow so that it ends up looking like a misshapen armadillo! I do not belong to either congregation but I am happy to contribute in celebrating the munificence of the land.

Market Place

Vegetables: aubergines, beetroot, broccoli, cabbages, carrots, cauliflowers, celery, ceps, chanterelles, Chinese leaves, courgettes, cucumbers, elderberries, fennel, garlic, globe artichokes, green beans, kohlrabi, leeks, lettuces, mangetout, marrows, onions, parsnips, peppers, pumpkins, radishes, swedes, sweetcorn, tomatoes, turnips.

Fruit and nuts: apples, Asian pears, blackberries, blueberries, damsons, figs, grapes, greengages, mangoes, melons, nectarines, peaches, plums, pomegranates, raspberries, strawberries.

Fish: cod, coley, Dover sole, grey mullet, haddock, halibut, herring, lobster, mussels, oysters, pilchards, plaice, prawns, red mullet, sea bass, sea bream, shrimps, skate, squid, turbot.

Meat: beef, chicken, duck, grouse, guinea-fowl, pigeon, pork, rabbit, venison.

Tips and Hints

Sweetcorn is available from July to October. Don't buy fresh sweetcorn if the corn is hidden and you cannot check that it is plump with a bright, golden colour. Season after cooking, not before, as salt toughens the kernels. To separate kernels, hold the uncooked cob upright and saw downwards with a sharp knife.

Free foods now are blackberries or brambles, elderberries and rowans. Don't forget either about fungi that can be picked from the wild – field, horse and oyster mushrooms, ceps and chanterelles – but, just to be sure, arm yourself first with a very good field guide.

Use some of the wealth of fruits available now to make ice creams (see the basic recipe on page 74). A tip from Mary Watts, my programme producer, is to freeze the ice cream in the dish from which you will serve it – I use a cheap glass bowl which comes to no harm. Stir the ice cream into an attractive whirl in the bowl, then freeze. When firm, cover with foil – and, allowing 20 minutes to soften, it can be taken straight to the table.

For "instant" seasoning, try Dorothy Sleightholme's salt and pepper mix. Mix 3 teaspoons of salt to 1 teaspoon of freshly ground black pepper. Keep in a screw-top or sprinkler-top jar.

To bake a pastry flan case blind – to cook it before the filling is added – line a flan case or ring on a baking sheet with the rolled out pastry. Prick the pastry base well, then put in a circle of greaseproof paper, greased side down. Cover with a layer of dried peas or haricot beans, about 1 cm/$\frac{1}{2}$ inch deep. Bake according to individual recipe directions. If using a rich shortcrust pastry, lay it on an upturned flan.

RECIPES

MUSHROOMS

Mushrooms cook fast, need almost no preparation, are packed with goodness, and are very versatile. Types available are button, cap and flat, the three stages of growth. Dried mushrooms make a good standby, and you can, of course, grow your own by buying a bag of compost containing the mushroom spores.

DEEP-FRIED MUSHROOMS

You could also deep-fry blanched celery chunks in this batter.

Serves 2 or more

Ingredients

125 g/4 oz button mushrooms
about 50 g/2 oz garlic and herb soft cream cheese
oil for deep-frying

Batter

50 g/2 oz plain or wholemeal flour
salt and freshly ground black pepper
½ teaspoon baking powder
1 egg, beaten
a scant 150 ml/¼ pint milk

Method

1 Remove the stalks from the mushrooms. Sandwich two mushrooms together with a little cream cheese, and secure with a cocktail stick. Repeat with remaining mushrooms.
2 To make the batter, put flour in a bowl with salt, pepper and baking powder. Make a well in centre and drop in the egg. Gradually beat in enough milk to make a smooth thick consistency.
3 Dip each pair of mushrooms into the batter and deep-fry in the hot oil until golden brown and crisp. Drain well, remove cocktail sticks and serve at once.

STROGANOFF

Make with either beef or pork.

Serves 6–8 (but easy to make less)

Ingredients

about 25 g/1 oz butter
a 900 g/2 lb single piece of beef or pork fillet, cut into thin strips about 5 cm/2 inches long
3 medium onions, peeled and chopped
225 g/8 oz mushrooms, wiped and finely sliced
a little chopped fresh parsley

Sauce

25 g/1 oz butter
25 g/1 oz plain flour
1 level tablespoon tomato purée
¼ level teaspoon freshly grated nutmeg
600 ml/1 pint beef stock
150 ml/¼ pint natural yoghurt or soured cream
salt and freshly ground black pepper

Method

1 Start with the sauce. In quite a large saucepan, melt butter, remove from heat and stir in flour, tomato purée and nutmeg, then gradually stir in stock.
2 Bring to the boil, stirring as sauce thickens, and simmer for 2 minutes, then stir in yoghurt or soured cream, and season with salt and pepper.
3 Now for the main part of the dish. Heat half of the butter in a large frying pan and quickly brown the meat on all sides. Remove from pan into sauce.
4 Add a little more butter to the pan if necessary and fry onion slowly until tender and light brown. Put in sauce.
5 In the last of the butter fry mushrooms for just 1 or 2 minutes. Put these with meat and onions.
6 Bring the stroganoff to the boil and simmer it for 15 minutes. Serve with boiled potatoes or rice, and garnish with the parsley.

MARROW RINGS STUFFED WITH CHICKEN AND MUSHROOMS

Marrows come into season this month, and are delicious cooked this way with mushrooms.

Serves 4

Ingredients

1 marrow, peeled, cut into thick rings, and seeded
1 tablespoon cooking oil
1 small onion, peeled and finely chopped
½ green pepper, de-seeded and sliced
125 g/4 oz cooked chicken, cut into small pieces
125 g/4 oz mushrooms, chopped
4 tomatoes, sliced
125 g/4 oz sweetcorn (optional)
125 g/4 oz peas (optional)
1 dessertspoon cornflour
300 ml/½ pint chicken stock
salt and freshly ground black pepper
15 g/½ oz butter or margarine
small sprigs of parsley

Method

1. Put marrow rings into a large flat casserole dish in one layer, and add 150 ml/¼ pint water. Cover dish and cook in a moderate oven, Gas 4, 350°F, 180°C, for about 20 minutes, or until soft, while you prepare the filling.
2. Heat oil in a large pan and fry onion and pepper gently till soft but not brown. Add chicken and mushrooms and toss together over low heat for 3-4 minutes.
3. Save a slice of tomato for the top of each marrow ring, and chop the rest. Add with the sweetcorn and peas. Stir together for 3–4 minutes.
4. Mix cornflour with a tablespoon of the stock. Add to the rest of the stock and pour this into chicken mixture. Add salt and pepper if necessary.
5. Take casserole from oven and drain off any liquid (keep it for making soup). Fill each marrow ring with chicken mixture. Lay a slice of tomato on each and dot with butter or margarine.
6. Cover casserole again and return it to the oven to cook for 20 minutes more. Serve with a sprig of parsley on each portion.

NUT AND MUSHROOM LOAF

A party dish. Delicious cold as a pâté or served hot in the style of a traditional Sunday lunch. When fresh chestnuts are available, you could use those instead; they won't need soaking.

Serves 8–10 (but easy to reduce quantities)

Ingredients

125 g/4 oz dried chestnuts, whole or kibbled (sold in small broken pieces)
50 g/2 oz butter
1 onion, peeled and chopped
2 cloves garlic, crushed
1 tablespoon chopped fresh parsley
2 teaspoons dried sage
¼ teaspoon winter savory
½ teaspoon paprika
2 tablespoons wholewheat flour
150 ml/¼ pint red wine
325 g/12 oz walnuts, ground
50 g/2 oz fresh wholewheat breadcrumbs
4 sticks celery, chopped
1 teaspoon salt
1 tablespoon Worcestershire sauce
225 g/8 oz mushrooms, sliced
1 beaten egg

Method

1. Soak chestnuts in 1.2 litres/2 pints boiling water for 1 hour.
2. Then cook them in the same water in a covered pan until soft. If whole this will take about 40 minutes; if kibbled, about 20 minutes. Save the cooking water as you drain them. Chop coarsely (not necessary with kibbled chestnuts).
3. Melt butter in a large frying pan and fry onion and garlic gently until transparent. Stir in herbs, paprika and flour and cook 2 minutes.
4. Add 150 ml/¼ pint stock from cooking chestnuts and the wine, and stir well. When sauce thickens, remove pan from heat.
5. Mix together in a bowl chestnuts, ground walnuts, breadcrumbs, celery, salt, Worcestershire sauce and mushrooms.
6. Mix in sauce and beaten egg. Check seasoning.
7. Grease a 1 kg/2 lb loaf tin and line it with greased greaseproof paper. Fill with mixture and press down well.
8. Bake in a moderately hot oven, Gas 5, 375°F, 190°C, for 1 hour until firm to the touch. Remove from oven. When serving hot, leave loaf in tin for 10 minutes before cutting.

AUTUMN FRUITS

Apples, damsons, greengages, plums (see August), pears, blackberries – there are so many home-grown fruits available at this time of year, to eat crisp and fresh, to cook, or to preserve in some way (see October).

Our huge pear tree has defeated me over the years – its sweet hazel pears do not cook well and are best eaten straight off the tree, but we cannot eat at that rate. Our solution to the windfalls is the use of three old golf putters with which we putt the fruit into the nearby shrubbery! The garden begins to smell very winey by the middle of September! But the birds enjoy it.

PEARS WITH STILTON SAUCE

A sophisticated starter for two. The sauce can be made in advance, but prepare the pear and assemble the dish at the last minute.

Ingredients

50 g/2 oz blue Stilton cheese
1–2 tablespoons cream or top-of-the milk
1 large ripe pear, peeled
2 tablespoons lemon juice
toasted flaked almonds
lettuce leaves and Melba toast (see page 14) to serve

Method

1 Grate the cheese and mix in enough cream or milk to make a thick, smooth sauce.
2 Cut the pear in half and remove the core with a teaspoon. Place each pear half flat-side down, cut it into thin slices, and brush thoroughly with lemon juice to prevent browning.
3 Arrange the slices like a fan on two small plates and spoon over the Stilton sauce. Scatter the almonds on top.
4 Garnish the plates with lettuce leaves and serve with toast.

SWEET PEARS AND CHEESE PIZZA

Serves 3 or 4

Ingredients

1 uncooked pizza base (see opposite)
3 dessert pears
rind and juice of ½ lemon
50 g/2 oz Lancashire, Cheshire or Mozzarella cheese, grated
25 g/1 oz plain cooking chocolate, grated
50 g/2 oz chopped walnuts
25 g/1 oz butter

Method

1 Lay the pizza dough base on a well-greased baking sheet.
2 Peel and core pears and cut into slices, about 3 slices to each quarter. Dip into lemon juice to prevent browning.
3 Arrange slices of pear on the dough, leaving a 1 cm/½ inch border all round.
4 Scatter on the lemon rind. Cover pears with cheese, sprinkle on chocolate and chopped walnuts. Dot with butter.
5 Cover lightly and leave aside in a warm place for the dough to rise.
6 Bake near top of a very hot oven for 5 minutes, Gas 7, 425°F, 220°C, then lower temperature to moderately hot, Gas 5, 375°F, 190°C, and bake for about 15 minutes more, or until pizza dough is brown.

FRESH PEARS (OR PEACHES) IN A FUDGE SAUCE

Serves 4 (but easy to make less)

Ingredients

4 soft ripe pears (or peaches)
a little butter

Fudge sauce

225 g/8 oz light soft brown sugar
15 g/½ oz butter
2 tablespoons milk

Method

1 Start with sauce. Put sugar, butter and milk in a heavy pan. Stir over low heat to dissolve sugar, then bring to the boil. Boil to the soft ball stage, 240°F, 116°C (when dribbles of sauce dropped in some cold water set to a soft ball, not crisp). Stir frequently.
2 Peel, quarter and core pears. (For peaches, peel, stone and halve.)
3 Place fruit cut side down in a buttered heatproof dish, and pour hot sauce over. Cool and serve really chilled.

BAKED APPLES WITH MUESLI

Serves 2

Ingredients

2 large Bramley apples, wiped and cored
25 g/1 oz raisins
2 heaped teaspoons golden syrup
250 ml/8 fl oz liquid (you can use apple juice, cider or water)
2 large tablespoons home-made muesli (see page 116)

Method

1 Using a sharp knife, score around the centre of the apples, just cutting the skin.
2 Stand the apples upright in a small ovenproof dish and fill the centres with the raisins. Spoon golden syrup over each apple and pour the liquid into the dish.
3 Bake uncovered in a moderately hot oven, at Gas 5, 375°F, 190°C, for about 40 minutes, or until the apples are soft. About 15 minutes before they are ready, put the muesli on to a baking sheet and cook in the oven until it is lightly browned.
4 Serve the apples and juice in individual bowls with the muesli scattered over the top.

BAKING

The word "baking" encompasses many skills, and due to space I can only give a limited selection of recipes here. There is a basic yeast-raised bread, which doubles as a pizza base; there is a savoury pie (there are other savoury flans elsewhere, on pages 44 and 45); and some delicious cakes and scones, which have many variations. Biscuit recipes can be found on pages 11, 33, 45 and 46.

SHORT-TIME BREAD OR PIZZA BASE

Ingredients

15 g/½ oz fresh yeast, or 7 g/¼ oz dried yeast
1 × 25 mg Vitamin C tablet (buy from chemist, also called ascorbic acid), crushed
about 150 ml/¼ pint warm water
½ teaspoon sugar
225 g/8 oz strong plain flour (or wholewheat flour, or half and half)
½ teaspoon salt
15 g/½ oz margarine

Method

1 Blend together the fresh yeast, crushed Vitamin C tablet and half the water. If using dried yeast, add sugar also and wait until it froths up before using.
2 Sieve flour and salt together, and rub in margarine. Pour yeast liquid into dry ingredients and mix well.
3 Add sufficient warm water to make a soft, beatable dough, then beat until the bowl is clean.
4 Turn dough out on to a lightly floured board and knead until smooth – about 10 minutes. Rest dough for 5 minutes, covered lightly.
5 *For the bread.* Shape into bread buns or cottage loaf, twist or plait, and put on a greased baking tray. Cover with a damp cloth or greased polythene, and leave in a warm place to rise until doubled in size.
For the pizza base. Divide the dough into four, and roll out to circles 18–20 cm/7–8 inches in diameter, and about 5 mm/¼ inch thick. Cover with the topping ingredients (see pages 83 and 92), then cover lightly and leave aside in a warm place until doubled in size or puffed up well.
6 *For the bread.* Bake near top of a hot oven, Gas 7, 425°F, 220°C. Bread buns take 10–12 minutes, loaves take 25–30 minutes.
For the pizzas. Start off baking near the top of a hot oven, Gas 7, 425°F, 220°C, for 20–30 minutes, reducing heat to moderately hot, Gas 5, 375°F, 190°C, after 15 minutes if browning too quickly.

PORK PIE

Freezes satisfactorily, but not longer than a month.

Serves 8

Ingredients

Hot water crust

125 ml/4 fl oz water
125 g/4 oz lard
275 g/10 oz strong plain flour
$\frac{1}{2}$ level teaspoon salt
1 small egg, beaten

Filling

450 g/1 lb pork from the shoulder, which should give roughly 325 g/12 oz lean and 125 g/4 oz fat
2 level teaspoons salt and pepper mix (see page 89)
$\frac{1}{4}$ level teaspoon powdered mace

Jelly

1 pig's trotter
1 bay leaf
6 black peppercorns

Method

1 Prepare jelly a day in advance. Boil trotter with bay leaf and peppercorns in 600 ml/1 pint water until quite soft and leaving the bone (about 3 hours). Strain liquid into basin – 150 ml/$\frac{1}{4}$ pint is enough for one pie – and leave overnight. Remove any fat from top. If jelly has not set, simmer gently to reduce. Discard trotter.
2 Now make the pastry. Boil water and lard, pour on to flour and salt. Mix with a knife (it will be hot) then knead with hands until quite smooth. Allow to cool a little before rolling out.
3 Now mix the filling. Trim gristle from pork which will reduce it to 400–425 g/14–15 oz. Cut it into very small pieces and season.
4 Roll out three-quarters of the pastry to fit a loose-bottomed tin, 15 cm/6 inches across and 8 cm/3 inches deep, pressing pastry round sides to make an even thickness. Pack filling in loosely.
5 Roll out lid to fit, brushing edges with beaten egg. Seal firmly. Cut away surplus pastry. Roll this out thinly and cut into leaves. Brush these with beaten egg and arrange on top. Flute edges of pie and brush all over top of pie with beaten egg. Make a hole in the centre.
6 Bake in a moderately hot oven, Gas 6, 400°F, 200°C, for 20 minutes. Reduce the heat if browning too quickly to Gas 5, 375°F, 190°C, and bake for a further hour. Turn out on to wire rack.
7 Boil up jelly, then allow pie and jelly to cool for 15 minutes. Using a small funnel, gently pour jelly through hole in centre, as much as it will hold. When jelly has settled into meat, add a little more for extra moistness. For best flavour, leave it 24 hours before eating.

FATLESS SPONGE

Serve the sponge filled with whipped double cream and sliced fresh strawberries in the summer. The mixture is sufficient for a 20 cm/8 inch tin 7.5 cm/3 inches deep, or for two 15 cm/6 inch sandwich tins; or for a sponge flan tin.

Ingredients

3 eggs
75 g/3 oz caster sugar
75 g/3 oz plain flour

Method

1 Grease tin(s) very well and put a circle of greased greaseproof paper in the bottom, or on the centre circle of a sponge flan tin (see page 29).
2 Using an electric mixer or a hand whisk, whip eggs and caster sugar together until very, very thick. It takes at least 5 minutes with an electric mixer – less time in a food processor.
3 Using a sieve, sprinkle about one-third of the flour over surface of egg mixture. Fold this in carefully with a spatula using a figure of eight movement. Do this twice more with the rest of the flour, taking care to cut through the mixture only with sharp edge of spatula in order to keep mixture as fluffy as possible.
4 When flour has been incorporated, pour mixture into tin(s).
5 Bake a 20 cm/8 inch cake in centre of a warm oven, Gas 3, 325°F, 160°C, for about 40 minutes until cake is well risen, golden, firm to touch and just shrinking from sides of tin. In 15 cm/6 inch sandwich tins, bake for about 30 minutes.

Chocolate Fatless Sponge

When flour has been weighed out, remove 2 teaspoons and replace with 2 teaspoons sifted cocoa (*not* drinking chocolate). Proceed as before.

SPICY APPLE LOAF

Makes two tasty, moist, small loaves. Serve sliced and spread with butter, margarine or cream cheese. They freeze well.

Ingredients
1 small egg
4 tablespoons oil
175 g/6 oz white or brown sugar
175 g/6 oz plain flour
¼ teaspoon bicarbonate of soda
½ teaspoon baking powder
½ teaspoon salt
1 teaspoon powdered cinnamon
25 g/1 oz chopped nuts
50 g/2 oz sultanas
2 dessert apples (about 250 g/9 oz), peeled, cored and grated

Method
1 Grease two 450 g/1 lb loaf tins and line the bases with greaseproof paper (see page 29).
2 Whisk the egg and oil together until foamy, then whisk in the sugar.
3 Fold in the sieved flour, bicarbonate of soda, baking powder, salt and cinnamon.
4 Lastly, stir in the nuts, sultanas and grated apples, and ensure that everything is well mixed.
5 Put the mixture into the prepared tins and bake in the middle of a moderate oven preheated to Gas 4, 350°F, 180°C, for about 50 minutes, or until firm to the touch.

DATE AND WALNUT LOAF

Eat cold, sliced and buttered. Ideal for picnics or packed lunches as well as teas. Keeps well.

Ingredients
225 g/8 oz chopped dates
125 g/4 oz caster sugar or vanilla sugar (preferable)*
a pinch of salt
1 level teaspoon bicarbonate of soda
50 g/2 oz margarine
175 ml/6 fl oz water
1 egg, beaten
50 g/2 oz chopped walnuts
225 g/8 oz self-raising flour
** 1 teaspoon vanilla essence (if vanilla sugar is not used)*

Method
1 Place dates, sugar, salt, soda and margarine (cut into small pieces) in a mixing bowl.
2 Boil water, pour over, and mix well to melt margarine. Cool a little.
3 Add beaten egg, walnuts and flour, and vanilla essence if used, and mix to a smooth, batter-type consistency.
4 Grease a 900 g/2 lb loaf tin and line base with greaseproof paper. Pour mixture in.
5 Bake in centre of a moderate oven, Gas 3, 325°F, 160°C, for approximately 1¼ hours until firm. Cool in tin 10–15 minutes, then turn out on to a wire rack.

OATCAKES

Delicious hot or cold with butter and cheese or honey. They keep well in a tin for about 10 days, and freeze well too.

Makes 10
Ingredients
175 g/6 oz medium oatmeal, plus a little extra
a pinch of salt
a pinch of bicarbonate of soda
1 tablespoon melted butter
4 tablespoons hot water
a knob of suet or a very little lard to grease girdle or pan

Method
1 Mix the 175 g/6 oz oatmeal with the other ingredients to a workable dough.
2 Form a round lump, sprinkle with oatmeal, and roll out almost paper thin.
3 Cut a large circle, using a dinner plate for guidance. Then cut this into triangles. You can get about 10 triangles.
4 Heat girdle (or a heavy-based frying pan) and grease it. Cook oatcakes, turning carefully until they are crisp but not brown.

BASIC SCONES

Ingredients
225 g/8 oz self-raising white flour
¼ teaspoon salt
50 g/2 oz margarine
5–6 tablespoons milk

Method
1 Sift flour and salt into a bowl, and rub in the margarine. Mix to a soft, but not sticky, dough with the milk.
2 Turn out on to a floured board, knead very lightly, and roll out just over 1 cm/½ inch thick.
3 Cut into 5 cm/2 inch rounds, re-rolling and cutting the trimmings, and place on a lightly greased baking tray.
4 Bake in a hot oven, Gas 7, 425°F, 220°C, for 12–14 minutes, until lightly golden and firm to the touch.

Herb scones
After rubbing in the margarine, add a shake of pepper and 1 level teaspoon mixed dried herbs. Mix and roll as above, then cut into about 10 fingers, place on tray and brush with milk. Bake as above.

Cheese scones
After rubbing margarine in, add ½ teaspoon dry mustard powder, a pinch of cayenne pepper, and 75 g/3 oz finely grated cheese. Finish according to basic recipe above.

Sweet scones
After rubbing margarine in, add 25 g/1 oz caster sugar and 50 g/2 oz sultanas. Finish according to basic recipe above.

DEVIL'S FOOD CAKE

This American-style cake is rich and chocolatey. It is traditionally covered with a chocolate cream icing but this white frosting is American inspired as well, and it looks very pretty.

Ingredients
75 g/3 oz plain good quality chocolate, broken in pieces
175 ml/6 fl oz strong black coffee
175 g/6 oz butter, softened
225 g/8 oz soft dark brown sugar
50 g/2 oz caster sugar
2–3 drops vanilla essence
3 eggs
275 g/10 oz plain white flour
1½ teaspoons bicarbonate of soda
175 ml/6 fl oz soured cream

Frosting
450 g/1 lb icing sugar
300 ml/½ pint water
2 egg whites, stiffly beaten

Method
1 Place the pieces of chocolate in a saucepan with the coffee. Stir over a low heat until the mixture is smooth.
2 Grease and line with greaseproof paper the bases of three 20 cm/8 inch sandwich tins.
3 In a roomy bowl beat the butter until pale and floppy, then beat in the sugars. Add vanilla essence and the eggs, one at a time, beating well after each addition. Stir in the chocolate mixture.
4 Sift the flour and bicarbonate of soda together into a small bowl.
5 Using a spatula, fold the sifted flour and soured cream alternately into the chocolate mixture.
6 Divide the cake mixture between the tins; use scales to check the weights are roughly even. Smooth over the tops.
7 Bake in a moderate oven, Gas 5, 375°F, 190°C, for about 25 minutes or until the mixture is beginning to shrink from the sides of the tins. Leave cakes in the tins for 5 minutes before turning out on to wire trays to cool.
8 To make the frosting, put the sugar and water in a roomy pan, and stir over a medium heat until the sugar dissolves. Brush away any sugar crystals that have formed on the sides of the pan with a pastry brush dipped in cold water. Increase the heat and bring to a boil. Cook to the soft ball stage, 240°F, 116°C. Remove the pan from the heat and set in a bowl of cold water to stop any further cooking.
9 Gradually whisk the syrup into the beaten egg whites. Continue beating until the icing loses its sheen. (Use an electric hand whisk to make a good job, but vigorous hand beating with a wire whisk will work just as well.) When the icing is thick and firm spread it immediately between the cake layers and over the top and sides.

SEPTEMBER MENU

HARVEST SUPPER

In my part of the world, harvest suppers are given in the village hall, with everyone contributing and helping. The main courses can be anything in the way of cold meats, served with salads and preserves; vol-au-vents, and things like sausage rolls help spin out the meats. The pudding is often a trifle, but apple pie served with cheese – a mild Wensleydale – is very traditional in Yorkshire. At several such suppers we have enjoyed home-made wines – one man bringing parsnip and blackberry for us to taste.

Forehock of bacon
Beef tomato salad
Endive salad
Coleslaw
Potato salad
Plum chutney
Apple pie served with cheese
Oatcakes

OCTOBER

It is difficult to select what to include or exclude in October as vegetables seem so good and cheap at this time, and many species of game and shellfish are just coming into season. To use up the proliferation of autumn fruit described last month, preserve them in October – a good month because there are so many apples about, and so many jams and jellies rely on the bulk of apples and on their pectin content.

Hallowe'en is the major festival on the last day, when witches, spirits and ghosts wish to return to their "homes". Country people would guard against unwelcome visitors by putting a protective rowan branch above doors, or by placing hollowed-out turnips or swedes lit by candles at their windows.

Market Place

Vegetables: aubergines, avocados, beetroots, broccoli, Brussels sprouts, cabbages, carrots, cauliflowers, celeriac, celery, chanterelles, Chinese leaves, courgettes, fennel, garlic, globe artichokes, green beans, kohlrabi, leeks, marrows, onions, parsnips, peppers, potatoes, pumpkins, swedes, sweetcorn, sweet potatoes, truffles, turnips.
Fruit and nuts: apples, Asian pears, blackberries, crab apples, cranberries, damsons, dates, elderberries, figs, grapes, hazelnuts, mangoes, medlars, pears, pomegranates, quinces, rowan berries, satsumas, sloes, walnuts.
Fish: carp, cod, coley, conger eel, Dover sole, eel, grey mullet, haddock, halibut, herring, mussels, oysters, pilchards, plaice, prawns, sea bass, sea bream, shrimps, skate, sprats, squid, turbot.
Meat: beef, chicken, duck, goose, grouse, guinea fowl, hare, partridge, pheasant, pigeon, pork, rabbit, venison.

Tips and Hints

When preserving, have your jam pots washed, dried and warming on a low heat in the oven – about Gas $\frac{1}{4}$, 225°F, 110°C. Fill warmed pots to the brim with preserve and seal immediately with a waxed disc, waxed side down. Make sure no bubbles of air are trapped underneath. Either put jam pot covers on at once, or leave until preserve is quite cold. Dampen one side and place dry side down, stretching and fixing with an elastic band. Always use vinegar-proof lids – i.e. not plain metal – with vinegar preserves. Label with name and date, and store in a cool, dark, airy place.

To make *dry breadcrumbs* lay slices of stale bread in a tin and place in the bottom of the oven. Remove when dry and crush with a rolling pin. They should keep in airtight jars for months. To make *fresh breadcrumbs*, use semi-fresh bread and grate by hand on a grater or in a processor. They keep in the fridge or freeze well.

Fried breadcrumbs are a delicious accompaniment to roast game birds. Simply heat 25 g/1 oz butter or margarine in a frying pan and brown in it 50–125 g/2–4 oz wholemeal or white breadcrumbs. Serve hot (or you can store when cold in a jar in the fridge).

Use the sloes abundant now to make sloe gin. Rinse and dry fruit, prick each several times, and pack into a clean bottle or jar. Use a funnel to pour in enough caster sugar to come one-third of the way up the level of the fruit. Pour in gin to cover, cover tightly and leave for 3 months. Turn every few days until sugar has dissolved. Decant the liqueur carefully and use the drained fruit, with more sugar and water, to flavour a light syrup for a fruit salad (throw the sloes away afterwards).

RECIPES

PRESERVES

I think the days are long gone when the store cupboard was filled to bursting with enough of everything to last a year until the next season. With a freezer we can easily stagger the preserving season into short bursts through the year, although October is a good month as mentioned above, because of the wealth of apples. If you make chutneys or relishes do try to leave them untasted until they have matured; the flavours are much more mellow.
We enjoyed preparing the preserves in the picture below for the *Farmhouse Kitchen* series.

SPICED VINEGAR FOR PICKLES

This can be used for most pickles – of onions, baby beets, cauliflower and red cabbage. Either brown or white vinegar can be used, depending on type of pickle – but white looks better with onions and cauliflower.

Ingredients
1.2 litres/2 pints best vinegar (keep bottles for your finished product)
7 g/$\frac{1}{4}$ oz cinnamon bark
7 g/$\frac{1}{4}$ oz whole cloves
12 black peppercorns
7 g/$\frac{1}{4}$ oz whole mace
7 g/$\frac{1}{4}$ oz whole allspice berries
1 or 2 bay leaves

Method
1 Place vinegar and spices (in a bag if you like) in a glass or china bowl (not metal or polythene) standing on a pan of water. Cover bowl and bring water slowly to boil. Remove from heat.
2 Allow to get quite cold – at least 2 hours. Remove bag of spices or strain vinegar and put back into original bottles.

PICKLED ONIONS

Select small even-sized onions, and place without peeling in a brine made from 450 g/1 lb salt to 4.5 litres/1 gallon water. Place a plate on top to keep onions submerged. Leave 12 hours, then peel and place in fresh brine for 24 hours. Drain thoroughly, pack into screw-top jars, and cover with cold spiced vinegar which should be 1 cm/$\frac{1}{2}$ inch above onions. Cover securely, and don't eat for 3 months.

PICKLED BABY BEETS

Wash young beetroots carefully and put in a saucepan with measured water – for every 1.2 litres/2 pints, add 1 dessertspoon vinegar and 1 teaspoon salt. Boil the beets for 30 minutes until tender, then dip in cold water, rub off the skins, and pack into jars. Allow 6 teaspoons sugar per 600 ml/1 pint of spiced vinegar, and bring to the boil, stirring to dissolve the sugar. Pour into the jars to cover beetroot, put lids on at once, and screw up tightly.

PICKLED CAULIFLOWER

Select sound, firm, white cauliflowers, and break heads into small pieces. Place in brine as for onions, and leave for 24 hours. Drain well, pack into jars, cover with cold spiced vinegar, and cover securely.

PICKLED RED CABBAGE

Choose a firm cabbage of good colour, and shred. Place on a large dish, layer with a good sprinkling of salt (approximately 50 g/2 oz coarse salt to each 450 g/1 lb cabbage) and leave for 24 hours. Drain well, rinsing away any surplus salt, and pack loosely into jars. Cover with cold spiced vinegar and screw tops down securely. Ready after 1 week, but loses its crispness after 3 months.

ELDERBERRY CHUTNEY

You could make a similar chutney using prunes or stoned plums instead of the elderberries.

Yields about 1.8 kg/4 lb

Ingredients

450 g/1 lb elderberries, removed from stalks by running a fork down stems
450 g/1 lb onions, peeled and finely chopped
450 g/1 lb cooking apples or windfalls (weigh after peeling and coring), chopped
125 g/4 oz dried fruit (raisins, sultanas or both)
1 teaspoon mixed spice
1 teaspoon ground ginger
1 teaspoon salt
$\frac{1}{4}$ teaspoon cayenne pepper
300 ml/$\frac{1}{2}$ pint malt vinegar
325 g/12 oz sugar

Method

1. Put elderberries, onions and apples in a large pan. Add dried fruit, spices, salt, cayenne and half the vinegar.
2. Bring to the boil and simmer until ingredients are soft.
3. Add sugar and remaining vinegar. Stir over low heat until sugar is dissolved.
4. Then simmer until chutney is thick. It is thick enough when you can draw a wooden spoon through the mixture and the trail of the spoon remains without filling with excess liquid. Stir frequently to prevent sticking.
5. Meanwhile warm jars as on page 99. Fill jars to the brim with hot chutney and cover as on page 99. Leave to cool, and when quite cold, label.

ROWAN AND APPLE JELLY

This is a lovely amber-coloured jelly to eat with game or pork. You could use blackberries or elderberries (the latter good with turkey instead of cranberries) in place of the rowan berries.

Yields 800 g/1$\frac{3}{4}$ lb

Ingredients

450 g/1 lb rowan berries
450 g/1 lb cooking apples or crab apples
1.1 litres/2 pints water
450 g/1 lb preserving sugar

Method

1. Strip the berries off the stalks, rinse and dry them on an old kitchen towel. Wipe the apples and chop into small pieces.
2. Put the rowans and apples into a roomy pan with the water. Stew gently. Mash until everything is soft and pulpy – about an hour.
3. Strain this mash through a double layer of muslin lining a nylon sieve. Do not push, and leave overnight for liquid to drip through into a bowl.
4. You should have 600 ml/1 pint juice. Weigh the sugar out, using 450 g/1 lb per pint of juice.
5. Heat the juice in a clean roomy pan, add the sugar and stir over a low heat without boiling until the sugar has completely dissolved.
6. Bring to a boil and boil until setting point is reached (see page 20). (Do not boil jelly quite as hard as you would jam. A steady boil is what is needed.) Pot and cover in the usual way.

LEMON CURD

The addition of custard powder helps to speed the thickening process.

Makes 225 g/8 oz

Ingredients

1 egg
$\frac{1}{2}$ teaspoon custard powder
75 g/3 oz sugar
25 g/1 oz butter
finely grated rind and juice of 1 lemon

Method

1. Use a basin that will fit nicely over a pan of simmering water. Do not let basin touch the water.
2. Beat the egg with custard powder. Then add sugar, butter, lemon rind and juice.
3. Set basin over pan of simmering water and stir mixture from time to time until it thickens. It will take about 15–20 minutes.
4. Fill a small jar and cool. Keep in fridge and use within 4 weeks.

GAME

Game is at its best in autumn, particularly during late October and November. It starts with the opening of the grouse season on August 12th, as before then it is illegal to shoot the birds. In some quarters there is a great race to have freshly shot birds on the menu that very day, which makes nonsense of the theory that all game should be hung before cooking. However, it's all a matter of taste. Grouse, partridge and, from 1st October, pheasant are now in season, and many other game species are available – pigeon, hare and rabbit. See also page 24.

ROAST PHEASANT

Hen birds are more tender and tasty, but cock birds are bigger.

Serves 4–5

Ingredients

1 pheasant, plucked, drawn and trussed
125 g/4 oz piece stewing beef, cheaper cut
2–4 rashers streaky bacon

Gravy

25 g/1 oz wholemeal or plain flour
hot vegetable water
salt and freshly ground black pepper

To serve

bread sauce (see page 123)
fried breadcrumbs (see page 99)
watercress

Method

1 Put the piece of stewing beef inside bird. This keeps the bird moist during cooking. It is not served up with the bird but do not throw it away: with the carcass it will make good stock.
2 Spread bacon over bird, put in a roasting tin, and roast in a moderate oven, Gas 4, 350°F, 180°C, for 45–60 minutes.
3 Remove on to a warmed serving dish and keep hot while you make the gravy.
4 Sprinkle the flour into the roasting tin and stir into the fat (there's not much) and the meat juices. Let cook for a minute on a low heat.
5 Pour in hot water, or water in which vegetables have been cooked, and stir well until gravy thickens, adding more water if necessary, to make a fairly thin gravy. Boil for 2–3 minutes. Taste and add salt and pepper if necessary. Strain into warmed gravy jug.
6 Serve the bird garnished with bunches of fresh watercress, breadcrumbs, potato crisps, braised celery or Brussels sprouts. A bread sauce (see page 123) may be cooked in the cooler part of the oven with the bird. Have a jelly on the table – the rowan and apple on page 101 is good.

CHESHIRE POTTED PIGEON

Will keep in a fridge or cold place for 1 month. Once open it should be used in a day or two. Eat like a pâté with toast or crusty French bread.

Fills at least 8 small ramekins

Ingredients

3 pigeons, plucked and drawn
salt and freshly ground black pepper
a dash of Worcestershire sauce
2–3 tablespoons melted butter

Method

1 Put the pigeons in a pan, cover with water and boil until the meat is leaving the bones.
2 Remove from the water and, when cool enough to handle, carefully remove all bones.
3 Put bones back into the saucepan and boil until the water has reduced to about 1 cupful stock.
4 Mince the meat finely and season with salt, pepper and Worcestershire sauce. Moisten with stock from the bones and a little of the melted butter.
5 Press into ramekins and run a layer of melted butter over the top to seal.

JUGGED HARE

This popular classic British dish is surprisingly cheap and not difficult to make. It is really only a glorified stew enriched with port, and thickened with a liaison – butter kneaded with flour – and the blood of the hare to give a really smooth sauce. Take care not to overcook the hare. Simmer it slowly. A young hare, leveret, will take about 2 hours, and serve six, whereas an older hare will take over 3 hours and be enough for eight to ten people.

Serves 6

Ingredients

1 young hare, cut into neat pieces
50 g/2 oz bacon fat
2 large onions, each stuck with 2 cloves
1 stick celery, cut in 2.5 cm/1 inch pieces
6 black peppercorns
rind of ½ lemon
a pinch of cayenne pepper
1 blade mace
1 bouquet garni (see page 144)
salt and freshly ground black pepper
1.2 litres/2 pints water

For the liaison

50 g/2 oz butter
50 g/2 oz wholemeal or white flour
150 ml/¼ pint port wine
1 tablespoons redcurrant jelly
the blood of the hare

For the garnish

salad oil for frying
4 slices bread
chopped parsley

Method

1 When cutting the hare, save as much of the blood as possible. Your butcher will do this for you and, more often than not, will put the blood in a tin for you to carry home.
2 Melt the bacon fat in a large frying pan and fry the joints briskly until they are a good brown colour; then remove them from the pan.
3 Pack the joints into a heavy ovenproof casserole with all the remaining ingredients, including the water, and cover with a tightly fitting lid. Bake in a moderate oven, Gas 3, 325°F, 160°C, for 2 hours or until the hare is tender.
4 Pour off the stew gravy juice through a sieve into a pan. Remove spices, lemon rind and herbs from the casserole and keep meat and vegetable warm.
5 To make the liaison, work the butter on a plate with a palette knife until it is soft. Then knead in the flour a little at a time to form a smooth paste.
6 Reheat the gravy, but do not allow it to boil, and add the kneaded butter in small pieces, whisking constantly until it has thickened.
7 Add the port and redcurrant jelly to the gravy and simmer gently until the jelly has dissolved.
8 Blend 2–3 tablespoons of the gravy with the blood and then add the blood to the rest of the gravy. Adjust the seasoning with more salt and pepper.
9 Strain the gravy over the hare. Cover bottom of a frying pan with oil, heat, add the slices of bread and fry until golden. Cut the fried bread into kite shapes and arrange on top of the hare. Sprinkle with parsley. Serve with redcurrant jelly and savoury forcemeat balls (see below).

FORCEMEAT BALLS

These savoury dumplings go well with many other casseroles – with a rabbit stew as well as the jugged hare above. They could be cooked separately, in about 600 ml/1 pint stock.

Ingredients

125 g/4 oz fresh wholemeal or white breadcrumbs (see page 99)
40 g/1½ oz shredded suet
1 tablespoon grated onion
2 teaspoons chopped fresh thyme, or ½ teaspoon dried thyme
½ teaspoon salt and pepper mix (see page 89)
1 egg, beaten
a little wholewheat or white flour

Method

1 Mix breadcrumbs, suet, onion, thyme and seasoning and bind together with the egg. Make into twelve balls and roll in flour. Fry lightly in oil to seal.
2 Place in the juices in the casserole, cover and cook for the last 30 minutes of the cooking time.

GREENS

A number of green vegetables are around in October, among them broccoli, Chinese leaves, courgettes, leeks and, primarily, cabbages and those harbingers of winter, Brussels sprouts. Sprouts need little cooking: steam or simmer them until still crisp, then toss in butter, and scatter with fried breadcrumbs (see page 99), with cooked chestnuts, or with pieces of fried bacon. There is no excuse either for cabbages to be the Cinderella of the vegetable garden. There are so many delicious varieties, and there are many exciting dishes which can be created with them. Cook cabbage very minimally as well – simmer in 3 tablespoons water for every 675 g/1½ lb cabbage, 5–6 minutes if shredded and 8 minutes if quartered.

BUBBLE AND SQUEAK

Serves 4

Ingredients

450 g/1 lb freshly boiled potatoes
225 g/8 oz freshly cooked cabbage or Brussels sprouts, drained
175 g/6 oz onions, peeled and finely chopped
oil or fat to fry (bacon fat is good)
25 g/1 oz butter
salt and freshly ground black pepper
25 g/1 oz plain flour

Method

1. While the potatoes and cabbage are cooking, fry the onion in a little of the oil or fat until transparent and soft.
2. Mash the drained potatoes with the butter in a large bowl. When this is fairly smooth, add the chopped cooked cabbage (or sprouts) and the onion. Mix and season well.
3. Divide the mixture into eight. Shape each piece into a round flattish cake and dust with flour. Fry each cake in hot oil or fat until brown and crisp on each side. Serve at once.

QUICK STIR-FRIED VEGETABLES WITH OYSTER SAUCE

Serves 2

Ingredients

325 g/12 oz leafy vegetable of your choice (cabbage, greens, Chinese leaves, celery, crisp lettuce or watercress)
2 tablespoons oil
1 clove garlic, chopped
1 tablespoon oyster sauce
salt, freshly ground black pepper and a pinch of sugar

Method

1. Prepare the vegetable, washing it thoroughly, and cut or shred it into bite-sized pieces. If it has thick stems separate these from the rest as they take longer to cook.
2. Heat the oil in a wok or large frying pan and quickly fry the garlic until lightly brown.
3. Add the stem pieces and cook for 3–4 minutes, tossing constantly over quite a high heat. Add the rest of the vegetable and stir-fry only until its colour begins to change to a more brilliant green.
4. Add the oyster sauce, a little salt, pepper and sugar; stir and cook for 1 or 2 minutes more. Serve the moment it is cooked.

COLESLAW

Serves 4

Ingredients

½ firm white cabbage
1 small onion, peeled and finely chopped
2 sticks celery, finely chopped
1 large carrot, grated
a few sultanas and chopped walnuts
4 tablespoons mayonnaise (see page 76)
2 tablespoons milk

Method

1. Mix the shredded cabbage together in a large bowl with the chopped onion, celery, grated carrot, sultanas and walnuts.
2. Lighten the mayonnaise with the milk, then mix into the salad ingredients, tossing well to coat thoroughly.

SHELLFISH

Although most seafood is available throughout the year, some species are at their best in autumn in the northern hemisphere. The season for oysters starts about September and lasts until April. Mussels start about September too, and last until March, although they're best until December. Scallops are available from September to March, but are best from December. Both crab and lobster are available from April to December, but are best in the summer months.

Prawns from North Atlantic waters are boiled in sea water and frozen. They are infinitely better in their shells than the packets of shelled prawns; I know they are more expensive, but you have the bonus of the heads and shells to make a good fish stock, or very superior sauces (see below). Mussels are my favourite shellfish – so easy, so bursting with flavour and, best of all, so cheap. Buy and eat on the same day if possible. Store for no more than 1 day, by leaving wet with a wet cloth over them. Do *not* leave in water. To prepare them, you need to wash them in lots of changes of cold water. I keep a bristle brush to brush round the "seam", and I use the back of an old knife to knock off any barnacles. Tear out the "beard" – the filaments at the seam. Discard any mussels that are gaping open before cooking and do not close when tapped, as well as any which stay shut after cooking.

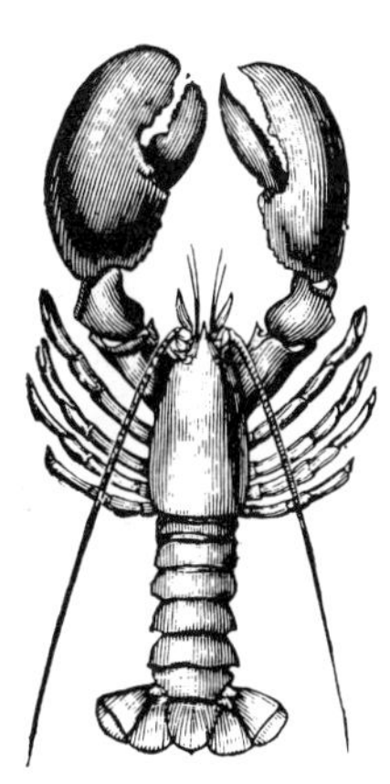

PRAWN COCKTAIL

I am not very fond of this name but it is so universally known that I think I should just try to improve its image rather than its title!

Serves 2

Ingredients

175 g/6 oz prawns in shell
1 teaspoon tomato purée
25 g/1 oz onion, peeled and finely chopped
1 small stick celery, finely chopped
150 ml/¼ pint double cream
1 dessertspoon fresh lemon juice
a pinch of cayenne pepper
salt and freshly ground black pepper

To serve

chopped lettuce
2 wedges fresh lemon
a few sticks of cucumber
grated carrot

Method

1. First peel the prawns and reserve them. Put the heads and shells in a saucepan with the purée, onion and celery. Barely cover with cold water, bring to a boil, then simmer for 20 minutes. Stir well two or three times, breaking down the shells as you do.
2. Put the contents of the pan through a liquidizer or food processor, then strain the stock through a sieve. Discard the shells.
3. In another pan mix the double cream and the prawn stock. Bring to a gentle boil and reduce this liquid until it is thick enough to coat the back of a wooden spoon. Allow to go cold before adding the lemon juice, cayenne pepper and adjusting the seasoning.
4. To serve, set the chopped lettuce in two glasses or flat bowls and divide out the reserved prawns. At the last minute pour the prawn sauce over, and serve each with a wedge of lemon, cucumber and grated carrot.

HOT MUSSELS AND TAGLIATELLE VERDI

Instead of serving with pasta and the vegetables as in the recipe, you can simply cook the mussels as below and then serve with lots of crusty bread to mop up the juices. They're so simple! Without the pasta, you might need *more* mussels to serve the same number of people – but it all depends on appetite, of course!

Serves 4

Ingredients

900 g/2 lb mussels, cleaned and prepared as overleaf
15 g/½ oz butter
2 tablespoons dry white wine
125 g/4 oz courgettes
125 g/4 oz mangetout peas, topped, tailed and stringed
275 g/10 oz tagliatelle verdi
50 ml/2 fl oz good salad oil
1 fat clove garlic, peeled and finely chopped
1 tablespoon chopped parsley

Method

1 Put the cleaned mussels in a roomy pan with the butter and wine. Set the pan over a high heat with the lid on, and cook, shaking the pan heartily from time to time, and holding the lid on. When the mussels have opened – about 4–5 minutes – they are ready (to eat or serve as below).
2 Strain the liquid through a sieve and reserve. Pick out the mussels and throw away the shells.
3 Cut the courgettes and mangetout into neat batons rather thicker than two matchsticks.
4 Now cook the pasta in plenty of boiling salted water until done but not soggy.
5 In the mussel pan, heat the oil and stir-fry the mangetout first for just a couple of minutes then add the courgettes. Stir well and add the mussels, about 3–4 tablespoons of the mussel juices, and the garlic. When all this is well heated stir in the strained pasta and parsley. Mix well, re-heat briefly and serve.

October Menu

CHILDREN'S HALLOWE'EN PARTY

In my home town of Dundee, we children dressed up and went "guising" round neighbours. The idea was to say a poem or sing a song in exchange for some sweets, nuts or, if very lucky, a silver threepenny piece. Tricks were also played on those reluctant to participate – I remember two door handles tied together and both doorbells pressed at once! After supper you could "dook for apples". Fill a baby bath with water and bob red apples in it; everyone tries to bite an apple with hands held behind. You could also hang treacley girdle scones from strings, for everyone to bite at similarly. We still have a row of cup hooks screwed into the ceiling of a conservatory where we did just that many years ago.

Cream of tomato soup
Sausages baked in the oven
Bubble and squeak with Brown plum sauce
Devil's Food Cake
Toffee apples

NOVEMBER

This is a month absolutely full of saints' days and special events. The 1st is All Saints' Day and the 2nd is All Souls' Day. The 15th commemorates St Catherine to whom you should pray if you want a husband. Sadly she herself was martyred on a wheel-shaped instrument of torture, and thus we have Catherine wheels on Firework Night, the 5th, a day on which the whole country burns in effigy Guy Fawkes who tried to blow up the King and Parliament in 1605. The 30th is the feast of St Andrew, patron saint of Scotland. November is also the month of remembrance for our dead in two World Wars. The most cheerful celebration is Thanksgiving Day in America; it is held on the third Thursday of the month.

Market Place

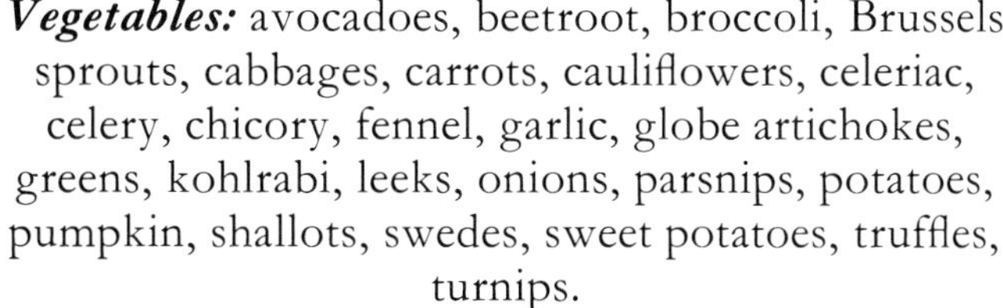

Vegetables: avocadoes, beetroot, broccoli, Brussels sprouts, cabbages, carrots, cauliflowers, celeriac, celery, chicory, fennel, garlic, globe artichokes, greens, kohlrabi, leeks, onions, parsnips, potatoes, pumpkin, shallots, swedes, sweet potatoes, truffles, turnips.

Fruit and nuts: almonds, apples, Asian pears, Brazil nuts, chestnuts, clementines, cranberries, custard apples, dates, figs, filberts, grapes, hazelnuts, kumquats, mangoes, oranges, pears, persimmons, pineapples, pomegranates, quinces, satsumas, sharon fruit, walnuts.

Fish: carp, cod, coley, conger eel, Dover sole, eel, grey mullet, haddock, halibut, herring, mackerel, mussels, oysters, plaice, sea bass, sea bream, skate, sprats, turbot, whiting.

Meat: beef, chicken, duck, goose, guinea fowl, hare, partridge, pheasant, pigeon, pork, rabbit, turkey, venison.

Tips and Hints

Now would be a good time to process the basic ingredients for pastry and store them in the freezer ready to be made into mince pies or whatever later on. Simply rub the fat into the flour and salt for the pastry. The dry crumbly mixture freezes well in plastic freezer bags in useable quantities. All that is needed thereafter is defrosting and the addition of water.

Dried fruit for mincemeat and puddings is always better if washed in hot water. Drain and spread out in a thin layer on kitchen paper to dry. Result is a much more moist cake or pudding.

Instead of ready chopped and mixed peel for puddings and mincemeat, I prefer to buy the candied fruit in big pieces (from a wholefood shop usually). I wash off all the sugar and if the peel is hard, I leave it in the water to soften. Then chop very small.

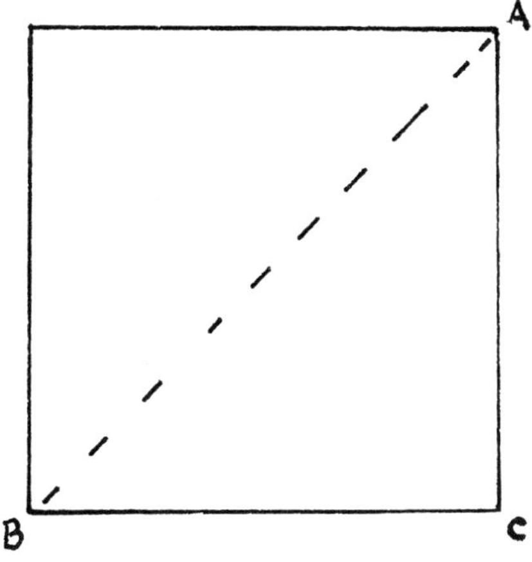

To make a paper icing bag, take a piece of greaseproof paper, 25 cm/10 inches square. Fold along the line A–B. Twist in point A to meet point C and hold it firmly in place. Then twist point B towards point C to complete the cone. Fold the points over firmly to secure the cone. Then snip off the tip so that the piping nozzle will project through.

To test boiling sweet mixtures without a thermometer, drop a teaspoon of mixture in a cup of ice-cold water. Always remove pan of mixture from heat when conducting the test. *Soft crack* (280–285°F, 140–142°C); when you remove from water and feel it between fingers and thumb, it is hard but not brittle. *Hard crack* (300°F, 150°C); when you remove from water and feel it between fingers and thumb, it is brittle. (For *soft ball* and *hard ball*, see pages 92 and 114).

RECIPES

ADVANCE PREPARATIONS FOR CHRISTMAS

This month there is Stir-up Sunday, traditionally the time when Christmas puds were mixed, but these are not the only pre-Christmas preparations you can do. Many things can be made in advance and put in the freezer if you have the space. The first thing *I* do is make and freeze lots of breadcrumbs (see page 99), but you could also make a special ice cream, a pâté, as well as a special soup. All freeze well, as do pastry crumbs, even the uncooked mince pies themselves. My mincemeat can be refrigerated, and the Christmas puddings keep very well in a cool place. The Christmas cake, if made now, will benefit enormously from several weeks in which to mature.

CHRISTMAS CAKE WITH ALMOND PASTE AND ROYAL ICING

Bake this cake very early in November (or even earlier) as it improves with keeping.

Ingredients
125 g/4 oz raisins, chopped
125 g/4 oz glacé cherries, chopped
125 g/4 oz mixed peel, chopped
450 g/1 lb currants
125 g/4 oz sultanas
2 tablespoons brandy, sherry or rum
225 g/8 oz butter
225 g/8 oz soft brown sugar
225 g/8 oz plain white flour
1 teaspoon mixed spice
125 g/4 oz ground almonds
4 eggs, beaten

Method
1 Put the raisins, cherries and mixed peel in a bowl with currants and sultanas. Pour over the brandy, sherry or rum and leave overnight.
2 Line a 20 cm/8 inch diameter round cake tin or an 18 cm/7 inch square tin, with greased, greaseproof paper (see page 29).
3 Cream butter and sugar together in a large bowl.
4 Sift flour and mixed spice into a separate bowl and add soaked fruit and ground almonds. Mix well together.
5 Add spoonfuls of egg then flour mixture to bowl of creamed ingredients. Mix well at each addition until all has been mixed thoroughly.
6 Put mixture into prepared tin. Wrap a double thickness of brown paper or newspaper around outside of tin. Let it stand up a good 5 cm/2 inches above tin. Tie it on with string. This will protect cake from browning on the outside before middle is cooked.
7 Bake cake for 3–4 hours in a cool oven, Gas 2, 300°F, 150°C, until firm, and fruit stops "singing" and "sissing".
8 Remove cake from tin on to a cooling rack. When cold, store in an airtight tin and let it mature as long as possible. It will keep for a year.

ALMOND PASTE

Make enough to cover top and sides of the cake opposite.

Ingredients
325 g/12 oz ground almonds
175 g/6 oz icing sugar, sieved
175 g/6 oz caster sugar
juice of ½ lemon
a few drops each of ratafia essence, almond and vanilla flavourings
1 teaspoon orange-flower water (buy it from the chemist)
2 teaspoons brandy, rum or sherry
1 large egg, beaten

To cover cake
1 egg white, beaten
icing sugar

Method
1 Mix ground almonds and sugars together.
2 Add lemon juice, ratafia, flavourings, orange-flower water and alcohol to the beaten egg.
3 Using a wooden spoon, mix the liquid carefully into almonds and sugar. Do not add it all at once because if mixture becomes too soft it will be difficult to roll out. Work it into a firm but manageable paste, kneading a little with hands.
4 To cover the cake, brush sides and top with a little beaten egg white (this gives a tacky surface to help the paste stick), and dredge a board with sifted icing sugar. Have more icing sugar ready for the rolling pin.
5 Take two-thirds of the almond paste for the sides of the cake. Measure the circumference – a piece of string will do – and the height of the sides. Your measurements will give a long, narrow rectangle.
6 Roll out the larger piece of paste just longer than this measurement and it will fit nicely round sides of cake. Press lightly with rolling pin at join.
7 For the top of the cake, shape remaining piece of paste into a round or a square and roll it out slightly larger than top of cake. Using the piece of string, check size of paste against size of cake top. Do not lift paste on to cake.
8 Turn cake upside-down on to the paste and trim neatly. Turn cake right side up again with paste in position. By doing it this way you get a nice flat surface to the paste.
9 Brush almond paste all over with egg white and leave to dry.

ROYAL ICING

This makes enough to cover the cake only, not for decoration. Mix the icing the day before you mean to ice the cake.

Ingredients
450 g/1 lb icing sugar
2 egg whites
2 teaspoons glycerine (buy at a chemist)
2 teaspoons lemon juice, strained

Method
1 Sieve icing sugar three times. This is necessary because the icing must not have any lumps in it – even tiny ones.
2 Put egg whites into a bowl and beat, but only lightly.
3 Add icing sugar to egg whites, a tablespoon at a time. Beat each spoonful in quickly with a round-bladed knife.
4 Add glycerine and strained lemon juice and mix in well. (Glycerine prevents the icing going rock hard.) Put a damp cloth over bowl of icing. Put bowl into a polythene bag and leave it overnight.
5 Next day, put cake on a board that is at least 7.5 cm/3 inches wider than the cake.
6 Put a first coat of icing on the sides. Use a plastic scraper, a hot knife or metal ruler. Dip it in a jug of boiling water, but wipe it dry before use. Never use a wet knife with this type of icing as it makes icing too soft and it may start to run.
7 Allow icing on the sides to dry overnight, then put a first coat on the top. It is better to use a hot knife or metal ruler for top, not a plastic scraper.
8 Allow time for icing to dry on top, then give the sides a second coat. Two coats of icing give a better finish. Finally, finish icing the top.

TO DECORATE CHRISTMAS CAKE

Ingredients
225 g/8 oz icing sugar
1 egg white
1 teaspoon lemon juice, strained
vegetable colouring

Method

1 Prick out the design on the cake top with a darning needle or hat pin.
2 Sieve sugar and add to beaten egg white as for royal icing above.
3 Add strained lemon juice and mix in well. Consistency should be very firm: it should form peaks in the bowl when you lift up the spoon.
4 Be very careful in colouring the icing. Add colour by dipping a skewer into the bottle and shaking it into icing.
5 Pipe on your design using a greaseproof paper bag (see page 109) or parchment bag with icing nozzles.

CHRISTMAS PUDDING

This is an excellent pudding, full of fruit. It can be made just a few weeks before Christmas but keeps for 6 months.

There is enough mixture for a 1.2 litre/2 pint basin plus a 300 ml/½ pint basin, *or* a 1 litre/1½ pint basin and a 600 ml/1 pint basin. Smaller puddings can be cooked with larger ones and removed from steamer slightly sooner. A 1.2 litre/2 pint pudding will provide ten to twelve helpings.

Ingredients
225 g/8 oz each of raisins, sultanas and currants, washed and dried
225 g/8 oz fresh breadcrumbs, wholewheat or white (see page 99)
50 g/2 oz almonds, blanched (see page 116) and finely chopped
1 apple, peeled, cored and finely chopped
grated rind and juice of 1 lemon
4 small eggs, beaten
250 g/9 oz moist brown sugar (try muscovado)
225 g/8 oz shredded suet
50 g/2 oz cut mixed peel
50 g/2 oz plain flour, wholewheat or white
1 rounded teaspoon mixed spice
3 tablespoons sherry or brandy

Method

1 Grease basins and place a circle of greaseproof paper or foil in the bottom of each. This will ensure puddings turn out easily.
2 In a very large bowl, mix all ingredients thoroughly. Make sure you get some help with the stirring!
3 Fill basins to 1 cm/½ inch below the rim. Do not pack the mixture in too tightly.
4 Cover basins with a piece of greaseproof paper, pleated along middle, and then with a piece of pleated foil. Tuck foil securely under rim of basin.
5 Steam the puddings 4 hours for 1.2 litre/2 pint basins and 2 hours for 600 ml/1 pint basins. The longer the steaming, the darker the pudding. If you do not have a steamer, stand basins on a trivet in a large pan of boiling water, put on the lid and boil. Do not let water go off the boil and remember to replenish with more boiling water from time to time. A pressure cooker will reduce cooking time considerably. Follow instructions in the handbook.
6 Remove puddings from steamer, take off paper and foil covers and leave to cool under a clean towel. When quite cold re-cover with fresh greaseproof paper and foil and store in a cool cupboard until required.
7 On Christmas Day, steam puddings 2 hours for the larger pud, 1 hour for the smaller. Or pressure cook to save time and fuel. Serve with rum sauce or rich brandy butter (see page opposite).

GRACE MULLIGAN'S MINCEMEAT

As mincemeat is liable to ferment, it is best if potted in a large jar and kept in the fridge – for up to 3 months.

Yields about 900 g/2 lb

Ingredients
225 g/8 oz seedless raisins
125 g/4 oz sultanas
125 g/4 oz eating apples, peeled and cored
125 g/4 oz mixed peel
50 g/2 oz shredded suet
225 g/8 oz currants
grated rind and juice of 1 lemon
125 g/4 oz soft brown sugar
1 tablespoon golden syrup
1 teaspoon mixed spice
1 teaspoon powdered cinnamon
$\frac{1}{4}$ teaspoon freshly grated nutmeg
4 tablespoons brandy or whisky

Method

1. Mince the raisins, sultanas, apple, peel and suet using the coarse mincing plates. Leave the currants whole.
2. Put all ingredients together and mix well.
3. Pot in cold jars, then cover as described on page 99. Keep in the refrigerator.

MINCE PIES

Mince pies are nearly always made with a double crust. The addition of cream cheese is not traditional, but it does make for a juicy pie. Freeze them *before* baking.

Makes a dozen

Ingredients
225 g/8 oz sweet shortcrust pastry (see page 116)
450 g/1 lb mincemeat
125 g/4 oz cream cheese
1 small egg, beaten

Method

1. Lightly grease the bun trays, and on a lightly floured board roll out the pastry thinly.
2. Stamp out twelve rounds using a 6 cm/$2\frac{1}{2}$ inch cutter. Re-roll the trimmings and cut twelve rounds using a 9 cm/$3\frac{1}{2}$ inch cutter.
3. Ease the larger rounds into the bun trays. Place a heaped teaspoon of mincemeat in each space and top with a small teaspoon of cream cheese.
4. Dampen the pastry edges with the beaten egg and press on the pastry lids, nipping the pastry rims together well. Brush over with beaten egg. Snip two or three Vs in each lid with scissors.
5. Bake in a moderately hot oven, Gas 6, 400°F, 200°C, for about 20–25 minutes until golden. Allow to rest in the tins for 10 minutes then cool on wire trays.

RICH BRANDY BUTTER

The mixture can be frozen well in advance or refrigerated for up to 4 days beforehand.

Ingredients
50 g/2 oz butter, softened
125 g/4 oz icing sugar
1 egg
50 g/2 oz ground almonds
150 ml/$\frac{1}{4}$ pint double cream
1 dessertspoon brandy

Method

1. Cream butter with icing sugar, then beat in the egg and ground almonds.
2. Whip cream separately until it holds soft peaks, then beat in brandy. Fold into the butter mixture.
3. Refrigerate for at least an hour before use, but preferably overnight. Serve with the Christmas pudding.

SWEET THINGS

I always associate things like toffee apples and cinder toffee with this time of year – I make the former for our church Christmas Fair every year, for instance, and cinder toffee is a must for a Bonfire Night party. Many other sweet things are festive and delicious at Christmas time, and can even be given as Christmas gifts. So many people appear to have everything, but a gift made especially for them is always appreciated. (Food gifts could also be some of your home preserves or liqueurs, but be sure to attach instructions on how they will keep or store, etc.)

TREACLE TOFFEE

For a good variation, substitute half of the treacle with honey.

Makes about 900 g/2 lb

Ingredients
450 g/1 lb Barbados sugar
450 g/1 lb black treacle or molasses
2½ tablespoons cider vinegar
125 g/4 oz butter

Method

1. Put sugar, treacle or molasses and vinegar in a large saucepan and stir over a low heat until sugar is completely dissolved.
2. Bring very slowly to boiling point. Keep it boiling for 10 minutes, stirring occasionally.
3. Carefully and gradually stir in the butter, in thin pieces, piece by piece.
4. Continue to boil to 284°F, 142°C, soft crack stage (see page 109).
5. Remove from heat and allow toffee to settle a minute. Pour gently into a well-greased tin. A tin 23 cm/9 inches square gives pieces just over 1 cm/½ inch thick.
6. When just cool, mark into squares. When cold, break into pieces. Wrap in waxed paper or store in an airtight container.

TOFFEE APPLES

For this you need a large heavy-based pan and a large greased baking tin. The sticks are not all that easy to find, so I have always used flat ice-lolly sticks. In fact I was persuaded about 10 years ago to bulk-buy – I still have hundreds left!

Ingredients
12 small eating apples
450 g/1 lb white or brown sugar
50 g/2 oz butter
1 tablespoon golden syrup
2 teaspoons vinegar
150 ml/¼ pint water

Method

1. Wash and dry the apples. Push a stick into each stalk end.
2. Put all remaining ingredients into a large pan. Stir over gentle heat until sugar is dissolved, then boil rapidly for 5 minutes. Stir just a little.
3. The syrup in the pan has to boil until it comes to the hard ball stage (265°F, 130°C) – when a little of the syrup dropped into a cup of ice-cold water forms a hard ball, which is still chewy. Go on boiling until this point is reached.
4. Remove pan from heat and, as quickly as possible, dip the apples. Twirl them around in toffee for a few seconds, shake off the surplus and put on to the greased baking tin to set. If the toffee starts to set in the pan, heat it gently again.

TOFFEE-GLAZED FRUITS

Fresh fruits such as strawberries, orange or mandarin segments, clusters of two grapes, etc., are dipped in caramel, giving them a shiny crisp coating. Canned fruit can also be used, including maraschino cherries, provided the syrup is dried off carefully before they are dipped in the caramel.

Lovely for a party, the fruits cannot be made too far ahead as they go sticky in a day or so, particularly if weather is humid. They'll stay crisp for 2–3 days.

The quantity of syrup given is enough to coat about twenty pieces of fruit. You will need tiny crinkled paper sweet cases which can be bought at good stationers. Also, several wooden cocktail sticks for dipping.

Ingredients

Syrup for caramel

125 g/4 oz sugar
60 ml/2½ fl oz hot water
1 teaspoon glucose (buy from the chemist)

Method

1 Brush baking trays lightly with some oil, and prepare fruit, making sure it is clean and thoroughly dried.
2 Put sugar in the hot water in a pan, stirring over a low heat until dissolved. Bring to the boil and add glucose.
3 Boil to 290°–300°F, 145–150°C, or until just before the syrup turns brown.
4 Set pan on a wet cloth to stop it boiling and, as soon as syrup has stopped bubbling, start dipping fruits, holding them by the stems or spearing them with a pair of wooden cocktail sticks.
5 Put each dipped fruit on the oiled trays to set, then place in small paper cases.

CINDER TOFFEE

This is something I always associate with bonfires. It is easy to make and is sometimes called sponge toffee in old recipe books, the reason being that the bicarbonate of soda added makes the mixture froth up to look like a sponge with lots of holes in it.

Makes about 900 g/2 lb

Ingredients
900 g/2 lb brown sugar (any kind)
175 ml/6 fl oz cold water
2 level teaspoons bicarbonate of soda

Method

1 Put the sugar and water in a very large pan with a heavy base and stir over a medium heat until all the sugar has melted.
2 Turn up the heat a little and boil for about 20 minutes or to the hard crack stage (see page 109).
3 Take the pan off the heat and immediately stir in the bicarbonate of soda. Check that there are no lumps in the soda. The toffee will froth up.
4 Pour into a well-greased tin – a big roasting tin is good. Leave to set, and mark while still warm. Break up before the toffee goes cold, and store as treacle toffee.

RICH RUM TRUFFLES

Makes about 12

Ingredients
75 g/3 oz dark cooking chocolate
1 teaspoon double cream
1 egg yolk
15 g/½ oz butter
rum to taste (1–2 teaspoons)
chocolate vermicelli

Method

1 Break chocolate into a small basin and melt over a pan of simmering water (do not let water touch basin). Remove from heat.
2 Add cream, egg yolk, butter and rum, and beat mixture until thick and like a paste.
3 When cool, form little balls of the mixture and roll them in chocolate vermicelli. Store in the fridge for up to a week (if you're able).

NUTS

Nuts come into the shops at this time, and I think they're almost as much a herald of Christmas and winter as Brussels sprouts! Their season, fresh, is very short – from November to January for almonds, Brazils and chestnuts, from October to January for walnuts, and only October and November for hazels. So, we should buy and eat and enjoy.

HOME-MADE MUESLI

This quantity makes enough for several days' healthy breakfasting. Buy ingredients in a good wholefood shop.

Ingredients
25–50 g/1–2 oz dried apricots
25 g/1 oz hazelnuts, walnuts or both
50–75 g/2–3 oz soft brown sugar
75 g/3 oz each of sultanas and raisins
325 g/12 oz porridge or rolled oats
25–50 g/1–2 oz each of wheat, rye or barley flakes
15–25 g/½–1 oz bran or millet

Method
1 Chop the apricots finely and the nuts (use *more* if you wish), roughly.
2 Mix all the ingredients together, adjusting the fruit, nut and sugar content to suit the quantity of cereal ingredients. Don't be mean with the fruit or nuts. Keep in a large covered bowl or tin to use when required.
3 To serve. The night before, place the quantity required in a bowl and pour on just enough milk. Next morning, add a little top of the milk. It is good to eat like this but even better with grated fresh apple, sliced bananas or stewed fruits.

FUDGE PECAN TART

This rich sweet shortcrust pastry is ideal for dessert flans and tartlet cases. Almost as rich as shortbread, it needs careful handling and blind baking, but the taste is quite magnificent.

Serves 4–6
Ingredients
Sweet shortcrust pastry
225 g/8 oz plain white flour
a pinch of salt
150 g/5 oz butter or margarine, softened
25 g/1 oz sugar
1 egg yolk
a squeeze of lemon juice
2 or 3 tablespoons cold water
Filling
50 g/2 oz butter
50 g/2 oz light soft brown sugar
200 ml/7 fl oz sweetened condensed milk
25 g/1 oz pecan nuts (or walnuts), roughly chopped
25 g/1 oz seedless raisins
25 g/1 oz glacé cherries, chopped

Method
1 Sieve flour and salt into a bowl, then rub in butter or margarine as lightly as possible. Add sugar.
2 Mix together egg yolk, lemon juice and 2 tablespoons water, and stir into flour with a round-ended knife.
3 Then use your hand to knead lightly to a firm dough, adding 1 or 2 teaspoons more water if necessary.
4 Rest pastry for about 15 minutes, then roll out carefully and thinly. Lay pastry on the *outside* of an upturned flan tin 18 cm/7 inches in diameter.
5 Prick the base and bake in a moderately hot oven, Gas 5, 375°F, 190°C, for 20–35 minutes. Leave to cool before turning out and while you make the filling.
6 Melt butter in pan. Add sugar and condensed milk. Stir over low heat until sugar is dissolved and mixture boils. Boil for 5 minutes, stirring all the time.
7 Take pan off heat. Stir in walnuts, raisins and cherries. Pour mixture into pastry case and leave to cool.

SALTED ALMONDS

Ingredients
125 g/4 oz whole almonds
15 g/½ oz butter
salt

Method
1 Blanch almonds as follows. Place in small basin, cover with boiling water, and leave for 5–8 minutes. Drain and press away the skin between finger and thumb. Pat the almonds dry.
2 Heat butter in small frying pan until just frothing. Tip in almonds, and stir over gentle heat until golden. Drain and salt.

November Menu

Guy Fawkes Barbecue

On coming to live in Yorkshire I learned that Guy Fawkes was born in York and that he was a pupil at St Peter's School there. Because of this the boys *never* have a bonfire to cremate their former pupil! However, the rest of us do, usually with a barbecue as well. I am a very nervous barbecue cook. I find it much less nerve-wracking to part-cook all the chicken drumsticks, sausages and anything with meat in advance; they can then go over the barbecue for a final browning and basting with a tangy tomato or other barbecue sauce. Potatoes I like to bake in advance too (for about 40 minutes) with each one wrapped in foil (at Gas 7, 425°F, 220°C). If the bonfire is big enough you could put the wrapped potatoes in the embers either to cook if the fire is hot enough or just to heat up. Start off with a hot soup in beakers (chop the fish chowder ingredients smaller) and finish off with cinder toffee.

Fish chowder
Chicken drumsticks marinated in Tangy tomato sauce
Baked jacket potatoes with grated cheese
Sausages
Cinder or treacle toffee

December

Christmas is a hectic time: there are all the traditional foods to be ordered, prepared and cooked; gifts and cards to wrap and send; decorations to be hung; and a tree to be erected and decorated. One can easily forget about the principal reason for the festival. However, we all seem to manage it every year, and I love it, although it's hard work. In my Scottish childhood, we saved all our energies and celebrations for Hogmanay the following week, the final day of December. I remember one Hogmanay tradition which has long since gone – the "first foot" gift of a kipper (once coal, bread and salt to symbolize warmth, hospitality and life). Our fish shop had rows and rows of kippers dressed up with coloured crêpe paper, bows for the "men", and skirts for the "girls"!

Market Place

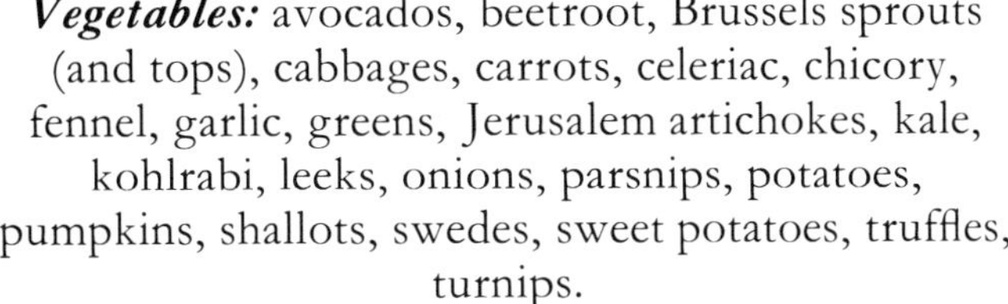

Vegetables: avocados, beetroot, Brussels sprouts (and tops), cabbages, carrots, celeriac, chicory, fennel, garlic, greens, Jerusalem artichokes, kale, kohlrabi, leeks, onions, parsnips, potatoes, pumpkins, shallots, swedes, sweet potatoes, truffles, turnips.

Fruit and nuts: almonds, apples, Asian pears, Brazil nuts, Cape gooseberries, chestnuts, clementines, cranberries, custard apples, dates, grapes, kumquats, lychees, mangoes, oranges, pears, persimmons, pineapples, pomegranates, rhubarb, satsumas, sharon fruit, walnuts, waterchestnuts.

Fish: carp, cod, coley, conger eel, Dover sole, eel, grey mullet, haddock, halibut, herring, lemon sole, mackerel, mussels, oysters, plaice, scallops, sea bass, sea bream, skate, sprats, turbot, whiting.

Meat: beef, chicken, duck, goose, guinea fowl, hare, pheasant, pigeon, pork, rabbit, turkey, vension.

Tips and Hints

The so-called Christmas celery – that which has had a touch of frost and is a bit dirty – is quite delicious, and every part of it can be used in some way. Its nutty flavour is far better than the pale green kind. As celery gets older, some of the outer leaves become stringy: just snap the stick in two and it will be easier to see and remove the strings.

Gather your holly early in the month to protect the berries from the birds. It will keep well with its stems forced into the soil, covered with a dustbin bag or an old nylon curtain.

A couple of days before the holiday, I prepare and chill a large bowl of eggs for sandwiches: hard-boiling about four, and scrambling four. I chop all together with plenty of seasoning and butter, and if too soft, I add 2-3 tablespoons fresh breadcrumbs. Served in soft baps (from the freezer), these egg sandwiches go down really well. Well covered, the eggs will keep in the fridge for 3 days.

If you don't want to make a proper cranberry preserve, you could simply stew some cranberries until soft in a minimum amount of water, sweeten to taste, and add some orange juice.

In advance of the big day, I make up 600 ml/1 pint stock (bone or giblet) and thicken it with flour or cornflour. It is then ready to go into the juices from the bird in the roasting tin to make the gravy.

I always put a heatproof bowl in the fridge so that I can pour in the fat from the bird. Returned to the fridge, the fat will rise in the cold bowl, can be skimmed off more easily, and I can rescue the juices for the gravy.

Save the copious fat from a Christmas goose – it makes for the most wonderful roast potatoes!

A SUGGESTED CHRISTMAS SCHEDULE

This is only an outline, obviously, but I hope it might help you plan ahead for what is, to many of us, a fraught time of year!

WELL IN ADVANCE

Make the Christmas pudding, the Christmas cake(s), the cranberry preserve, the brandy butter, the mincemeat, sweets – all the traditional items that can either store or freeze well (see November). Make and freeze some soups (see January) which can be defrosted for the odd lunch or supper.

THE WEEK BEFORE

Make sure your shopping lists are carefully adhered to, and collections from the butcher and greengrocer are well organised. The public holiday itself seems to get longer each year, so make sure you have enough basics to last while the shops are shut – freeze loaves of bread, for instance, in case you run out (or make your own, of course!), and buy more salad vegetables than usual so that there is always the makings of a quick, healthy meal.

THE DAY BEFORE

Make the stuffings and, after you collect your bird, make the giblet stock. Chill overnight. Take anything you need for tomorrow out of the freezer. Lay the table if possible. Make the brandy butter to serve with the Christmas pudding.

We enjoy ourselves on the TV set at Christmas.

THE BIG DAY ITSELF

1. Stuff the bird. Preheat the oven.
2. Depending on the size of the bird, start cooking at least 3–4$\frac{3}{4}$ hours in advance of the designated meal time. Baste often.
3. Allowing time for eating the starter and main course, put Christmas puddings on to boil 1–2 hours before the designated meal time. Prepare a fresh fruit salad now if liked.
4. Peel potatoes, boil and then roast at the top of the oven for about 1 hour alongside the bird (slightly longer than recommended on page 42 because of the lower oven temperature).
5. Prepare the bread sauce and put in oven alongside turkey for 20 minutes before the designated meal time.
6. Prepare vegetables. Grill cocktail sausages and rolls of streaky bacon (three from each rinded rasher, and easier to turn over if threaded on to skewers).
7. Take bird out of the oven and its tin and place on warm dish 10–15 minutes before serving the meal. This allows it to "rest".
8. Make the gravy and cook the vegetables briefly.
9. Carve and serve on to hot plates, passing bread sauce, cranberry preserve and gravy separately.
10. Sit down, eat and relax!

RECIPES

CHRISTMAS STARTERS

I feel these should be as simple as possible. In fact we often omit this course, but one tradition in our family is just a glass of Buck's Fizz – real orange juice, freshly squeezed, and chilled champagne. Sometimes we are sent smoked salmon from the west of Scotland, and that is splendid, simply served with plenty of fresh lemon juice and buttered brown bread. Something like Parma ham, wafer thin and served with chilled slices of melon, could not be easier. Another simple favourite of mine is slices of chilled melon cut thin and laid out like a fan; a sprig of watercress or curly endive and a dressing made of 2 tablespoons mayonnaise, 3 tablespoons double cream and 50 g/2 oz Roquefort cheese blended together. The strong flavour of the cheese tempered with cream is perfect with juicy ripe melons. If you can get two melons, one with green flesh, and one with gold, this would also make for a pretty picture. The following two pâtés would also be fairly light and they're very flavourful.
(They make good Christmas gifts too!)

SMOKED MACKEREL PÂTÉ

For this you need a liquidizer or food processor.

Serves 6

Ingredients
325 g/12 oz smoked mackerel
2 thick slices wholemeal or brown bread
3 tablespoons wine or cider vinegar
½ tart eating apple, about 125 g/4 oz, peeled and cored
freshly ground black pepper

Method

1 If using home-smoked mackerel, proceed straight to Step 2. Otherwise proceed as follows. Soak fish in water for an hour or two to relieve strong smoky taste. Wash thoroughly and cook in water just to cover, simmering for 5 minutes. Drain.
2 Remove bones and skin from fish.
3 Soak bread with vinegar.
4 Place all ingredients in liquidizer or food processor and switch on until all is blended and smooth.
5 Press into a 450 g/1 lb loaf tin or a 13 cm/5 inch round tin or a soufflé dish. Chill.
6 Turn out on to an attractive plate to serve – with Melba toast (see page 14) and butter, a nice salad or plain watercress.

SMOKED COD'S ROE PÂTÉ

Do not use an electric mixer or blender for this pâté as it would break up the tiny eggs.

Serves 4

Ingredients
225 g/8 oz smoked cod's roe
juice of 1 lemon
150 ml/¼ pint double cream, or 75 g/3 oz butter mixed with milk made up to 150 ml/¼ pint
a pinch each of ground ginger, cayenne pepper and paprika

Method

1 Remove skin and put the cod's roe into a bowl.
2 Put in half of the lemon juice and mash well with a fork. Add rest of lemon juice and beat again.
3 Gradually beat in cream, or the butter and milk.
4 Season to taste with the ginger and cayenne pepper.
5 Transfer to a serving dish, sprinkle with paprika, and refrigerate. Serve with hot buttered toast.

THE CHRISTMAS MAIN COURSE

Three of the most traditional Christmas foods are turkey, goose and ham. Turkeys were once driven into town in flocks for Christmas (and still are in parts of Europe), often equipped with boots to keep their feet in good condition or with their feet dipped in tar then sand to give them instant shoes! However, with modern turkey production, the birds are no longer bred only for Christmas (in America for Thanksgiving), and are now available and popular all year round, thanks to small breeds and deep freezing.

Geese are enjoying a slight revival, and are nothing like as fatty as they used to be. (This fat was much prized in the north for rubbing on an uneasy chest in order to relieve the lungs!) A goose at Christmas or New Year makes a delicious change from turkey.

A piece of ham is always a really good standby to eat cold for a salad or just for sandwiches. It accompanies cold turkey well too. There's a good recipe for a forehock of bacon on page 71.

TO ROAST A TURKEY

Always try to time the cooking so that the turkey is removed from the oven on to a warm dish 10–15 minutes before serving the meal. This will allow time to make the gravy and also to "rest" the bird.

Cooking Time: This method is recommended unless instructions given with the bird differ. Always make sure that a turkey that was frozen has defrosted *completely* – this can take over 24 hours with a big bird.

Stuffed Weight kg	lb	Total cooking time in hours
2.7–3.6	6–8	3–3½
3.6–4.5	8–10	3½–3¾
4.5–5.4	10–12	3¾–4
5.4–6.3	12–14	4–4¼
6.3–7.2	14–16	4¼–4½
7.2–8.1	16–18	4½–4¾

Method

1 Choose and prepare two suitable stuffings for neck end and body cavity (see below). The body cavity takes more than the neck end. Any stuffing left can be put in a pie dish, covered securely and cooked in the bottom of the oven. It will take no harm there for 1½–2 hours.
2 Remove giblets from turkey, wash them and place in pan with sufficient water to cover. Add 6–8 peppercorns and a small bay leaf. Bring to boil and simmer for at least 2 hours. Strain and keep stock for gravy. The giblets can now be discarded. (Preparation and cooking of giblets can be done the day before.)
3 Wipe inside of turkey and stuff to a plump, even shape.
4 Truss with skewers and fine clean string, folding wings under body and tying legs tightly together.
5 Place on rack in a large roasting tin. Cover well with good dripping or pieces of fat pork or bacon. Press foil around legs as they are inclined to dry before being cooked.
6 Place in a moderately hot oven, Gas 6, 400°F, 200°C, for 20 minutes. Then lower heat to moderate, Gas 4, 350°F, 180°C, for remainder of cooking time. Baste frequently, turning bird on its side once or twice during cooking time. If breast browns too quickly cover with foil. Test to see that the bird is cooked by piercing the thickest part of the thigh through to the bone. If the juices run clear it is ready.
7 Remove turkey on to a warm dish and make gravy with giblet stock and sediment from roasting tin. Serve with bread sauce and cranberry preserve (both opposite), small sausages, bacon rolls, roast potatoes (see page 42) – or indeed, new potatoes (see page 59) – and Brussels sprouts (or other green vegetable).

TWO STUFFINGS FOR TURKEY (OR CHICKEN)

Adjust quantities for size of bird and cavity to be filled.

Corn and Bacon Stuffing

50 g/2 oz butter
1 large onion, peeled and finely chopped
225 g/8 oz bacon pieces
1 can sweetcorn, approx. 300 g/11 oz
4 tablespoons chopped parsley
2 teaspoons salt and pepper mix (see page 89)
1 teaspoon mixed herbs
1 small loaf bread, crusts removed
2 small eggs, beaten

Method

1 Melt butter in pan. Fry onion and chopped bacon to soften.
2 Place in bowl, add sweetcorn, parsley, salt, pepper and herbs. Cut bread into cubes and add as well.
3 Mix eggs in lightly. Do not pack stuffing into bird too tightly.

Sausagemeat Stuffing

450–675 g/1–1½ lb pork sausagemeat
1 teaspoon mixed herbs
1 onion, peeled and finely grated
1 apple, cored and grated
a little freshly ground black pepper
fresh breadcrumbs (see page 99)

Method

1 Mix together all ingredients, adding 1–2 tablespoons breadcrumbs if mixture is too soft.
2 Stuff into the bird. Do not pack too tightly.

BREAD SAUCE

Ingredients
1 medium onion, peeled and stuck with 2 cloves
450 ml/¾ pint milk
½ level teaspoon salt
6 black peppercorns
a small piece of bay leaf
175–225 g/6–8 oz fresh wholemeal or white breadcrumbs (see page 99)
15 g/½ oz butter

Method

1 Put the onion in saucepan with milk, salt, peppercorns and bay leaf. Cover, place over very low heat and bring to just below boiling point.
2 Remove from heat and set aside for 30 minutes or longer.
3 Strain milk, bring it to the boil, pour over the crumbs, add butter and stir.
4 Place in heatproof dish. Cover and place in oven on low shelf under meat for 20 minutes.

CRANBERRY AND ORANGE PRESERVE

This sets like jelly and is delicious with roast turkey.

Yields about 900 g/2 lb

Ingredients
450 g/1 lb granulated sugar
450 g/1 lb fresh or frozen cranberries
finely grated rind and juice of 1 orange
water

Method

1 Put sugar to warm in a very cool oven, Gas ¼, 225°F, 110°C. Put clean 225 g/8 oz jars into oven at same time.
2 Pick over fruit and discard any that is bruised. Put cranberries into a roomy saucepan.
3 Mix orange juice with water to make 300 ml/½ pint. Add to pan with rind.
4 Bring to the boil over gentle heat and simmer for 10 minutes, stirring occasionally. Cranberries will cook down to a thick pulp.
5 Push pulp through a nylon sieve to make a purée, scraping as much as possible from under the sieve.
6 Put purée in a clean pan, add sugar and stir over low heat until sugar is dissolved.
7 Now turn up heat and boil for 4–5 minutes.
8 Pour hot preserve into prepared jars. Cover as on page 99.

COOKING THE GOOSE

Time the cooking as for the turkey, allowing 10–15 minutes to "rest".

Cooking time: 20 minutes to each 450 g/1 lb weight after stuffing plus 20–30 minutes extra.

Method
1 First make the stuffing (see next recipe).
2 Make giblet stock as for turkey.
3 Wipe inside of goose and fill with stuffing, not too tightly packed.
4 Truss goose neatly with skewers and fine clean string. This is simply to keep the stuffing in.
5 Place goose on a roasting rack in oven tin. Rub with salt and sprinkle on a little flour. The breast can be pricked with a fork to help the fat escape.
6 Place in centre of oven preheated to moderately hot, Gas 6, 400°F, 200°C, for 20 minutes to crisp skin. Then lower heat to moderate, Gas 4, 350°F, 180°C for remainder of cooking time and cover goose with greaseproof paper or foil to prevent excess browning. Remove paper for last 20 minutes if goose is not brown enough. (You may need to remove excess fat from the tin from time to time.) Test with a skewer as for the turkey.
7 Remove goose on to warm dish and make the gravy, using giblet stock, and onion liquor reserved from preparation of stuffing. Serve with roast potatoes and green vegetable as for turkey (or with braised red cabbage, see page 16), perhaps with a slice or two of apple fried in a little butter.

SAGE AND ONION STUFFING

This quantity is sufficient for a 3.6–4.5 kg/8–10 lb goose.

Ingredients
900 g/2 lb onions, peeled and chopped
25 g/1 oz butter
125–175 g/4–6 oz fresh breadcrumbs
2 teaspoons salt and pepper mix (see page 89) and 3 teaspoons dried sage

Method
1 Cook onion in a little water until just softening, about 15–20 minutes. Drain well, reserving liquid for gravy.
2 Add butter, crumbs, seasoning and sage to taste, using sufficient crumbs to make mixture hold together. Do not stuff too tightly.

CHRISTMAS DESSERTS

The traditional dessert for a Christmas Day meal is that pudding which you made in November. Serve it with brandy butter (see page 113). Or you could also try the ice cream below. If you prefer a lighter finale, serve a compôte of fresh oranges – citrus fruits are at their peak now – or a simple fruit salad. This could consist of segmented oranges, chunks of banana and apple (toss the latter in citrus juice to prevent discoloration; prepare and add the banana at the last minute), some chopped or sliced nuts, or any other exotic fruit around at this time of year (December marks the beginning of the short lychee season, for instance).

COMPÔTE OF FRESH ORANGES

Serves 4

Ingredients
3 large or 4 smaller oranges
water
125 g/4 oz sugar

Method
1 Scrub oranges and score the skin into four sections. Cover with boiling water and leave 5 minutes. Peel.
2 Reserve four to five sections of peel, cut away white pith and discard. Cut the remaining rind into very fine strips.
3 Place strips of rind in a small pan of water, bring to the boil, drain and half-fill the pan with fresh water. (This is to remove any bitterness.) Simmer about 30 minutes until the rind is really tender. Drain and discard water.
4 Place sugar and 150 ml/$\frac{1}{4}$ pint fresh water in pan. Dissolve sugar over a low heat then bring to boil and simmer for 3–4 minutes until looking syrupy.
5 Add shredded peel and simmer 2–3 minutes. Leave to cool. (A couple of tablespoons of sherry or even a tablespoon of Grand Marnier, Orange Curaçao or brandy can be used to cool syrup, and adds a very special flavour.)
6 Peel away any white pith from oranges, and cut into thin slices, removing pips.
7 Place orange slices in a serving dish, then pour over syrup and shredded peel when quite cold. Chill a little before serving.

ICE CREAM CHRISTMAS PUD

It is worthwhile making up the whole quantity, then dividing the mixture between a variety of small basins or old teacups. Once frozen, the puddings can be released from their containers by dipping momentarily into hot water. Then refreeze them on a tray and in polythene bags for storage. The full quantity fits a 1 litre/$1\frac{1}{2}$ pint pudding basin.

Ingredients
a 495 ml/$17\frac{1}{2}$ fl oz carton vanilla ice cream (or chocolate if you want the pud to look dark)
75 g/3 oz each of raisins, sultanas and currants
2 tablespoons sherry or brandy
40 g/$1\frac{1}{2}$ oz broken walnuts, chopped
50 g/2 oz glacé cherries, red, green and yellow, chopped

Method
1 Overnight soak the raisins, sultanas and currants in the sherry or brandy.
2 Turn out the ice cream to soften very slightly.
3 Mix everything together very swiftly. Pack into pudding basins or teacups, and re-freeze.
4 To serve, allow to soften slightly, turn out into a deep dish and top with a sprig of holly.

CHRISTMAS LEFTOVERS

Most of us face the Christmas bird leftovers with enthusiasm at first – and then with some despair! There are a few good and different ideas here which won't allow the family to become bored. Don't forget the variety of salads that can accompany cold turkey, goose or ham (see pages 71, 122, 124), nor the delicious sandwiches that can be made. When the bird is finally picked clean, use the carcass to make lots of good strong stock (see page 12) for soup.

TURKEY (OR CHICKEN) RISSOLES

Makes 8 small rissoles

Ingredients

1 rasher bacon, rind removed
125 g/4 oz cooked turkey, finely minced
50 g/2 oz fresh brown breadcrumbs
salt and freshly ground black pepper
1 egg yolk or 1 tablespoon white sauce
1 egg, beaten
dried breadcrumbs to coat rissoles
fat or oil to deep-dry

Method

1. Fry the bacon until really crisp, then crush into small pieces.
2. Mix turkey, bacon, fresh breadcrumbs and seasoning with enough white sauce or egg yolk to bind it together.
3. With floured hands, shape mixture into short fat sausages. Leave aside to firm up.
4. Dip rissoles in beaten egg, then in dried breadcrumbs. Leave aside to firm up.
5. Heat fat or oil until really smoking. Fry rissoles until golden. Drain on kitchen paper.

TURKEY (OR CHICKEN) KEBABS

Makes about six kebabs. The kebabs freeze well before they are fried and can be cooked straight from the freezer.

Ingredients

2 cloves garlic
½ green chilli, de-seeded
a 5 mm/¼ inch cube fresh ginger
325 g/12 oz cooked turkey meat, skin and bones removed
1 small egg
½ teaspoon garam masala
½ teaspoon cumin powder
¼ teaspoon grated nutmeg
½ teaspoon salt
oil for deep-frying

Method

1. Put the garlic, chilli and ginger into a food processor and process until it is finely chopped (or, of course, chop or mince by hand).
2. Add the turkey, egg, spices and salt and process until everything is smooth and well mixed.
3. Brush your hands with a little oil and form shapes with the turkey mixture about 1 cm/½ inch thick. Put them on an oiled tray in the refrigerator for 2 hours. They are easier to fry when very cold.
4. Deep-fry the turkey kebabs in hot oil for a few minutes each side, then drain them on kitchen paper. Serve them hot with tangy tomato sauce (see page 83) and salad, or as a snack with some yoghurt *raita* – natural yoghurt mixed with diced cucumber and some freshly chopped or freeze-dried mint.

TURKEY (OR CHICKEN) IN SHERRY SAUCE

Serves 4

Ingredients

325 g/12 oz cold cooked turkey
75 g/3 oz butter
1 small onion, peeled and chopped
2 lean rashers bacon, rinded and chopped
50 g/2 oz button mushrooms
2 level tablespoons wholemeal flour
salt and freshly ground black pepper
300 ml/½ pint turkey stock
3 tablespoons dry sherry
chopped parsley and toast

Method

1. Fry bite-sized pieces of turkey (or chicken) in hot butter until golden. Drain meat, place it on a hot serving dish and keep warm.
2. Fry onion and bacon in same pan for about 2 minutes, add mushrooms and cook for 2 minutes.
3. Stir in flour and a shake of salt and pepper. Cook for 1 minute, then add stock and simmer for 2 minutes.
4. Add sherry, bring just to boil, and pour over chicken. Sprinkle on the chopped parsley and serve with toast, cut into triangles.

DECEMBER MENU

CHRISTMAS LUNCH

With long experience I've got this Christmas lunch more or less taped, but I still think that any kind of a roast is one of the most difficult meals to bring together on time: with veg, gravy, accompaniments etc! Added to all this, our entire family used to have to be at one of our local hospitals for 11 am on Christmas Day – my husband Brian is a GP and the old tradition survived that a doctor carves the turkey. I never had time to worry about how my own turkey was getting on!

Buck's fizz
Melon with Parma ham or Blue cheese dressing
or
Smoked salmon
Roast Turkey or Goose with Stuffing
Sausages and Bacon rolls
Roast potatoes
Green vegetables
Bread sauce
Cranberry and orange preserve
Gravy
Christmas pudding with
Rich brandy butter
and/or Fresh orange compôte
Coffee and Toffee-glazed fruits

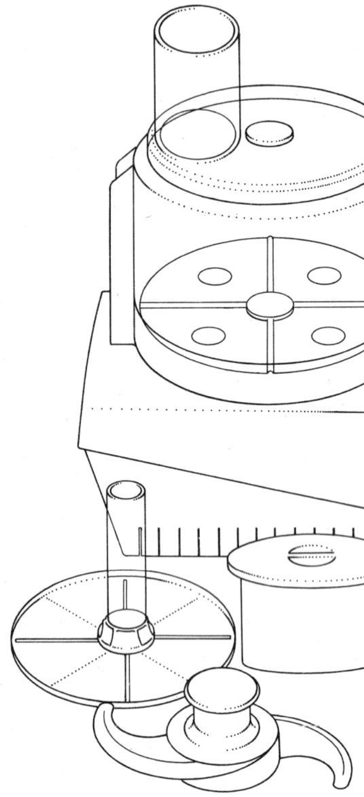

Food processor

KITCHEN APPLIANCES

Undoubtedly electrical kitchen appliances are a great help to the busy cook. Many are expensive, so only invest in a particular piece of equipment if the cost can be justified. The ultimate kitchen appliance is, of course, your cooker, and I haven't got space here to go into all the ins and outs. However, one question I'm always being asked is whether I have any preference for cooking with gas or electricity. I cannot say I do. I used nothing but gas for 15 years, then nothing but electricity for the next 15. I now use gas *and* electricity at the television studio, as well as a halogen hob at home. I find the halogen rings – that is, heat by light – are as immediate as gas. Any cooker must have a good grill attached – this is vital. Other than that, the selection below is of appliances that I believe are good to have in the kitchen.

REFRIGERATORS AND FREEZERS

These are now as essential to the modern kitchen as a cooker. I give a few tips on choosing and using freezers on p. 136, and with refrigerators many of the same rules generally apply: they should be big enough to contain the perishable stores for all your family needs at the height of summer; the doors should open the right way; cleaning and defrosting should be simple; there should be adjustable shelves and plenty of standing room for a number of tall bottles. I, myself, find the mini compartments in many refrigerators are pretty useless. Hygiene is very important, so check your refrigerator stores regularly and throw away outdated supplies. Also check the bottom shelf temperature pretty regularly. Thermostats are not always accurate, and I find it is best to keep to around 5°C. Much higher, say 8°C, and the milk does not keep any time at all.

The combined fridge/freezers come in a wide variety of sizes, but do check on the star ratings of the freezer compartments, so that you are sure of the freezing capacity.

MIXERS AND PROCESSORS

This is another regular question: which is more useful, a mixer or a processor? The answer depends on the kind of cook you are. If you are a keen baker then there is nothing to beat the big mixers with stands and bowls, and which have heavy-duty motors. One of my daughters is still using my original mixer, now 35 years old, and I have a smart new one to use on the set. Then of course there are all the gadgets which go with mixers. Most have a blender, so useful for puréeing soups, pâtés etc, and a mincer. I have used mine a lot recently, to make my own sausagemeat and sausages (this way I know exactly what goes into them). The three beaters with a big mixer are extremely useful to the home cook:

the ordinary one for creaming butter and sugar; the dough hook for bread dough; and the wire whisk for meringues, fatless sponges, etc.

A food processor is a wonderful gadget for chopping meat and breadcrumbs, etc. The various blades are splendid for shredding vegetables, both for stir-frying and for salads. I am not so impressed with their ability to cream or whisk.

Hand-held Electric Whisk
This is a good alternative to an expensive big mixer. It is capable of doing most of the whisking a big mixer can do, but in smaller quantities – especially good for less heavy mixing jobs like whipping cream, mayonnaise, fruit purées, etc.

Hand-held Electric or Battery Stick Whisk or Creamer
Smaller still, this is a handy gadget for whisking a small quantity of mayonnaise, cream or baby food, and some models will handle mashed potatoes, purées and pâtés.

Electric Kettle
This is a necessity for almost all of us, and there is a huge range of finishes and sizes to choose from. Those which cut-out automatically when the water has boiled are probably best. Look after both the outside and the inside, de-scaling regularly if you live in a hard-water area.

Electric Deep-fryer
If you deep-fry a lot, one of these can be useful. It keeps the temperature of the oil constant to whichever setting you select, and helps to control smells. It is also much safer.

Electric Frying Pan
These have lids, retain a constant heat rather like a slow-cooker (see below), and could be the ideal solution for a single person or student. In fact it is like a miniature cooker: not only can you fry in it, but you can also casserole chicken pieces and meat. On some, there is a stoneware dish which fits inside the pan for cooking slowly.

Slow Cooker
The extremely low heat used over a long period to cook stews or a very tasty pot roast makes this gadget a good investment. Switched on as you leave for work the food will be ready the minute you get home. Because of the controlled heat, there is no fear of spoiling. The electricity used is minimal too, so it is an economical way of braising tougher cuts of meat (you have to pre-fry/sear, etc, separately though).

Pressure Cooker
Still a most useful addition to any kitchen. I use mine for soups, stocks and stews. There is absolutely no danger if you follow the instructions in the handbook. In fact, you can now get a pressure cooker which makes hardly any noise.

Microwave Cooker
Comparatively, this is one of the newest kitchen appliances. They are heavy and should not be moved unnecessarily, and models with drop-down doors take up less work surface space. Once you have mastered the microwave cooker's many features you can cook entire meals, and thaw and reheat food straight from the freezer. I do think, though, that they are more practical for small meals – the larger the quantity the more inefficient they become. Cooking and reheating individual meals for the latecomer is an added bonus. Apart from meals, a microwave cooker helps with a number of other tasks such as softening butter or cream cheese, melting chocolate and gelatine, and also blanching vegetables before freezing.

Combination Microwave Cooker
These combine the speed of microwave cooking with conventional heat, but they are heavy on power and involve more complicated programming.

Electric Toaster
These come in many varieties, for two slices and for four slices, and often you can dictate the shade of brown of the toast. Make sure the slots are wide enough to take bread you have sliced yourself – bought or home-made – and that there is a crumb tray for easy cleaning.

Electric Sandwich Maker
This excellent gadget can turn a simple sandwich into a hot tasty meal.

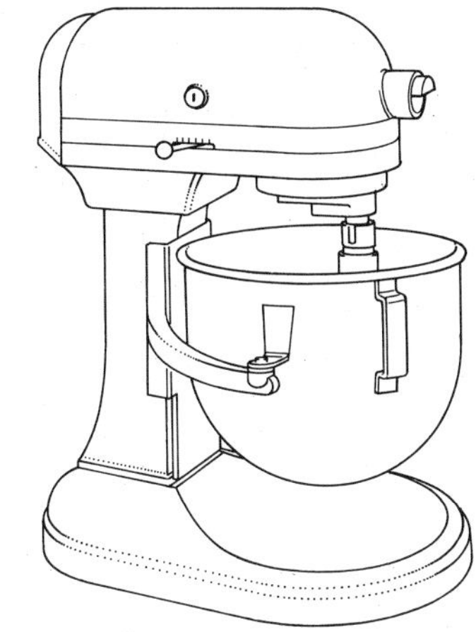
Heavy duty blender

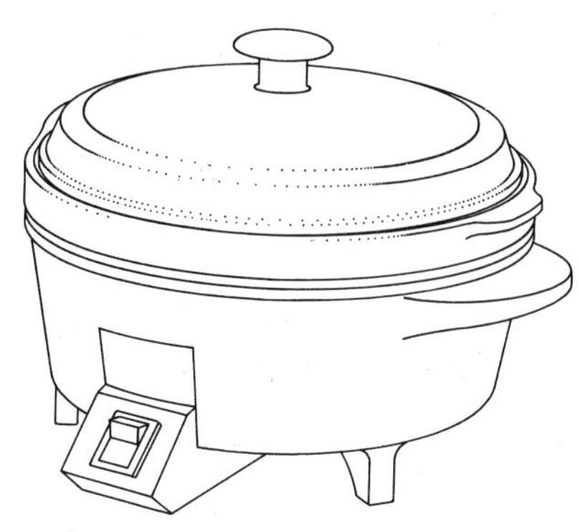
Slow cooker

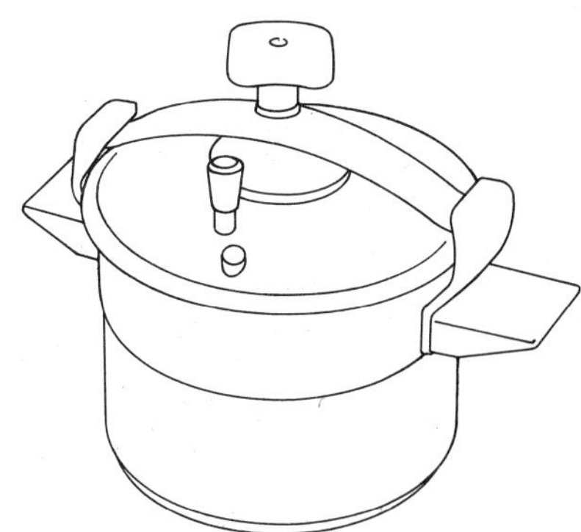
Pressure cooker

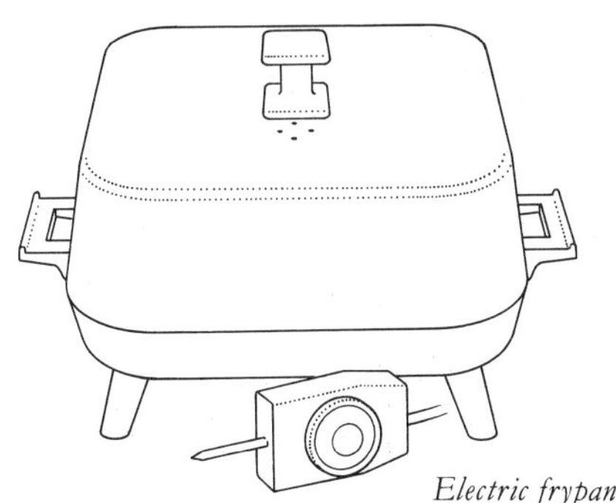
Electric frypan

It will seal in sweet or savoury fillings, and many can also cook steaks and burgers very efficiently.

Electric Carving Knife
These can be useful for slicing meat (or vegetables) more evenly than is possible by hand, or for coping with difficult joints, though bones present problems. They're also good for slicing smoked salmon to the required thinness – and most come with a blade suitable for cutting through frozen foods.

Electric Yoghurt Maker
If you like yoghurt, and use it in cooking, a yoghurt maker is a good investment. You can make yoghurt at home in various other containers (see page 75), but it's easiest with a kit – basically a temperature-controlled or insulated flask and thermometer. There are many varieties available, and all have easy-to-follow instructions.

A final word: none of the electrical parts of any of the above appliances must be immersed in water when washed.

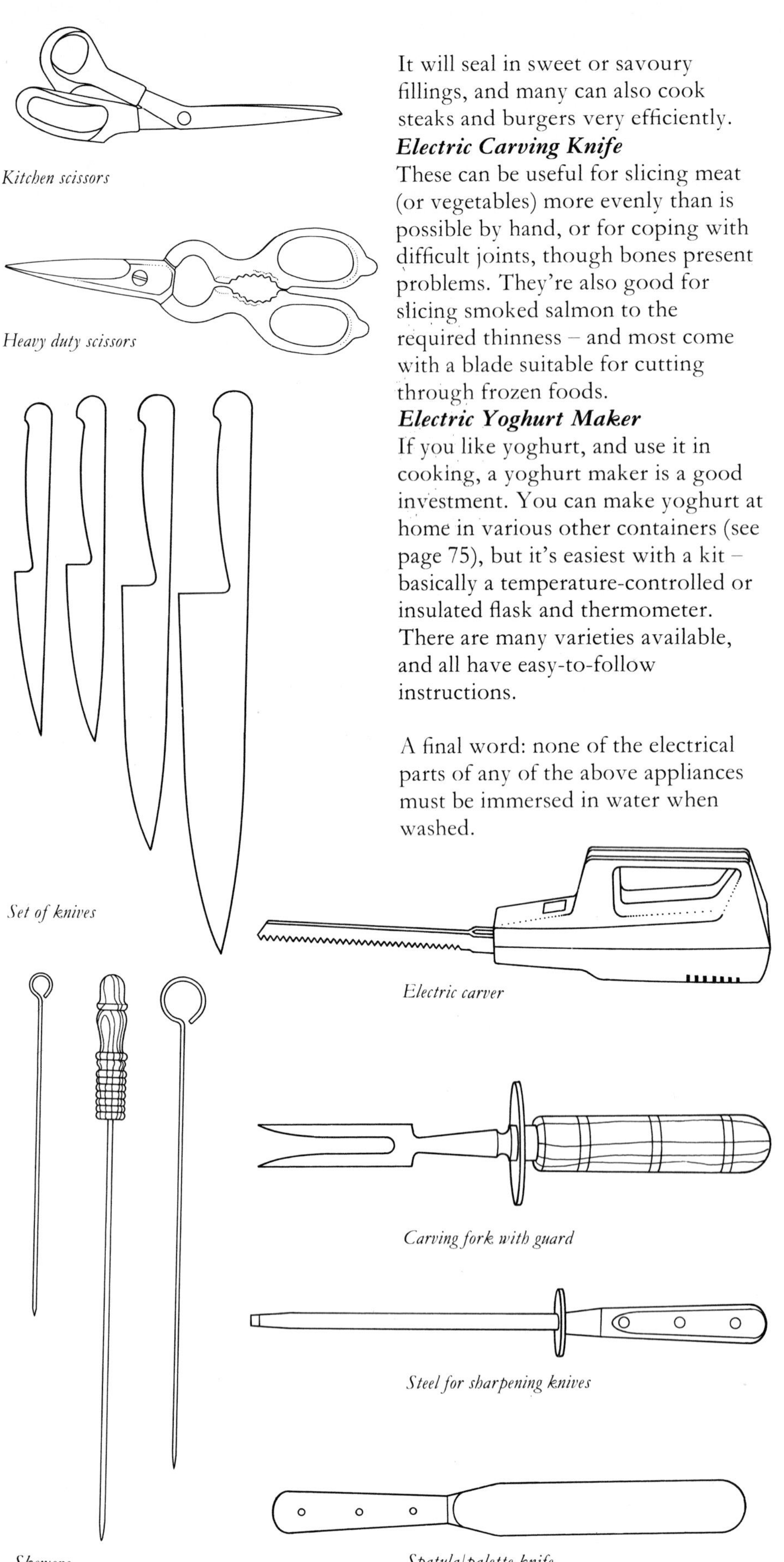

Kitchen scissors

Heavy duty scissors

Set of knives

Electric carver

Carving fork with guard

Steel for sharpening knives

Skewers

Spatula/palette knife

KITCHEN TOOLS

The big items or appliances may be the most expensive "tools" in the kitchen, but there are a host of other things that are vital – the tools with which to chop, mix, measure, store, and in which to do the actual cooking! The following are a selection of those which I consider of value.

CUTTING AND CHOPPING

A frustrated cook is often a cook using a blunt knife or knives – and it is bluntness that usually causes accidents, not sharpness.

Knives Good easy slicing depends on well balanced, razor-sharp knives. Carbon steel knives have the edge over stainless steel ones which, although bright and hard-wearing, cannot be sharpened to the keenness of their flexible, stainable rivals. I am still using a knife I bought in a cutlery shop at Les Halles, the famous meat market in Paris, over 30 years ago. Its carbon-steel blade is very thin and does have to be cleaned regularly, but I would not be without it. The handle split last year but the director of *Farmhouse Kitchen*, Graham Watts, is a craftsman with wood; he fitted a beautiful smooth teak handle to the old blade and I expect it to go on for another 30 years! The other knife I bought at the same time for paring, broke in two some time ago. My children detected my sadness at the loss of an old friend and when I went out to the garden they had organized a funeral, with the knife in a shoe box and a suitable memorial "stone" made out of cardboard!

Knife blades must be firmly riveted to the handles. Wooden handles give the best grip of all, but, unlike plastic ones, must not go into the dishwasher. Carbon steel knives should be washed by hand immediately after use, and stored like all knives in a rack when they cannot be blunted by other utensils. If carbon steel *does* stain – and it is very susceptible to foods with a high acid content, like tomatoes, lemons and rhubarb – rub with a cork dipped in abrasive cleaning powder.

The number of knives you need depends upon individual needs. I suggest a basic collection of two cook's knives with 7.5 cm/3 inch and 20 cm/8 inch blades, one paring knife for vegetables and a carving knife. A serrated knife is always good for slicing bread.

Steel for Sharpening Knives This should be used often, and choose the hardness of the steel to suit the type of knives you have. One with a hand guard is best. Hold the steel at a 20° angle to the blade of the knife, and draw lightly down the front first then the back. Knife sharpeners are easier to use and more popular than a steel, but they can ruin a true edge.

Stainless Steel Carving Fork Invaluable for all sorts of "holding" jobs while you're cutting. Choose one that has a guard, and two strong tines.

Spatula A spatula or palette knife is not strictly for cutting, but is very useful for turning omelettes, spreading soft mixtures and sliding under pastry to prevent it sticking. Choose one of stainless steel, and make sure it's flexible.

Potato Peeler Those with one central blade are very useful for stripping skin off most vegetables, as are the swivel-action peelers which rotate according to different surfaces and cut either way with their double-edged blades. Better and healthier than a knife to use on potatoes as a thinner layer of the nutrient-rich skin is cut away.

Plastic Mouli-grater Even if you've got the electrical appliances, one of these, with alternative metal attachment for coarse or fine grating, is useful for cheese, chocolate, nuts and carrots in small quantities.

Box Grater There are a number of styles, but those with three kinds of perforations and a sharp split for slicing vegetables, are best – for grating cheese, lemon peel and bread. Special graters are available for nutmeg, some even have compartments to hold the whole spice.

Kitchen Scissors These should be light, comfortable to use, and chosen for left- or right-handed use. I use scissors for many jobs, from a fine shower of green chives, to cutting meat into manageable pieces and removing skin and gristle. Some tougher kitchen scissors can be dismantled for cleaning, and others are designed with dual roles, such as nut-cracking!

Can and Bottle Opener Those which have both functions in one are cheap enough to throw away and replace often. Many people swear by the more expensive wall-mounted can openers. Whichever type you use, always be careful of the sharp edges of an opened tin.

Chopping Board One of thick beech is probably best. It needs to be cleaned carefully, and can mellow as it matures if nourished by olive oil.

Skewers There are many available – long, metal and decorative for kebabs, and shorter for trussing birds or testing to see if something is done. Flat ones are better than round for kebabs, as the food doesn't slip off so easily.

MIXING AND MEASURING

It is always worth paying out a little more for good quality tools – wooden spoons that won't split, sieves that won't give in to pressure.

Weighing Scales This is the first necessity, and a good set of precision or balance scales (the latter are much more attractive in the kitchen) should weigh up to at least 1 kg/2 lb in metric and Imperial. Plastic scales are available which weigh up to 2.5 kg/5 lb in metric and Imperial. Choose which is more appropriate to the type of weighing you want to do – and according to the space in and look of your kitchen, etc.

Measuring Jugs These are available in clear polypropylene with 600 ml/1 pint or 1.2 litre/2 pint capacity, or in toughened glass at 600 ml/1 pint or 1.2 litre/2 pint or in a French model

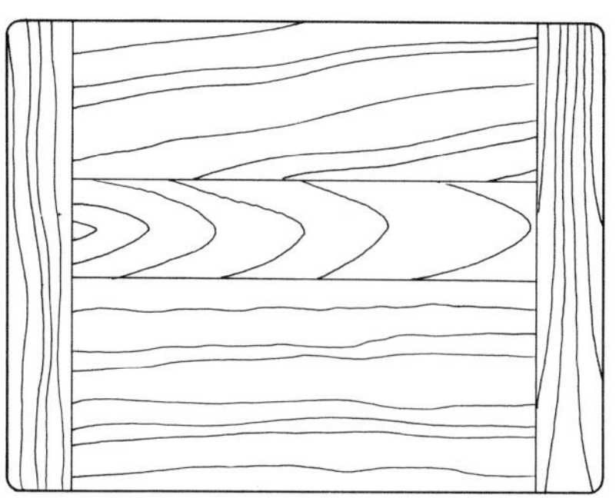

Chopping board

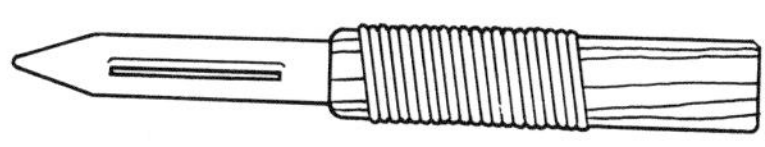

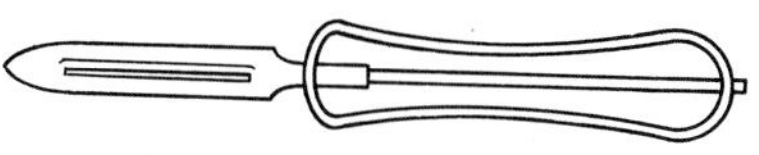

Potato peelers

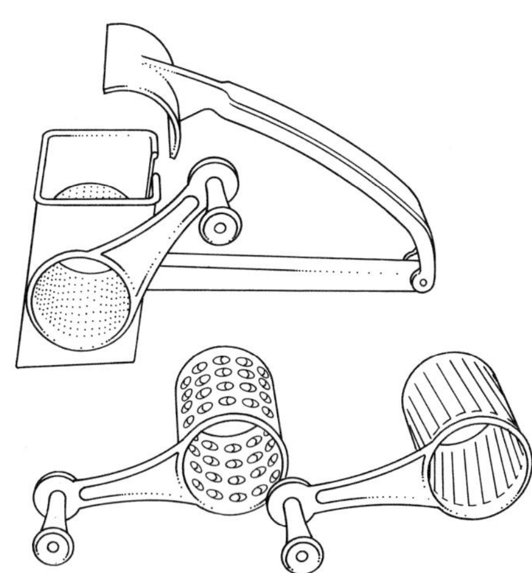

Mouli grater with fittings

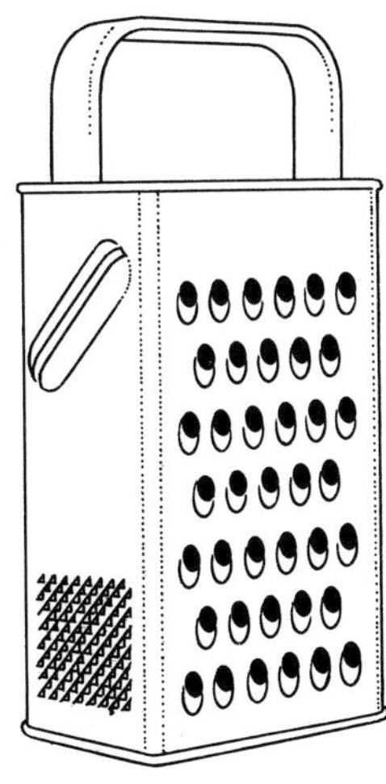

Box grater

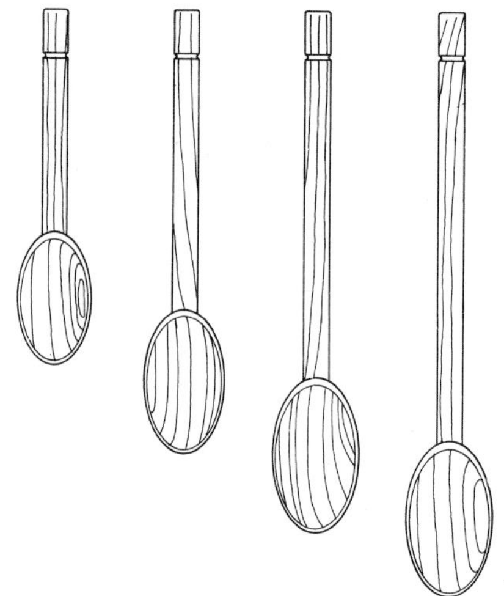

Boxwood spoons

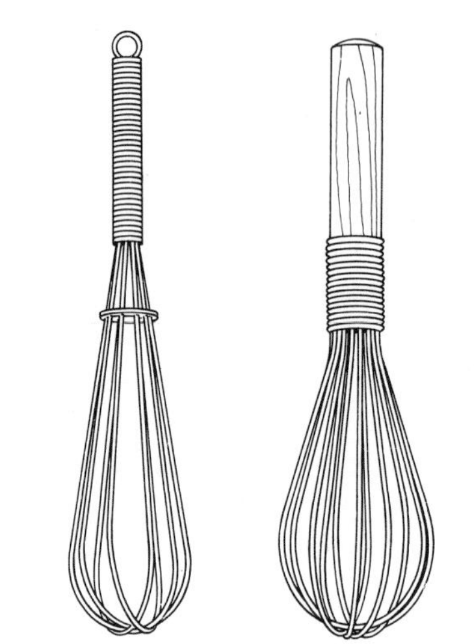

Balloon whisks

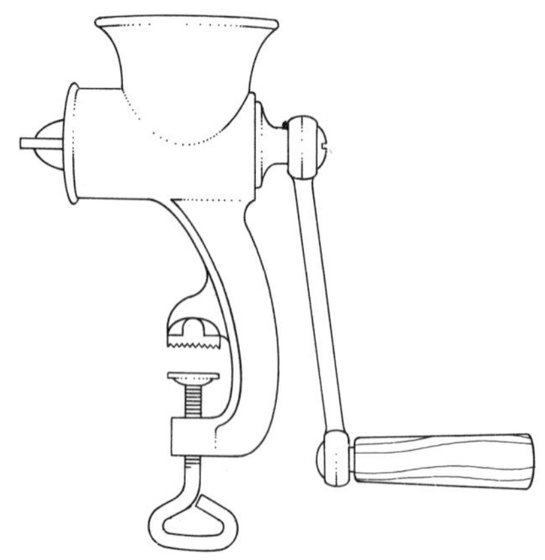

Traditional mincer

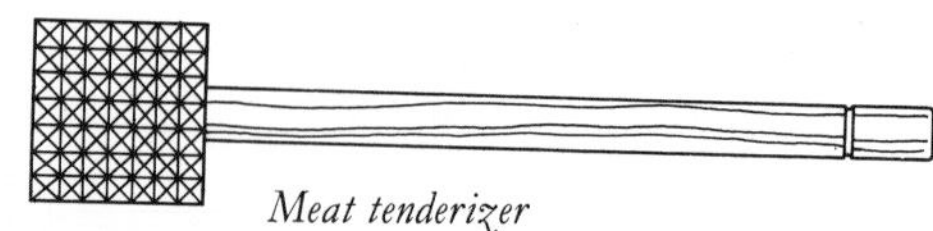

Meat tenderizer

at 300 ml/½ pint capacity.

Measuring Spoons These are available in sets of four plastic spoons which measure from ¼ teaspoon up to 1 tablespoon. They measure much more accurately than metal spoons; the ingredients should be levelled off with a knife unless the recipe specifies a heaped spoonful.

Wooden Spoons You need a set of hard and well seasoned boxwood spoons, which will not split or splinter. Have some long handled, some short, and try to keep some for savoury mixtures, some for sweet – to prevent the curry affecting the custard! Beechwood spoons with one pointed edge are useful for scraping round the edges of pans, and the ones with holes in the middle are for blending mixtures like batter. Wood is a bad conductor of heat, so you'll never burn your hands (although wooden spoons themselves often get burned); wooden implements are also vital to avoid damaging your non-stick pans. Wooden forks are useful too.

Metal Spoons Large metal spoons are needed for some mixtures, for folding whipped egg white into something, for instance, or for basting roasts. Many metal spoons are used as measures – tablespoons, dessertspoons and teaspoons – but these are not so accurate on the whole as the special measuring-spoon sets. Perforated metal spoons are good for picking foods out of boiling water or deep fat. Ladles of various sizes are useful, small for sauces, larger for soups.

Bowls Mixing bowls, and indeed bowls of many kinds, are vital in the kitchen. You need a large china, glass or plastic one for large mixings, smaller ones for smaller mixtures. Stainless steel bowls have their uses too. Heatproof pudding bowls or basins, ranging from 300 ml to 1.2 litres/½ to 2 pints in capacity, are necessary for steaming puddings, for some ice cream dishes, and for summer pudding.

A set of serving bowls or dishes, at least some of which are ovenproof, are a necessity. Many people like to have wooden salad bowls (and servers).

Sieves Stainless steel mesh wire sieves should be strong enough for puréeing cooked foods as well as for straining liquids. You should have at least two plastic sieves which are light and easy to wash and dry; these are useful for sieving dry flour, icing sugar, etc, and for certain foods that react against non-stainless steel metal sieves (fruits).

Whisks Light wire balloon whisks with coiled wire handles are good for beating batter and egg whites, and for sauces like mayonnaise. There are various sizes. A less usual whisk is a spinning-top whisk which operates exactly like a child's top, to whip up a dollop of cream or a single milk shake in moments. I also like the loop top whisks – they come in two sizes and are very handy for small quantities like a single egg or in microwave cooking. Using a rotary whisk is less tiring than using a balloon whisk, but both hands are occupied which can be a disadvantage.

Thermometers Measuring heat is as important as measuring ingredients. If your oven is reliable, you won't need a separate oven thermometer, but a middle-range thermometer is good for preserves, and a sugar or deep-fat thermometer for frying or sweet-making. Thermometers should always be introduced gradually to extreme heat, and a good tip is to stand them in boiling water prior to putting them into the hot substance.

Timers Many ovens have clocks and automatic timers, but the portable timers are particularly useful if you're gardening when a cake is baking! Traditional egg timers are attractive, and time a soft-boiled egg to perfection. (But you need to know where your eggs are coming from if you eat them soft-boiled.)

MASHING AND GRINDING

Several tools are useful for grinding, mashing and generally pulverizing ingredients. The most valuable are listed below.

Pepper Mill The wooden ones are the best – the plastic seem to lose cutability quite quickly. Salt mills look similar and can grind down coarse sea salt grains.
Meat Hammers These can be useful. Made of beechwood or metal, one side is notched to tenderize tough meat, but don't use them on your best wooden boards; the other is smooth to slap something like a steak or escalope flat.
Pestle and Mortar The best ones are invariably the most expensive – those of hard, pure white porcelain. The handle end of the pestle should be of strong wood, and the join between wood and porcelain should be very firm.
Citrus Squeezer Glass ones can be found – often in antique shops – and there are electrical appliances available. The least expensive are made of plastic, with an inner dome for lemons and a domed cover which is for oranges.
Garlic Press There are a variety of shapes available, all with a foot which squashes both peeled and unpeeled cloves.
Potato Masher These are useful for other vegetables as well, squashing lumps as it is pumped up and down. Choose one with a rounded mashing plate to get more easily into sides of pans. I also use a "ricer", which operates rather like an oversize garlic crusher and makes very good creamed potatoes.
Meat Mincer Vital if you haven't got a processor for mincing foods. Those made of heavy iron and which clamp on to the table won't budge as you grind meat. It must come apart completely so that it can be thoroughly cleaned.

BOILING AND STEAMING

Good pans are the cook's first requirement (after a good cooker) and there are many to choose from – copper, iron, steel, enamelled iron and steel, aluminium, stainless steel, non-stick surfaced metal, and porcelain and glass.

Pans I would choose a set of three heavy stainless steel pans with good lids for normal, everyday cooking. They should have sturdy, good handles too. I would also have a double lipped milk pan.
Stock Pot Your largest saucepan may do, but a special pot is useful if you make lots of soups – they can double as stewpots and steamers as well, some actually having inner wire baskets to lift out. Some come with a top pan which turns them into a capacious double boiler (but a smaller version is more useful generally, for sauces, keeping things warm, etc.).
Steamer Some are like a double boiler, but have perforations in the top pan; some are perforated "fans" of metal to fit any size of saucepan.
Colander An enamelled colander can be used over water as a steamer, or it can fulfil its normal function as something through which to drain cooked foods.

FRYING AND GRILLING

The first necessity for grilling, of course, is a good grill; the second is probably a good pair of scissor-action, stainless-steel tongs for gripping without piercing. (The same, very roughly, applies to charcoal-grilling on the barbecue!)

Frying Pans Again choose a selection of sizes to suit family or purpose. A large lidded frying pan is very useful for all sorts of things, but nothing beats the black iron ones (clean with oil and salt to preserve the appearance, *never* soapy water or abrasives). There are omelette pans and special crêpe pans, and there are some useful little skillets with metal handles which can go in the oven too.
Deep-frying Pans If you haven't got an electric one, and you're keen on deep-frying, a special pan with a wire mesh basket is very useful (or you could use one of those collapsible wire baskets in an ordinary pan – very good for whirling the salad dry too!).

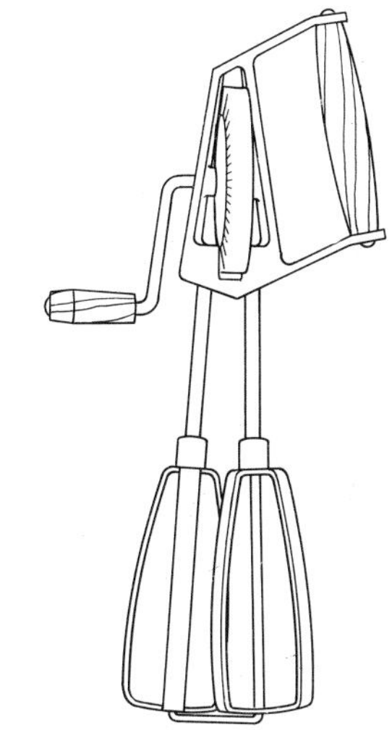

Rotary hand whisk

Citrus squeezer

Pestle and mortar

Garlic press

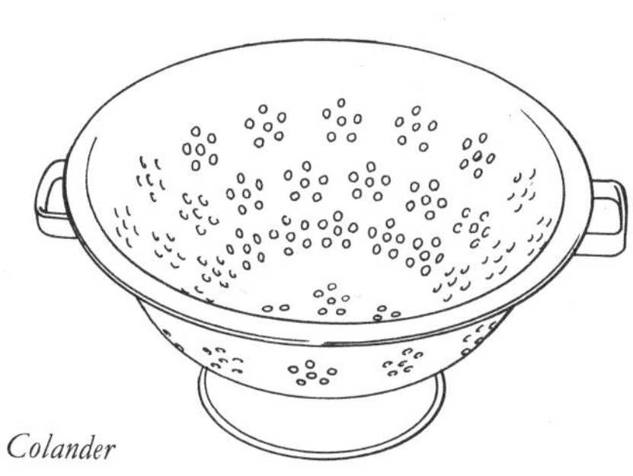

Colander

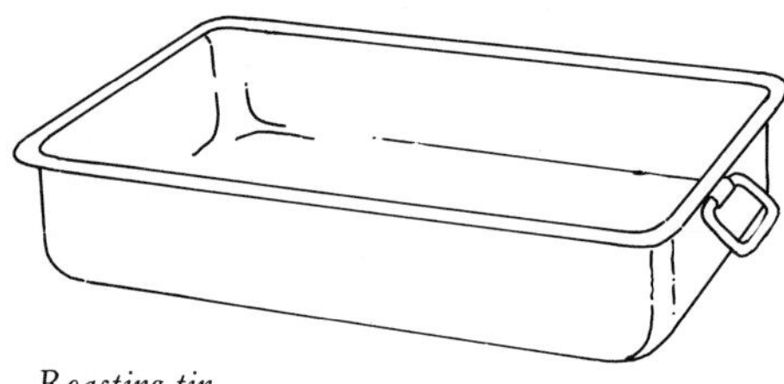

Roasting tin

Square cake tin

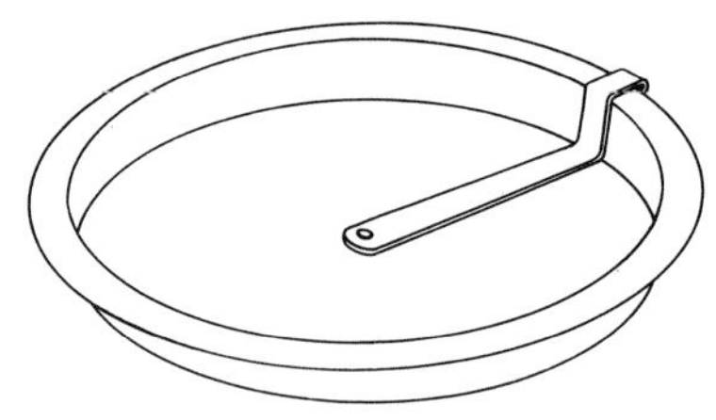

Sandwich tin with sliding lever

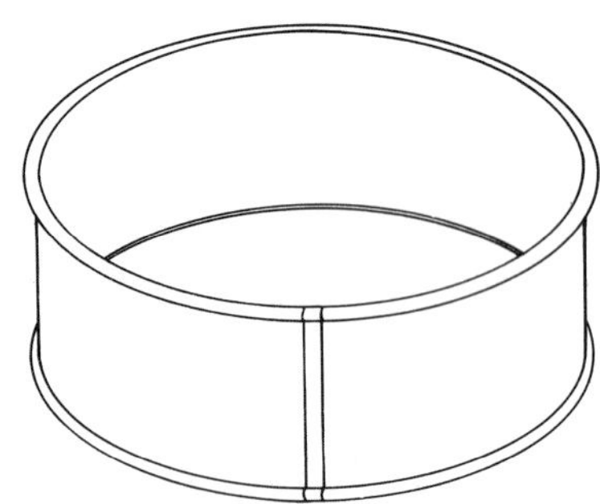

Deep round cake tin

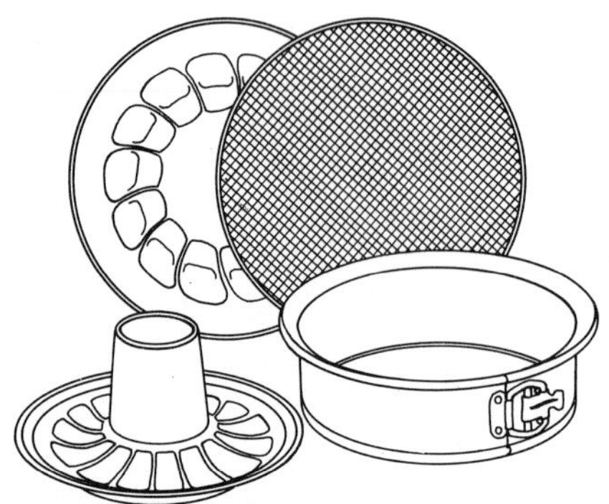

Three-in-one, spring form tin with alternative bases

Griddle or Girdle Not strictly necessary, of course, but wonderful for traditional drop scones or Scotch pancakes.

ROASTING AND CASSEROLING

Choosing dishes, trays and pans that will go in the oven, will depend on your budget to a large extent. There is a great deal of choice.

Roasting Tins Those made of metal which will not buckle in the oven or over direct heat are best – large for such as a turkey, smaller for a more compact joint or for the roast potatoes. Cast-iron dishes are good too, as are some non-stick surfaced tins.

Meat Rack One of these set in the roasting tin keeps the meat out of its own fat – vital for fatty birds such as duck and goose.

Casseroles There is a huge number of types, but those which will conduct heat evenly, both in the oven *and* on top of the cooker, will be best. Enamelled ironware is good for this, but some earthenware for lovely country stews can be used – carefully – over direct heat. Whatever casserole you choose, it must have a good lid, which fits well. Choose carefully according to size – larger if you have a family to feed, and small if dealing with a small quantity of vegetables.

Oven Dishes These come in various materials, but cast-iron ones are useful for gratins, and dishes like moussaka or lasagne.

BAKING

Although the weekly ceremony of baking day has gone, baking still ranks high among kitchen skills. The apple pie, mincemeat tarts and sponge cake still survive to gladden our senses. Even bread-making is enjoying a bit of a revival. Baking equipment has not changed much over the years, but pans, trays and tins are now made in materials that clean easily and don't stick like they used to. Refinements like removable bases and non-stick linings help enormously.

Cake Tins These come in tin plate, aluminium, or non-stick silicone, and in various shapes and sizes. What you choose depends on your needs, ambitions and skills. For round cakes, those sized between 15–23 cm/6–9 inches are useful, particularly those which are loose-bottomed. Square cake tins come in the same sizes (a large one is ideal for a rich fruit cake). For sandwich cakes, choose tins of 15–20 cm/6–8 inches; some come with levers to ensure easy detachment of sponge or pastry from the base. Flan rings or flan tins of 18–20 cm/7–8 inches are handy. An innovation is a three-in-one spring-form tin with spring-apart sides; this has a trio of separate bases for baking a variety of shapes – plain, moulded and a shape with a hole (good for puddings, savoury mousses or jellied rings as well).

Other tins are shallower. A tin of approximately 27 × 18 cm/11 × 7 inches is good for any Swiss roll mixture, and 18–23 cm/7–9 inch square tins are good for mixtures like gingerbread.

Loaf Tins There are a variety of finishes and materials but you should have a couple of 450 g/1 lb capacity and one of 900 g/2 lb capacity.

Pie Dishes, Pans and Plates Pie dishes can range in capacity up to about 1.2 litres/2 pints, and they should be deep with a wide lip. Pie plates can be of enamel, and come in a variety of sizes; they too should have wide lips. Pyrex or enamel pans, oblong in shape, are useful too.

Small Tins and Cutters A patty tin with twelve holes is good for small cakes and Yorkshire puddings. Cutters of various sizes, crinkled or plain, are good for tartlets and small pastry pie cases, and tiny ones are useful for biscuits. There is a variety of other small tin sizes – boat-shaped are good for pastry cases.

Baking Sheets At least a couple of good solid baking sheets or trays are vital for baking and for a variety of other things. They must be strong enough not to buckle or warp at high temperatures.

Soufflé and Ramekin Dishes A pyrex soufflé dish can be used for a number of things, not least soufflés, and the miniature version, the ramekin, is good for baking eggs, for fruit brûlées, and for individual dips or starters. Ovenproof china or pottery versions are also available.
Rolling Pin There are many, but the best for the serious pastry cook is a good wooden one without handles.
Pastry Board Cold is helpful in rolling pastry, and marble retains its chill well, though it is expensive and heavy. A good clean working surface can do!
Cooling Tray A good wire mesh tray is useful if you bake a lot – otherwise use the grid from the grill pan.
Piping If you want to pipe whipped cream, choux pastry or icing, you'll need several bags (or make them yourself, see page 109), and a selection of nozzles.

BINS, JARS AND RACKS

Sensible storage is all-important in the kitchen – for both convenience and hygiene. A few ideas are listed below.

Wine Racks For small quantities of wine, a wooden wine rack which folds flat or expands concertina fashion is very handy.
Cheese Dish Nothing beats the traditional china dishes which now come in such a wonderful array of patterns and colours. The shape fits perfectly over a wedge of cheese, but store cheese in a cool place, not in the fridge.
Garlic A special wire bulb keeps garlic fresh – it can be hung up too. Terracotta containers with large holes are also useful for storing garlic.
Hooks It may seem simplistic, but these are useful all over the kitchen – on shelves for cups or jugs, on doors, etc. Butcher's hooks, too, can be arranged along a rail to store pots or strings of onions etc.
Refrigerator Containers Plastic lidded boxes of all shapes and sizes are useful both in the fridge and freezer. Save old margarine and yoghurt containers for the same purpose.
Tea Towel Holder Useful to keep towels out of the way but within reach.
Cookery Book Stand The final requirement, a perspex stand, if you want to keep your precious cookery books free of stains!

GADGETS

There's a new one invented every week, I'm sure – but some are useful and do earn their kitchen space.

Corkscrew There is an enormous number of styles, but one I can recommend is made of boxwood with a bit that fits over the cork; screw in the top handle and twist out the cork with the bottom one.
Bottle Stopper An expanding stopper which fits any bottle neck. Several would be useful.
Milk Saver A toughened glass ring which rattles on the bottom of the pan before the milk starts to foam.
Spike Murphy A metal stand for baking potatoes more quickly – the heat conducts through the spikes. Metal skewers also work well.
Egg Pricker A hole at each end will prevent an egg from cracking in boiling water.

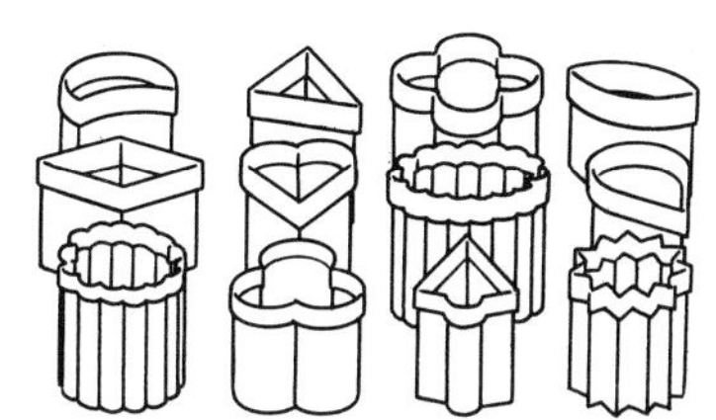

Shaped cutters

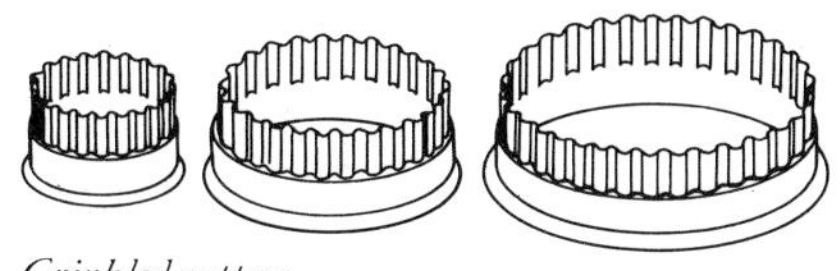

Crinkled cutters

Rubber grip tea towel holder

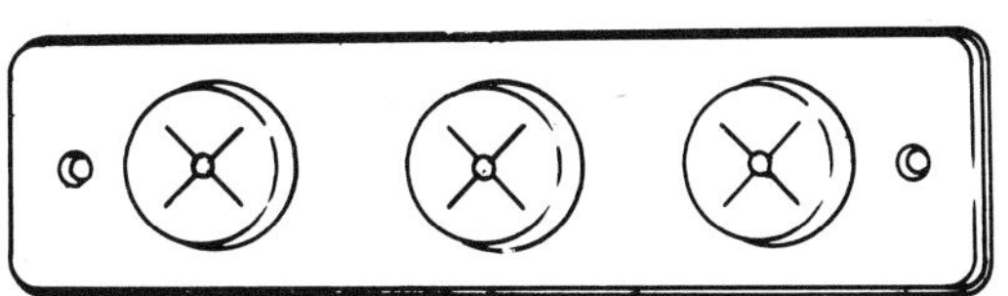

Pot hook *Baked potato stand*

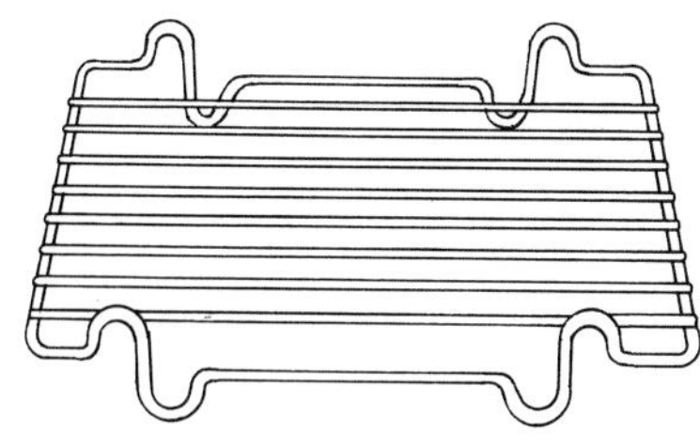

Meat rack

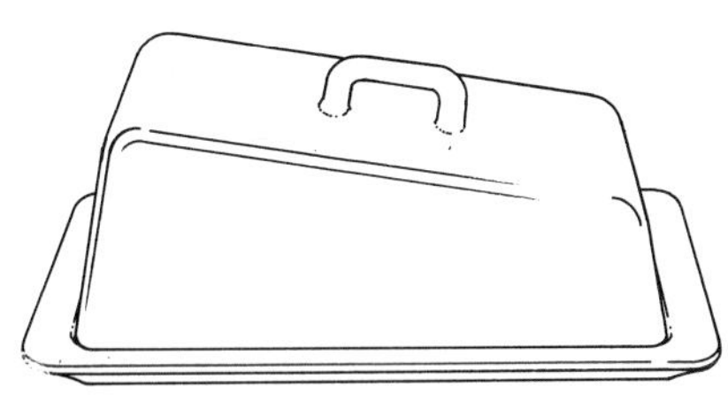

Traditional cheese dish

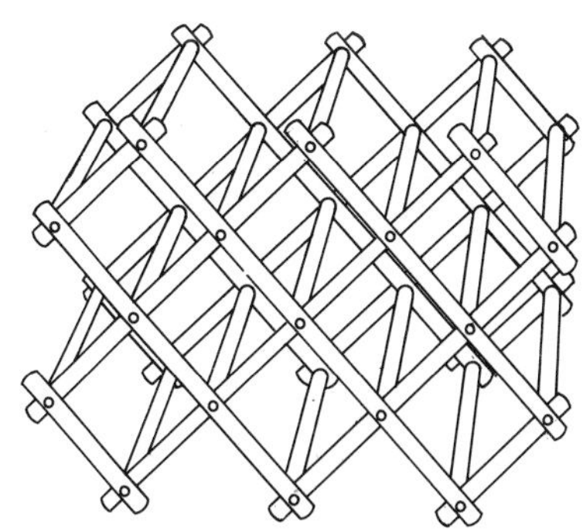

Wine rack

Egg pricker

FREEZING

The earliest form of freezing was in ice houses built in the grounds of great houses of the eighteenth and nineteenth centuries. Ice hacked from frozen lakes in the winter was stored in these underground brick structures, and this kept meat fresh (a change from dried or salted, the only forms of preservation until then). It wasn't until the twentieth century that household refrigerators and freezers became common.

Freezer compartments in refrigerators are marked with one to three stars, to correspond to the stars marked on frozen food packets, and are a guide to storage (see below).

STAR	TEMPERATURE	STORAGE LIFE
★	**21°F/ − 6°C**	**1 week**
★★	**10°F/ − 12°C**	**1 month**
★★★	**0°F/ − 18°C**	**3 months**

Unless they have four stars – one large white and three small dark stars – these freezer compartments are for storing frozen foods only. The four stars indicate that any freezer has the ability to freeze fresh, unfrozen food at a lower temperature than 0°F/ − 18°C. To do this, about 2 hours in advance turn the freezer thermostat or control to colder, so that the fresh or cooked food does not raise the temperature of the already frozen food inside (which would cause deterioration). When the food is frozen, the thermostat can be returned to the normal storage setting of 0°F/ − 18°C.

BASIC TIPS

Choose your freezer according to the size of your family and the amount of space available. Chest freezers take up more space than uprights, but generally have lower running costs, are cheaper to buy, and don't lose their coldness so readily when opened. Upright freezers fit more easily into modern kitchens, often on top of or below a refrigerator. I must admit, though, that I find my chest freezer far more difficult to keep tidy than my upright one.

Site your freezer in a cool dry place. It mustn't be *too* cold though. One of mine is in my garage, and it was raided last year, so a resolution I have had to make is to keep the garage locked. Many people use their garages, so be warned: the days are long gone when doors can safely be left unlocked.

Open the freezer up as seldom as possible. It's more economical in energy terms (yours as well!) to make one trip to take stuff out for three meals (store in the freezing compartment of the fridge) than to make three trips on three separate days.

Rotate the stock carefully, and don't let ancient packages lurk at the bottom. Try to keep a list of what's there – I always *try* – and mark things off in rotation.

Most freezers operate best when about two-thirds full. If yours is continually emptier than that, the freezer is either too big, or you're not using it as sensibly as you might.

When freezing freshly cooked food, do make sure it's quite cold before placing it in the freezer.

If you don't set the freezer to a lower setting when putting fresh or cooked food in to freeze, your food may not taste so good later. The faster a food is frozen, the better. If the process is prolonged, the cell structures of the food may be damaged.

Make sure that all food is packed and labelled properly before freezing. Inept packaging can spoil the food too, and if it lacks labels, how on earth will you be able to tell what it is a few months or even weeks later?

Freeze only foods that are in perfect condition. What comes out is only as good as what is put in.

For maximum efficiency, defrost your freezer according to manufacturers' instructions – chest freezers once or twice a year usually, upright two or three times.

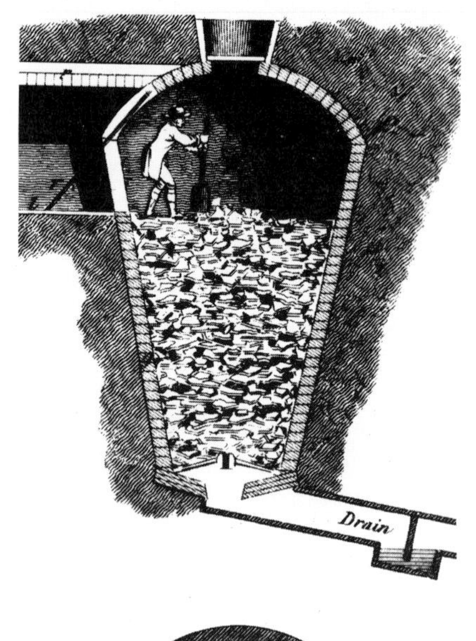

The ice-house became a feature of the grand country estates in the 18th century. The ice was taken from frozen lakes in winter and then stacked in deep underground pits.

PACKAGING FOR THE FREEZER

Strong wrappings are needed for the freezer to protect the food from the cold air, and there is a wide range available. There are waxed cartons, plastic containers of all sizes, foil containers, special freezer-to-microwave containers, freezer foils, polythene sheeting and cling film, and heavy gauge polythene bags. You can save your old ice cream, margarine and yoghurt cartons to use too, but they must have tight-fitting lids. All containers and bags need to be waterproof and airtight to avoid freezer burn, and it is vital to exclude all air before freezing. One easy way with bags is to suck the air out with a straw!

I find plastic carrier bags handy for storing small packets in the freezer. I have one for meat, things like chops, slices of ham or liver; in another are packets of frozen vegetables; and in a third, packets of breadcrumbs.

Some freezer bags come with their own labels, other bags and containers will need to be labelled with special freezer labels that still stick at low temperatures. A freezer log book is useful if you're going to be efficient!

MEAT, POULTRY AND GAME

The meat must be as fresh as possible. Cut off all visible fat – which reduces freezer life – and wrap chops or steaks in film, plastic or foil. Overwrap bone ends with foil to prevent them breaking through wrappings, then pack, in meal-sized portions, in thick polybags. Chicken is available already frozen, but, if you're lucky enough to get a fresh game bird, it can be hung, plucked, cleaned and then covered with foil and plastic and overwrapped with heavy polythene.

Cooked meat, poultry and game dishes may be frozen. Cook thoroughly, then cool quickly and freeze. Many casseroles can be frozen in their dishes (as long as they're freezer-proof – enamelled metal is good), then removed from the dish, packed in a heavy polybag, and returned to the freezer. This frees the dish for further use in the kitchen, and the frozen stew shape can be popped back into the same dish when you want to defrost and reheat.

FISH AND SHELLFISH

Unless you know the fish is fresh from the hook or net, it is better not to freeze fish from the fishmonger; it will be good enough to eat, but not quite good enough to freeze.

VEGETABLES

Most vegetables will freeze successfully either in their natural, raw state or in some other form (in stews or casseroles, or as soups and purées, for instance). There's nothing quite like a vegetable harvested from the garden, frozen at its freshest, and enjoyed months later after the season is long gone.

As a general rule, vegetables that are difficult to freeze successfully are those with a high water content or a soft delicate texture; the look and the structures of these vegetables will alter quite considerably with freezing. Salad vegetables, for instance, go limp when frozen because of their high water content: a glut of lettuce *could* be frozen, but they would only be suitable for using in soups afterwards; and tomatoes should only be frozen as juices, purée or sauce.

Vegetables to be frozen should be young and tender, and at their peak. Most have to be blanched before freezing – i.e. cooked at a high heat in the boiling water (or *over* boiling water) which stops the workings of enzymes (chemical agents in plants) which affect quality, flavour and colour, and nutritive value during storage in the freezer. (Scientific tests have proved that blanching preserves colour and flavour, helps retain Vitamin C, and kills micro-organisms.) With water blanching, bring a large pot of water – about 4.5 litres/8 pints – to the boil, and put 450 g/1 lb prepared vegetable (see below) into a wire basket. Immerse the basket in the boiling water, cover tightly and time the blanching from when the water returns to the boil. As soon as the time is up, remove the basket and plunge the vegetable into iced water to cool. Dry well before freezing. (To steam blanch, the vegetables are steamed over the boiling water in a steamer, which takes half as long again as water blanching. Cool and dry as above.)

Asparagus Trim and sort into similar lengths and thicknesses. Tie in bundles. Blanch for 2–5 minutes according to thickness. Pack in rigid containers or polybags. Store for up to 6 months.

Aubergines Slice, blanch for 4 minutes, then interleave slices with freezer paper in a rigid container, and store for up to 12 months.

Avocado Freeze as purée with lemon juice, or as soup.

Beans, Broad Pod and blanch for 2–3 minutes, pack in a polybag, and store for up to 12 months.

Beans, Haricot/French Blanch whole for 1–2 minutes, pack in polybag and store for up to 12 months.

Beans, Runner Slice, blanch, pack and store as for haricots.

Beetroot Boil and skin, and freeze whole, sliced or diced, in rigid container for up to 6 months.

Broccoli Separate into florets, blanch for 2–4 minutes, then open-freeze (on a tray, uncovered). Pack frozen florets into polybags and store for up to 12 months.

Brussels sprouts Blanch whole for 2–4 minutes, then open-freeze, pack and store as broccoli.

Cabbage Shred any type, blanch for 1 minute, then pack in polybags. Store green or white for up to 6 months, red for up to 12.

Carrots Blanch baby new whole for 3 minutes, then pack in a rigid container or polybag and store for up to 12 months. Slice old carrots, blanch for 2 minutes, and pack and store as new.

Cauliflower Freeze as broccoli.

Celeriac Dice or slice and blanch for 1 minute then store in polybags for up to 6 months.

Celery Blanch chunks for 3 minutes,

wrap in polybags and store for up to 6 months.
Courgettes Slice large ones, or leave small ones whole. Blanch for 1 minute, open-freeze, then store in polybags for up to 12 months.
Cucumber Freeze as soup or purée.
Fennel Cut bulbs in quarters, blanch for 3–5 minutes, then store in polybags for up to 6 months.
Greens Freeze as cabbage.
Jerusalem Artichokes Freeze as a cooked purée.
Kohlrabi Slice large ones then blanch for 2 minutes, pack in polybags and store for up to 6 months. Small whole ones can be blanched whole for 4 minutes, then packed and stored as sliced.
Leeks Slice large ones, leave small ones whole. Blanch for 3 minutes, pack in polybags and store for up to 6 months.
Marrow Blanch chunks for 2 minutes, then store in rigid containers for up to 6 months.
Mushrooms They can be open-frozen whole without blanching, but keep better if sliced and sautéed in butter. Pack in rigid containers and store for 1–2 months.
Parsnips Slice then blanch, pack and store as for sliced kohlrabi.
Peas Pod, blanch for 1 minute then open-freeze. Store in polybags for up to 12 months.
Peppers Blanch slices for 2 minutes, open-freeze then store in polybags for up to 6 months. Blanch whole de-seeded peppers for 3–4 minutes then pack and store as slices.
Potatoes Old ones should be cut into chips and part-fried for about 4 minutes. Pack in polybags and store for up to 3 months. They could also be mashed with butter and stored. New potatoes should be blanched for 4 minutes, then stored in polybags for up to 3 months.
Pumpkin Freeze as a purée or soup.
Shallots Blanch whole for 2 minutes, then open-freeze and store in polybags for up to 3 months.
Spinach Freeze as a cooked purée in a polybag, for up to 12 months.
Swedes Dice, then blanch, pack and store as for kohlrabi.
Sweetcorn Blanch whole cobs for 2–8 minutes, depending on size, then open-freeze, wrap in polybags, and store for up to 12 months.
Sweet Potatoes Freeze as a purée.
Turnips Freeze as for kohlrabi.

Many vegetables can be thawed at room temperature then used virtually as you would fresh: among them aubergine slices, red cabbage, sliced courgettes, kohlrabi, sliced peppers and shallots. Some need a little further cooking from frozen to be served as a vegetable – beans, broccoli, Brussels sprouts, white or green cabbage, cauliflower, whole courgettes, fennel quarters, whole leeks, marrow, parsnips, peas, small turnips. Or many frozen vegetables can be decanted frozen into casseroles – peppers, carrots, celeriac, celery, sliced leeks, parsnips, swedes and turnips. It's all common sense really.

FRUIT

Most fruit will freeze successfully, but their structures do, on the whole, change. Fruits can be frozen in so many different forms that if you are a keen fruit grower – even if you only have one plum tree and a small patch of strawberries or raspberries – a freezer is a great asset. Your own home-grown raspberries with cream at Christmas time is a wonderful reminder of summer!

Soft Fruits If you grow your own soft fruit or make use of a local fruit farm you really should also invest in a freezer. Most soft fruits freeze well whole, with the possible exception of strawberries, which defrost into a rather wet mush and are much better made into a purée for a sauce and then frozen. (However, I always freeze some perfect small whole strawberries, with calyxes still attached, which I use for decorating a gâteau, for topping individual strawberry mousses and also for adding to fruit salad. The trick is to use them just before they collapse into that mush.)

There are one or two golden rules to follow if you are picking soft fruit for the freezer. Gather the fruit only when the weather is dry since wet fruit goes mouldy very quickly. Freeze it as soon as possible and if you are intending to make jam, make this as soon as possible too. The pectin quality of fruit, which is what makes the jam set well, deteriorates the longer it sits about. For this same reason, when you are making jam from frozen fruit you should add 10 per cent more fruit than the recipe states to make up for pectin loss.

Most soft fruit is easier to handle if it has been open-frozen first, laid out in a single layer on trays. When frozen hard, put the now free-flow berries into polybags and label clearly with name of fruit, date and year. I usually do about half of my rasps like this and the other half go straight into bags; the latter will be used for jam, while the open-frozen fruit keeps its appearance well and can be used as fresh.

Loganberries freeze similarly to raspberries, as do blackberries (or brambles as I prefer to call them). I gather the latter early for freezing for jam, as the seeds get so big later on.

Currants also freeze perfectly. It is really better not to wash them or any soft fruit unless you don't know where they've come from.

Redcurrants and whitecurrants are easier to pick in bunches. Open-freeze these bunches on trays then run a fork through each bunch and force the berries downwards. See that you have a large basin underneath because they jump about a lot.

Cranberries, bilberries, blueberries and elderberries can be treated like currants, although the latter should have a prior blanching of about 30 seconds.

Grapes and gooseberries can be treated as soft fruit. Open-freeze, then put into polybags.

Some of these soft fruits can be made into purée which can be frozen for various uses – for fools, fruit sauces, etc. Gooseberries will need to be cooked, all the other berries are pushed uncooked through a sieve.

A nice idea is to freeze whole

raspberries or strawberries in ice-cube trays with water to make decorative cubes for summer drinks.

Stone Fruit These fruits are treated rather differently, many of them being frozen in a sugar syrup. Plums I have already discussed (see page 79), and damsons and greengages can be frozen in exactly the same way.

It is very rewarding freezing peaches, nectarines and apricots. Although the texture changes, they retain much of that fresh flavour which is so altered when the fruit is canned. Peaches and nectarines can be peeled and frozen as they are, but apricots usually respond to being gently poached in a sugar syrup first to soften them slightly (stone before cooking, then cool). Peel the peaches and nectarines by pouring boiling water over to soften the skin, peel, then run a knife round the equator of the flesh part of the fruit. Twist the two halves in opposite directions and remove the stones. You can leave the fruit in halves or slice it.

The syrup used to poach the apricots is the same mixture as the one you should use to pour over the fresh nectarines, peaches and, of course, the poached apricots before freezing. Make the syrup in plenty of time so that it can go cold. Dissolve 175 g/6 oz sugar in 600 ml/1 pint water and boil briefly. Stir 1 tablespoon of lemon juice or $\frac{1}{4}$ teaspoon of ascorbic acid into the cold syrup. This light syrup helps to keep the fruit a good colour. The fruit goes into a freezer box, the syrup is poured over and then it is all frozen. To keep the fruit submerged, one tip is to crumple a sheet of greaseproof paper and lay this on top; my own solution is the knife one on page 79.

Apples and Pears There are very many ways of freezing these. Choose firm, ripe fruit with a good flavour. Have lots of lemon juice on hand as you prepare them as they will go brown very quickly. Although this does you no harm, it doesn't look very attractive.

Apples

1 Mix 450 g/1 lb sugar to 1.8 kg/4 lb fruit, peeled, cored and sliced. Pack in lidded plastic box.
2 For free-flow pack apples, blanch slices, 225 g/8 oz at a time, for just 1 minute. Pat dry, then open-freeze and pack in polybags.
3 Mix blanched slices with sugar, 450 g/1 lb to 1.8 kg/4 lb fruit. Pack in bags or boxes.
4 Pack unblanched slices in a medium syrup – 275 g/10 oz sugar boiled with 600 ml/1 pint water and cooled – in plastic boxes. Leave a headspace of 1 cm/$\frac{1}{2}$ inch, and keep fruit under syrup until frozen.
5 Purée sliced apples with a little sugar and a knob of butter until soft. Freeze in rigid container.
6 Poach peeled, cored and halved apples until just soft in the above medium syrup. Cool and freeze in a rigid container, leaving 1 cm/$\frac{1}{2}$ inch headspace.

Pears

1 Skin, halve, core, then poach as for apples above (no. 6). Add a piece of vanilla pod to the poaching syrup to give extra flavour.
2 Another nice poaching liquid for pears consists of honey and water – 1 tablespoon honey to 150 ml/$\frac{1}{4}$ pint water. Freeze as for apples.

Citrus Fruits All can be frozen whole. With Seville oranges frozen in January/February, I can stagger my marmalade making throughout the year (remember to add the extra 10 per cent). By freezing lemons when they are really cheap, I can save money when they are expensive towards Christmas! You could freeze the juice in small containers, and don't forget you can freeze the half shells too, for use as a container for ice cream perhaps, or for grating purposes as on page 19.

Rhubarb Look for unblemished red or reddish green stalks of around 2.5 cm/1 inch thick. Don't forget to use a stainless steel knife as you cut stalks into chunks. Blanch for about 1–2 minutes, drain and dry, and pack without sugar.

HERBS

A cooking herb is any plant which adds flavour to food. It is easier now to buy fresh herbs but for delicious scent and flavour you can't beat those fresh-picked from the garden. However, in the summer you can prepare and freeze some for use in winter, when your plants have died down.

Pack and freeze the herbs as soon as you can. Leaves and sprigs just need to be rinsed, dried with kitchen paper and packed into small tubs or cartons. For larger sprays lay them flat and interleave with freezer paper so that they do not freeze together. Pack chopped herbs in ice-cube trays or tiny plastic containers, cover with water and freeze. Once frozen the cubes can be shaken from the ice trays and stored in clearly labelled polybags. These individual cubes of herbs are a very handy size for use in stews, etc. throughout the year. Chopped mint is best covered with sweetened hot water and cooled before freezing. To reconstitute the mint for mint sauce just add it to warm vinegar.

You can freeze any herb as a savoury butter for making herb bread etc (see page 59).

Frozen sprigs and leaves are easy to use straight from the freezer. Simply crumble, chop or grate straight on to the food. Another thing I like to do for the freezer is reduce a huge bunch of rinsed and dried parsley heads in a food processor. I then sit down and make up dozens of foil packets with about 1 tablespoon of parsley in each.

Fresh herbs are best frozen as whole leaves, whole sprigs or chopped as listed below. When chopping, do it by hand as it is easy to over-process in a machine and turn them into a mush.

Basil – leaves
Bay – leaves
Chervil – sprigs
Chives – snipped with scissors, they don't keep their flavour long
Dill – feathery leaves
Horseradish – grated root
Marjoram – sprigs
Mint – sprigs and leaves

Oregano – best dried rather than frozen
Parsley – sprigs and chopped
Rosemary – sprigs
Sage – leaves
Sorrel – leaves
Tarragon – sprigs and leaves
Thyme – sprigs, both lemon and sweet

STOCKS

These are extremely useful to have in the freezer. Stocks can be frozen as they come from the pot (after cooling, of course) in large plastic rigid containers, but a way of economizing on space is to reduce the stock by boiling down to about, say, 600 ml/1 pint, then pouring into ice-cube trays and freezing that way. The cubes can be decanted into polybags and stored for up to 6 months. One cube adds flavour to gravies, sauces or casseroles, a few form the basis of a soup. They can be diluted.

SOUPS

Soups can be a life-saver in the freezer when you run out of supplies, or some unexpected guests arrive.

Take soup recipes up to virtually final stages, but do not add thickening, eggs, cream, yoghurt or milk (these could cause unsightly curdling when the soup is reheated after thawing). Season minimally as well. Pack in rigid containers allowing about 2.5 cm/1 inch headspace (frozen liquids expand and rise). Store for up to 3 months. Reheat block of soup very gently in a heavy-based saucepan or in a double boiler.

OTHER FROZEN FOODS

I have talked throughout the book about many things which can be frozen. I really do think it's a good idea to make more than you need for one meal, and to freeze the remainder for a meal in the future. Certain ingredients, such as breadcrumbs, are worth freezing. I put leftover bread into the processor and to make the crumbs. I then freeze these in 125 g/4 oz packs. They are endlessly useful for stuffings, crumbles and fish coatings. A spacious freezer is a boon before Christmas or a special large party. But they are just as invaluable for storing small portions for individual, quick meals.

Happy freezing!

Pastry freezes very well whether cooked or uncooked.

PRESERVING

The easiest method of preserving today is freezing, but many of us still cling to old traditions and enjoy using the seasonal fruits of the garden to make jams, jellies, chutneys and preserves of all kinds. There is nothing more satisfying than seeing row upon row of carefully labelled jars containing home-made gooseberry jelly, strawberry jam, tomato relish or pickled onions. And it's very easy, too, if you follow recipes and instructions carefully.

JAMS, JELLIES AND MARMALADE

Most of the equipment needed for jam, jelly or marmalade making you will already have in your kitchen. The real necessity is a preserving pan, preferably made of stainless steel as it then can be used for pickles and chutney as well. The pan must be roomy as preserves rise very high and spit during the final boiling. Aim to have your pan not more than half full before you start. If you are making jellies you can buy jelly bags, but a piece of sheeting or even old blanket can be used. In each case scald it before using by pouring boiling water through it and wringing it out. Special stands are available, but you can improvise with the four legs of an upturned tall stool.

There are a number of basic stages in the making of jams, jellies and marmalade.

1. Choosing and preparing the fruit For jams and jellies always use dry, fresh fruit. It should be slightly underripe because the riper and older a fruit gets, the more it loses its pectin content. Try to make the preserve on the same day as the fruit is picked because, again, the pectin content does decrease even if the fruit is left overnight. Frozen fruit, if it has been frozen in perfect condition, is excellent, but will also have lost a little pectin, and to counteract this add a little extra fruit, about 10 per cent more than specified in the recipe, or 1–2 oranges to a marmalade.

Pick over the fruit, discarding any that are not perfect, wash and dry carefully.

2. Simmering the fruit The gentle simmering of the fruit in water breaks down the fruit, softens it, and extracts the pectin. The amount of water varies with the fruit, little being needed with fruits that contain a lot of juice. Jams may need to be stirred from time to time, and with jellies the fruit needs to be crushed well with a potato masher during this simmering.

While the simmering is going on, the sugar content of most recipes and the requisite number of clean jam jars should be warming through in a very low oven, Gas $\frac{1}{4}$, 225°F, 110°C.

3. Testing for pectin content If you are unsure of the pectin content of your fruit – and this is what makes your jam or jelly set (see below) – you can test the pulp of your preserve before the sugar is added. Take a teaspoon of juice from the pan of simmered fruit, put it in a glass and cool it. Add 3 teaspoons of methylated spirit and shake gently. If plenty of pectin is present, a clear jelly clot will form. If a medium amount of pectin is present several small clots will form. If a poor amount of pectin is present, no real clot will be formed. If after further cooking, no clot is formed, additional pectin should be added in the proportions, 50–125 ml/ 2–4 fl oz per 450 g/1 lb of fruit. That means you should add 2 tablespoons lemon juice, or $\frac{1}{2}$ level teaspoon citric or tartaric acid, or 150 ml/$\frac{1}{4}$ pint redcurrant or gooseberry juice. Commercially prepared pectins, liquid and powder, are also available and when using these you should follow manufacturers' instructions.

The lemon juice needed for additional pectin with some fruit is added during the simmering stage, the acid helping to extract what natural pectin content there is in the fruit. In marmalade-making, the pips and pith are put in a muslin bag with the chopped fruit; this is because both pips and pith are rich in pectin.

Good Pectin Content
Blackcurrants
Cranberries
Damsons
Gooseberries
Some plums
Quince
Freshly picked raspberries
Redcurrants
Seville oranges

Medium Pectin Content
Fresh apricots
Early blackberries
Greengages
Lemons
Limes
Loganberries
Sweet oranges

Poor Pectin Content
Late blackberries
Cherries
Elderberries
Grapefruit
Marrows
Medlars
Pears
Rhubarb
Strawberries
Tangerines
Tomatoes

4. For jelly only As soon as the fruit has cooked to a pulp and the juices are running freely (and you have tested for pectin), tip the contents of the pan into the scalded jelly bag, with a wide basin beneath. Leave the pulp to drain for several hours, and never squeeze it if you want a clear jelly. Measure the juice and have ready the recommended amount of sugar per 600 ml/1 pint of juice.

5. Adding the sugar Granulated sugar is excellent, but proper preserving sugar crystals are said to give a brighter result when making jelly. Caster and brown sugar produce a lot of extra froth. Warming the sugar before adding it to the mixture enables it to dissolve more quickly.

Always use exactly the amount of

sugar specified in the recipe. Stir the preserve constantly while adding the sugar, and continue stirring until it has dissolved completely, when there are no sugar crystals visible on the spoon.

For marmalade, remove the bag of pith and pips before adding sugar. Cool a little and press well against the side of the pan to extract as much pectin-rich juice as possible.

6. Boiling When the sugar has completely dissolved, bring the preserve to boiling point, and continue boiling for the recommended time in the recipe, up to 20 minutes depending on the type of fruit. The boil must be fast and rolling to obtain a set quickly which will give the preserve the best flavour and the brightest colour.

7. Testing for setting point Do this after 10 minutes if fruit is on the high pectin list above; after 15 minutes if it is on the medium pectin list; after 20 minutes if on the poor pectin list. For ways in which to test, turn to page 20.

8. Removing the scum When preserve is ready for potting take pan from heat and leave to settle for a few minutes, and stir in a knob of butter. This helps disperse the foam. If it still persists, scoop it off into a bowl and use it in the kitchen – it is just jam with a lot of air in it.

9. Potting and storing See page 99. Strawberry jam and marmalade may be left for a few minutes before potting to prevent fruit and rind rising in the jars. Jelly is best potted into small jars so that, once opened, it is eaten up quite quickly. In large jars it tends to "weep" after opening.

PICKLES AND CHUTNEYS

The main objective of pickling is to preserve colour, shape and texture of the individual vegetables, therefore vegetables should be young, fresh and crisp. With chutneys, however, the fruits or vegetables are chopped or minced, mixed with other ingredients and cooked to a pulp: the ingredients therefore can be of less immaculate quality.

The equipment required for both is, once again, virtually the same as that for jam-making and much of which will already be in your kitchen. The large preserving pan is vital, and it must never be of copper or brass as vinegar is highly corrosive and will react with them, spoiling the preserve. Use only wooden spoons, nylon sieves and stainless steel knives.

For both pickles and chutneys, a good quality malt vinegar should be used, one with a 5 per cent acetic acid content for a good flavour and keeping quality. It can be brown malt or white distilled malt, depending on taste and the look you want for your finished preserve.

PICKLES

Method

1 The spiced vinegar can be prepared up to a month in advance (see page 100) in order to give the spices time to permeate the vinegar thoroughly.
2 Prepare the vegetables as advised in the recipes. Some are improved by salting, either by immersion in a brine or by packing with salt, before pickling. Use coarse salt rather than table salt. This salt needs to be well rinsed off after the recommended time.
3 Pack the vegetables into clean dry jars, leaving 2.5 cm/1 inch headspace, and cover with spiced vinegar. Those vegetables to be kept crisp should be covered with cold vinegar, softer types with hot vinegar.
4 Seal the jars with vinegar-proof lids – metal twist tops with plastic inner coating, soft plastic snap-on type, or hard plastic screw-on type. Cellophane jam-pot covers are not suitable because the vinegar would evaporate. Plain metal tops will corrode and rust and impart a metallic taste.
5 Leave to mature for up to 3 months.

CHUTNEYS

Method

1 Prepare the ingredients by peeling, coring, topping and tailing as appropriate. Then chop or mince as instructed.
2 The fruits or vegetables are cooked first to soften in a covered pan with very little water (or some of the recipe vinegar). Dark-coloured chutneys are made by cooking the sugar with the other ingredients, or by using brown sugar. For light-coloured chutneys, add the

Cold meats and cheese make good companions to pickles and chutneys, as shown here on the television set.

(white) sugar when the fruit or vegetables are well softened.

3 The vinegar is added, and the chutney is cooked gently and regularly stirred to avoid sticking until thick. When a spoon drawn through the mixture leaves its trail, and does not at once fill with excess liquid, the chutney is ready to pot into clean, dry warm jars, filling to the brim.
4 Seal the jars and leave to mature as for pickles.

DRYING FRUIT AND HERBS

Drying and salting were once the only methods of preserving – meat and fish as well as fruit and herbs. In many parts of the world – among them Australia, Africa and California – drying by the sun is still carried out with grapes, figs, dates, apricots, peaches and apples. You can do it at home too, but, sadly, without the sun! I have had my greatest successes with apples.

FRUIT

You need trays with slats, or wire baking trays. Stretch muslin over the tray and lay the fruit on top. The idea is to get heat all round the fruit. Whatever type of tray you use, be sure to check that it fits into the oven!

Gas, electric or solid fuel ovens can all be used for drying provided that the oven can be set to a very low heat. If using gas or electricity you will have to prop the door open (a wooden spoon will do this) because the ventilation will help the drying process as well. The temperature should be about Gas 0, 110–130°F, 44–55°C; or, put another way, if you can hold your bare hand in the oven comfortably for 30 seconds, then that oven will do. The plate-warming oven of a solid fuel or oil-fired cooker can also be used, as can a warm airing cupboard.

Store the dried fruit in wooden boxes, paper bags, or cardboard cartons. Do not put it in anything absolutely airtight.

It does not matter if the drying process is interrupted, the fruit will not be changed in any way. Allow all the fruit to cool down overnight before packing away.

To reconstitute, just pour boiling water over to cover well. Soak for 24–48 hours, then simmer and sweeten if need be.

Apples Peel, core and slice into 5 mm/$\frac{1}{4}$ inch thick rings. Drop immediately into salted water (1 teaspoon to 600 ml/1 pint water is about right). Rinse and pat dry with kitchen paper before drying. Apart from the tray method, apple rings can be threaded on to wooden dowelling cut to fit your oven slats. Another way is to thread on to fine string. This results, after about 4–6 hours, in very dry and leathery soft rings which are good for chopping small and putting into muesli. Bramley apples are excellent for drying.

Apricots, Nectarines, Peaches The fruit must be in absolutely perfect condition and fully ripe. Halve and remove stones. No need to skin. Lay on muslin-covered trays with cut side up. The result is very dry and shrivelled, after quite a long time – 16–24 hours.

Bananas Peel and slice down two or three times lengthways. Dry for 3–4 hours. Finished, they will be very brown with a wavy edge, and not nearly as sweet as the kind you buy.

Pears Peel, halve and cut out core and thread. Drop into brine as for apples. Rinse and pat dry before drying – for 16–24 hours, depending on size. (If very large, cut in quarters.)

Plums, Cherries, Grapes Dry whole, but be sure to pick big, fat, juicy fruit in perfect condition. Plums will take about 16–24 hours, cherries and grapes about 8–12 hours.

Don't forget that grated citrus peel can be dried too (see page 19).

HERBS

All herbs are best used fresh from the garden, but a few jars or bunches of dried herbs are an excellent standby in winter. Herbs intended for drying should be picked on a warm, dry day before the sun has got to them. (The sun is said to evaporate the essential oils.) Pick them also before they come into flower, as the leaves start to toughen after flowering.

There are two ways of drying herbs. The first is to tie the picked-over herbs in small bunches. Dunk in boiling water for 1–2 minutes. Shake and leave to dry on kitchen paper or an old towel. Tie up to dry above the cooker or in an airing cupboard, but away from strong sunlight. Some people advise covering the bundle with muslin, but I feel this is over-doing it a bit. In an airy kitchen above a cooker the process may take just a few hours; in an airing cupboard with no draught the process might take 3–4 days. The herbs are dry when they become crisp.

The other method is for the larger-leaved herbs like sage or mint. Strip the leaves from their stems. Pick over for any discoloured or yellow leaves, then pack into a bowl and pour over boiling water. Drain it off after 2–3 minutes, and pat dry. Spread the leaves on trays, as for fruits, and place in a very cool oven, Gas 0, 110–130°F, 45–55°C, and dry until crisp. An hour should be enough.

Parsley has to be dried rather more quickly. Wash and tie up into small bundles: Hang the bundles in the oven and dry at Gas $\frac{1}{4}$–$\frac{1}{2}$, 240°F, 115°C for about 1 hour. Switch off the heat and leave the parsley in the cooling oven until cold.

After drying, the herbs should be crushed with a rolling pin and the stalks discarded. Store in airtight containers away from light, and use up quickly.

CHERVIL

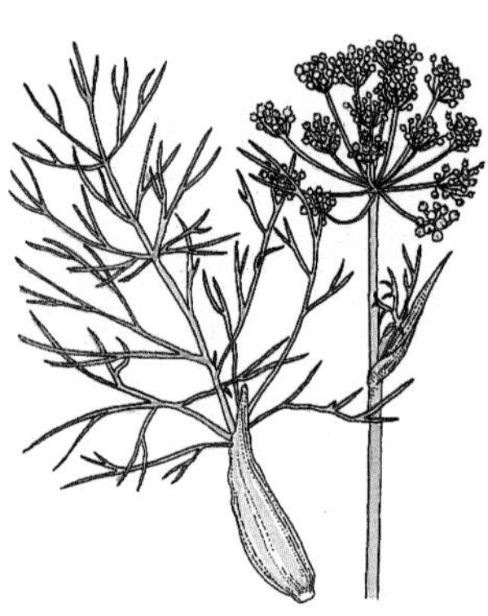

DILL

CHIVES

AN ABC OF HERBS

My herb garden is handy at my back door, and Brian, my husband, replants it from time to time. Here are notes about the herbs I find most useful.

ANGELICA

The botanical name for this 2 metre/6 foot high plant is *Angelica archangelica.* It is an umbellifer and likes partial shade – ours is half under a maple tree. It is a biennial but ours seems to come up year after year and vanishes completely in winter. The young stems can be candied and used as an edible decoration – its pale green colour making good imitation leaves. I like to use the large feathery greenish flower heads for big flower arrangements. These heads also dry very well. The young aromatic leaves are used when poaching fruit and fish.

BASIL

This is one plant I always have and it is kept in a pot on my window sill. We have tried it outside in several places but I feel our cold climate and heavy soil just does not suit. *Ocimum basilicum* is a native of Greece. One variety grows to 20 cm/8 inches, the other to 60 cm/2 feet. Plant the seeds in spring, prick out seedlings into pots, and plant out in the summer. The bright green or purple leaves are excellent in anything with tomatoes (particularly the tomato salad described on page 59), egg dishes, poultry and fish.

BAY

This evergreen shrub seems to stand up to a lot of tough treatment. I cut long branches to hang up and dry and they are sold at our autumn fair. I mostly use fresh leaves to make up *bouquets garnis*; I use a big leaf so that I can wrap it round the parsley, thyme and chervil, and tie it up with fine string to use in marinades, casseroles, stocks and sauces. Leaves can be used to infuse milk along with onion and cloves, etc in béchamel sauce. *Laurus nobilis* will grow from cuttings in early autumn or can be bought as a pot plant and trained by trimming into fancy shapes.

BORAGE

The bright blue flowers of this attractive plant look wonderful floating in summer drinks. The flowers and young leaves are used in salads. *Borago officinalis* is an annual. Sow the seeds in April in a sunny spot and they will seed everywhere quite quickly. The flowers are often crystallized to use on cakes and puddings (as are primroses, violets, pansies, geraniums, mint leaves, etc). Just beat lightly the white of a small egg. Use a small brush to paint the petals of the flowers back and front. Shake caster sugar all over and, when well covered, set aside to dry until crisp on non-stick paper or foil. They will store for weeks in an airtight tin.

CHERVIL

Just think of a finer, more feathery version of parsley, and you have *Anthriscus cerefolium*. Sow the seed in partial shade in succession from May to summer. Thin to 20 cm/8 inches apart. Use in a *fines herbes* mixture (with parsley and chives) in salads, sauces and creamy soups.

CHIVES

I use vast handfuls of *Allium schoenoprasum*. It belongs to the onion family and likes sun or partial shade. This is also a good "doer" in a pot if fed. Plant bulbs or divide the bulb clusters in the spring. Cut off the pretty thrift-like mauve flowers as soon as you see them. The more you cut chives the more vigorous they become. Use the bright green leaves for a delicate onion flavour in salads, sauces, dressings, stuffings and soups. Cut it in a bunch with scissors and snip off the browned ends made by the previous chop.

CORIANDER

This herb is used far more in Indian cookery than ours. It grows to 45 cm/18 inches tall, looks like flat-leaved parsley, and has a very distinctive smell. You can use the fresh, spicy leaves in curries and the dried seeds as a spice in meat dishes including curries, as well as breads and biscuits. The Latin name is *Coriandrum sativum*.

DILL
This herb is a bit like fennel, with feathery leaves and pale lemon flowers. Sow the seed of this annual plant in a sunny sheltered spot in the spring. It can grow to 60 cm/2 feet. The leaves are good in sauces, salads and vegetables. The feathery fronds are often used to decorate pieces of fish, chicken or pâté. Its Latin name is *Anethum graveolens*.

The seeds are used too, as a spice, and they're good with fish too.

FENNEL
This herb is grown for its feathery leaves. (The fat white bulbous root variety is properly called Florence fennel.) Sow the seeds in April and thin to 30 cm/12 inches apart. It can grow to 2 metres/6 feet high. The leaves go well with all kinds of fish and cheese dishes. The leaves are also used a great deal in decoration. The dried stalks are wonderfully aromatic strewn over the hot charcoal in a barbecue. I mainly use *Foeniculum vulgare* in a sauce for fresh salmon.

The seeds are used too, as a spice, mainly in Indian cookery, and are chewed after meals to sweeten the breath.

LOVAGE
Levisticum officinale is also tall, 2 metres/6 feet high. Sow seeds in boxes in autumn and plant out about 60 cm/2 feet apart in the spring in a sunny position. The large cut leaves are used in soups, stews and sauces; I never use more than two leaves at a time. It seeds very vigorously all over the garden, and I keep trying to banish it, but it springs up all over the place.

MARJORAM
One of the most used plants in my herb garden, *Origanum spp* is a most versatile plant and very easy to grow. There are three varieties including the wild one, oregano. All of them give an authentic Mediterranean flavour to salads, dressings, rice, pastas and stuffings.

MINT
I grow several of the sweet-smelling *Mentha spp* – apple mint, Bowles mint, eau de cologne mint, peppermint and spearmint. Most of these I use in flower arrangements and, in spite of the opinion of others in favour of Bowles mint, I still prefer my old green, pointed mint leaves for mint sauce. I know it is riddled with disease every year, but there is something about the woolly leaves of both apple and Bowles mint which I do not like. We plant our mints in sunken pots to try and contain them. It is a constant battle. Mint in cheese dishes and pasta sauces is delightful. The leaves crystallize well and are delicious with ice cream and crushed into syllabubs.

PARSLEY
One of my daughters called parsley my "green rain" because I use it in so many things. The botanical name *Petroselinum crispum* hides a large number of varieties from tight curly parsley to the flat-leaved variety. The plant is best bought as a container-grown plant. It is a biennial and the seed is tricky to germinate. Best way of all is to cover the row of sown seeds with a long narrow plastic trough. This brings the temperature up very well. I use parsley in all savoury dishes, and as a beautiful garnish, either chopped or in sprigs.

ROSEMARY
An evergreen shrub which grows to 1.2 metres/4 feet high, and has tiny pale blue flowers. Plant a container-grown plant or a cutting in a sunny spot. Chop the spiky, needle-like leaves finely for casseroles, stuffings, soups, stews, sauces, milk puddings, cakes and biscuits. We always use small sprigs to press into

MINT

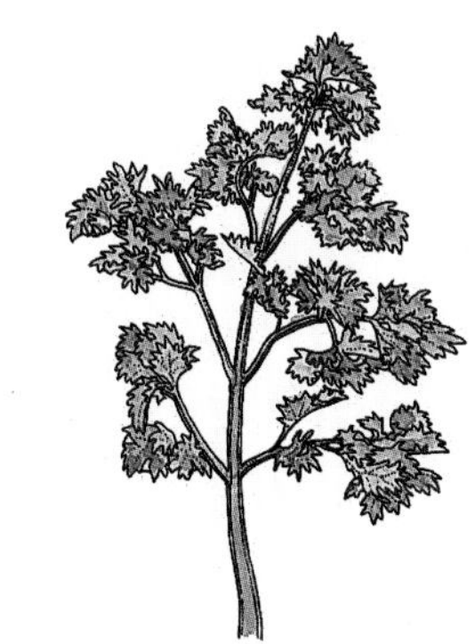

PARSLEY

ROSEMARY

SAGE

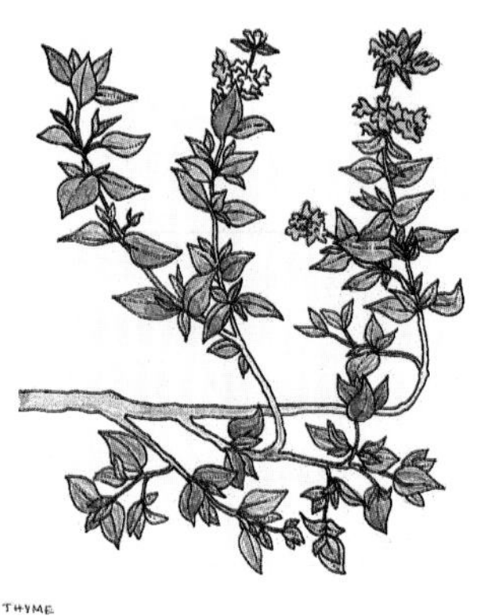

THYME

TARRAGON

slits in lamb to be roasted along with slivers of garlic. The Latin name is *Rosmarinus officinalis*.

SAGE
Salvia officinalis is another evergreen shrub which can reach 60 cm/2 feet. Take cuttings in late summer or sow seeds in pots in spring and set out at 45 cm/18 inches apart. When the bush gets woody – about every 4–5 years – it is time to renew it. Sage and onion stuffing is very English – chop the grey small leaves finely. I'm very fond of whole sage leaves to flavour lightly fried calves liver.

TARRAGON
Artemisia dracunculus is the Latin name of a pungent delicious herb which I first tasted in the Dordogne in France. Grown from cuttings this perennial is used to flavour fish, poultry and egg dishes. It is often used to flavour oil or wine vinegar. Choose French tarragon – the Russian one is very poor in comparison. One of my favourite recipes is breast of chicken poached in a chicken stock flavoured with onion and tarragon. The cream sauce is simple too: double cream heated and flavoured with fresh chopped tarragon, with a little of the poaching liquid stirred in as well.

THYME
We have to grow all our thyme in a wall near to the herb garden – our heavy clay soil is no good at all for *Thymus spp.* It is a low-growing perennial which should be cut back often to prevent it becoming too woody. I use thyme with other herbs in bouquet garnis for sauces, stews, casseroles and stuffings. Lemon thyme goes well with chicken.

A FEW SPICES AS WELL

Exotic spices are enjoying a new lease of life with the current interest in ethnic cuisines, but several have been traditionally used in our cookery for years.

CLOVES
These are the flower buds of a tropical tree (*Eugenia caryophyllus*), and have a very powerful scent and flavour. One or two imbedded in an onion will flavour a stew or bread sauce; they're used as well in rice for curries, in apple pies, and on hams.

CINNAMON
The sticks are the young bark of a tropical tree (*Cinnamomum verum*). They're good for flavouring milks for puddings, rice for curries, hot punches and some pickles. Cinnamon toast is delicious for tea – mix 1 teaspoon ground cinnamon with 2 teaspoons caster sugar, and 40 g/ $1\frac{1}{2}$ oz butter and spread on toast.

GINGER
Zingiber officinale is available in several forms – fresh, dried, powdered, and stem preserved in syrup. Fresh is best for Chinese and Indian cooking; the dried is used in chutneys; powdered in sweet dishes, cakes and biscuits.

MACE AND NUTMEG
Both come from the same tropical tree (*Myristica fragrans*). Inside the large fruit is a seed which is the nutmeg; this is encased in a net-like aril, which is the mace. Mace, more usually available in powder form, is good in cakes, sausages, potted meats and pâtés. Nutmeg, which is best ground freshly, has similar uses, but is wonderful too grated over mashed potatoes or milk puddings.

SAFFRON
Once grown in England, true saffron is expensive and it is used to colour and flavour a great many Spanish dishes, particularly the rice for paella, and in fish soups, cakes and puddings.

VANILLA
The pods come from a South American vine (*Vanilla planifolia*). Wonderful for flavouring milks for puddings and ice cream. After heating, the pods can be washed and stored (preferably in a jar of sugar to create vanilla sugar) for future use.

SAFETY IN THE KITCHEN

More accidents occur in the home than anywhere else, particularly to children and old people, and the kitchen is the most dangerous room of all. If you are lucky enough to be able to plan your kitchen from scratch in consultation with your kitchen designer, architect or builder, you should take account of all the safety factors. But it is important to be fully aware of the most notorious hazards so that you can avoid all unnecessary accidents.

COOKER

This should be sited carefully, with cooker, work top and sink in an unbroken line. This cuts down on the hazards involved in carrying pans of boiling liquid from place to place. There should, ideally, be heatproof work tops on either side of the cooker – safer and much more convenient. There should be no danger of anything near the cooker becoming too hot or catching fire: this means no cupboards above the cooker, no hanging of cloths above the cooker, no trailing flexes, and nothing nearby, a blown window curtain for instance, which could accidentally ignite.

If there are children in the house, a cooker guard is a good investment. This is a rail that fits in around the cooker top and prevents hot pans from being pulled down by a curious child (which can and does result in horrendous burns). In the absence of this, try to get into the habit of turning pan handles towards the sides or back of the cooker. Cooker controls are irresistable to a toddler, and could mean electricity burning pans or dishes, or gas escaping (automatic gas ignition is safer in this respect). Failing stern warnings and constant vigilance when a child is in the kitchen, the best solution might be to have a cooker top – one of those that is inset into a work surface – which has controls on the top, out of reach of most small children. Another cooker hazard is the oven itself: most conform to manufacturers' and governmental safety standards, but the outside of the oven doors of some have been known to reach temperatures which burn. Check carefully and thoroughly before you buy.

FIRE

This is one of the greatest hazards in any kitchen, so be prepared by having a small CO_2 fire extinguisher handy and a fire blanket. Fat fires, for instance, must never be extinguished with water (they blaze up even more); instead the supply of oxygen to the flames must be cut off by smothering them with a lid, a tray, a damp cloth, the fire extinguisher or a special fire blanket. Both the latter can be bought for wall mounting.

Explosions, major or minor, often cause fire. Aerosol cans may explode if they become hot, so store them well away from any source of heat. Even boxes of matches left too near heat can ignite and lead to a worse fire. A gas build-up from a leak or from accidental turning-on, can explode and ignite if a flame is struck or something gives off a spark. If you suspect there is gas escaping, check the controls first, then the pilot light. Open outside doors or windows to allow excess to escape, and if you cannot see where the problem lies, turn the gas off at the mains and get expert advice immediately. (Surprisingly few householders know where the gas main enters their homes, or how to turn the gas off: find out now!)

APPLIANCES

Electricity is another potential source of danger in the kitchen if it is not handled properly or respected. I am afraid that we are all guilty of acquiring ever more kitchen appliances to help us cook, chop, toast, boil, etc, and we never seem to consider how the electricity supply will cope. This must be geared to the number of appliances, which means installing additional sockets (expensive, yes, but very much safer). Many of us rely on adaptors to take up to four plugs, but this is not recommended by electricians, and indeed can be highly dangerous. Overloading of circuits can cause considerable damage.

Fixed electrical machines, specifically the cooker, must be wired in separately by professionals, preferably controlled by those wall mounted units with switches and light indicators. Other sockets for the more mobile appliances should be away from the cooker – and from water – and sited at the back of the work surface in a place where trailing flexes will not get burned or wet, or be in the way. In fact, it's best to have *short* flexes on most appliances.

Many appliances themselves can be dangerous if not handled properly. Avoid the razor-sharp blades of a processor or blender whether in the machine or in the wash; site toasters where nothing can be heated or ignited by them. Don't have a kettle steaming away beside a socket outlet, and always switch off and unplug a kettle before pouring (unless it is one which automatically switches off when it reaches boiling point). Kettles can become very hot, and some can jet out small amounts of boiling water if filled too full, so never have them near the edge of the work surface where a child could be within range. Washing machines and dishwashers should be "lockable" – i.e. with doors that can't be pulled open by a child when in operation.

Always check the flexes of appliances to ensure they are not wearing thin. And always follow manufacturers' recommendations when fitting plugs on appliances, using the correct fuses, etc.

FLOOR

The kitchen, which is where many of us spend a great deal of our time, must have a good, sensible floor covering which is non-slip even when wet. It must be in good condition, must be level, and any damaged places should be quickly repaired to prevent tripping. Get into the habit of wiping up any spills immediately – whether of water, oil or grease which can lead so easily to skidding and sliding. Any floor covering should be kept immaculately clean – hygiene is vital in the kitchen – so it is worthwhile planning flooring carefully, allowing as few places and spaces as possible in which dirt and germs can lurk.

The kitchen floor is often an area on which children play – in order to be within sight and reach of mother – but unless space is really limited, this should be discouraged. Children (and pets) can get under foot, as can toys, and this could be lethal when pans of boiling liquid are involved. If there are any electrical sockets near floor level in the kitchen, and there are children around, they should be secured from inquisitive fingers by dummy plugs that children cannot pull out.

LIGHTING

When dealing with heat, you must be able to see very clearly what you are doing, so you must never skimp on kitchen lighting. All work surfaces and storage areas should be brightly lit.

STORAGE

This should be planned carefully in the kitchen. Insufficient cupboards can mean dangerous over-crowding of work surfaces, and unplanned areas at ground level can lead to more nooks and crannies where dirt and germs can accumulate. Store the items you use most – appliances, pots, pans, china, etc – at a level which is easy to reach. Reaching, stretching, bending and twisting – which can be daily occurrences in a less than well planned kitchen – can cause back problems. Always store heavier items at ground or waist level: if stored too high up accidents can occur when climbing up to get them – slipping off a stool or stepladder, or the item could actually fall down on to you or a child. Open cupboard doors, whether at ground or head level, can trip up or bang a head.

Food storage should be dark, cool, well ventilated and out of reach of pets, rodents and flies – perhaps even of marauding children too. The most used items, again, should be easily accessible to you.

Cleaning materials – which can include such poisonous substances as bleach, caustic soda and acid oven cleaners – should be stored in a cupboard that can be locked if there are children in the house. Special security latches can be bought to fit on drawers as well as cupboards, vital if you store sharp kitchen utensils in a drawer which could be raided by small vulnerable fingers. And do try to store your sharpest knives in a block or on a magnetic wall-mounted rack – you too could cut yourself disastrously while rummaging around in the drawer for something.

HYGIENE

Nowhere is this more vital than in the kitchen because of the fear of food contamination and poisoning. Foods must be kept fresh (rotting foods attract bacteria and flies); hands, surface and utensils must be kept immaculately clean. Pets can contribute to dirt and germs; cat litter trays and animal feeding dishes must be washed often, as should the floor, especially is there is a crawling baby or toddler in the house. The most recent contribution to kitchen hygiene is probably the automatic dishwasher which washes at high temperatures and hot-air dries: however, many utensils, cutlery and indeed older pieces of china cannot withstand that intense heat. In that case hot water washing (at 150°F/65°C) and drip drying (more hygienic than using a drying cloth) is the best alternative.

Waste disposal should be carefully planned, and bins should never be open to flies, pets or children. They should be kept immaculately clean and emptied very regularly. Take particular care with plastic bags, whether small or large waste-bin ones, or indeed those which encase virtually everything we buy: they can suffocate small children and pets.

OTHER CONSIDERATIONS

In a busy kitchen, where you or children are rushing to and fro, sharp corners on furniture can catch or knock, so choose units or tables with rounded edges. (Special protective corners made of plastic can be bought to slot on.) Try not to have trailing cloths on a table, as a child – or indeed a playful cat – could pull this off, plus accompanying china, cutlery or hot food.

As the kitchen is so full of potential danger, perhaps this is the best place to keep the first-aid box – but have it out of reach of children.

INDEX

ACKNOWLEDGEMENTS

Many of the recipes in the book are my own, a lot of which have not been published before. But many are reprinted from our previous books – *The Farmhouse Kitchen Books 1, 2 and 3* (published by Yorkshire Television, and in 1984 additionally as a single volume by Collins, *The Complete Farmhouse Kitchen Book*), *Cooking for One and Two* (Yorkshire Television, 1988) and *Farmhouse Kitchen Baking Book* (Collins, 1988) – and are the work of our talented and generous contributors and viewers. I list their names below, and thank them once again. I should also like to mention a unique book which has proved invaluable in our seasonal research – *The Independent Cook* by Jeremy Round (Barrie & Jenkins, 1988). Finally, I want to say how very much I have enjoyed working with Susan Fleming, the editor of this book. Her ability to crystallize my waffling comments into just a sentence was inspiring. I thank her for all her many skills and unstinting help.

Contributors: Judith Adshead, Mottram St Andrew, Cheshire; Mrs M. Alderson, Leeds, Yorks; Mrs Doreen Allars, Welbourn, Nr Lincoln; Mrs Stella Boldy, Sykehouse, N. Humberside; Mrs Thelma E. Boyne, Aberdeen; Alan Briggs, Batley, W. Yorks; Sarah Brown, London; Mrs A. Bucknell, Bisley, Glos; Mrs Cynthia Cooksey, Cofton Hackett, Worcs; Yvonne Coull, Sea Fish Industry Authority, Edinburgh; Miss G.S. Davies, Flintshire; Simon Dunn, Bickley, Kent; John Firrell, Piddletrenthide, Dorset; Mrs Kay Fussey, Denby Dale, Yorks; Mrs A. Greenwood, Boroughbridge, Yorks; Joan Guy, Tavistock, Devon; Mrs Eunice Heath, Thirsk, N. Yorks; Angela Henderson, Fleet, Hants; Margaret Heywood, Todmorden, Yorks; Janet Horsley, Leeds, Yorks; Mrs Hunter, Hessle, N. Humberside; Isabel James, McCarrison Society; Mrs Joyce Langley, Shoreham-by-Sea, W. Sussex; Dr Doug McEachern, Stirling, S. Australia; Elizabeth Mickery, Pudsey, W. Yorks; Grainne Mulligan, Madrid; Sybil Norcott, Irlam, Nr Manchester; Mrs Olive Odell, Hartlebury, Worcs; Mrs Powell, Enfield, Mddx; Mrs Joyce Powell, Llanddewi Rhydderch WI, Gwent; Mrs Phyllis E. Roche, Normanton, W. Yorks; Jennie Siew Lee Cook, York; Anne Wallace, Stewarton, Ayrshire; Mrs Lynda M. White, Wroot, Nr Doncaster; Priya Wickramasinghe, Cardiff; Mrs Emily Williams, Moggerhanger, Beds; Debbie Woolhead, Boston Spa, W. Yorks.

PICTURE CREDITS

Dover Pictorial Archive Series for all b & w prints except those listed for Star Services and Mitchell Beazley below. E.T. Archive, 55; Fine Art Photographic Library Ltd., 1, 2–3, 8–9, 17–19, 21, 28, 35, 37, 38, 43, 48, 52, 58, 64, 68, 78, 88–9, 98–9, 108, 118–119, 124B; Mitchell Beazley, 41, 59, 128–134, 136, 144–6; Star Services, 33, 91, 113, 123, 125B Yorkshire Television Enterprises Ltd., 4, 6, 100, 106, 120, 140.

Storage check list

Storage life for fresh meat and fish

Fresh meat	Freezer 0°F/ − 18°C	Refrigerator 35–45°F/2–7°C
Joints: beef	*8 months*	*3–5 days*
lamb	*6 months*	*3–5 days*
pork	*6 months*	*3–5 days*
veal	*8 months*	*3–5 days*
Minced meat	*3 months*	*1–2 days*
Kidney, liver, etc	*2 months*	*1–2 days*
Bacon	*2–3 months*	*7–10 days*
Sausages	*2 months*	*1–2 days*
Poultry	*6–8 months*	*2–3 days*
Game	*6–8 months*	*2–3 days*
Chops	*3 months*	*3–5 days*
Steaks	*3 months*	*3–5 days*
Stewing meat	*3 months*	*3–5 days*
Fresh fish		
Oily fish: mackerel, salmon, herring	*2–3 months*	*1–2 days*
White fish: plaice, sole, cod	*6 months*	*1–2 days*
Shellfish	*1 month*	*1 day*

Fish off the fishmonger's slab may be several days old; only fish caught that day should be frozen.

Recommended thawing times for frozen meat and fish

	In the refrigerator	At room temperature
Joints under 1.3 kg/3 lb	*3–4 hours per 450 g/lb*	*1–2 hours per 450 g/lb*
Joints 3 lb and over	*4–7 hours per 450 g/lb*	*2–3 hours per 450 g/lb*
Thick cuts of meat	*5–6 hours*	*2–4 hours*
Poultry	*2 hours per 450 g/lb*	*1 hour per 450 g/lb*
Fish	*8 hours per 450 g/lb*	*4 hours per 450 g/lb*

Fish must be covered and slowly thawed in the refrigerator.
Thawing in the refrigerator is recommended when time allows.
In emergencies only, thaw by immersing in cool (not warm) water in a watertight wrapping.
Cook thawed foods as soon as possible.

Cooking from the frozen state

May be cooked frozen	Must be thawed first
All beef joints on the bone	All boneless joints
All lamb joints on the bone	All boiling joints
Pork joints weighing 1.8 kg/4 lb or more	Pork joints on the bone under 1.8 kg/4 lb
Chops, steaks, stewing meat	Poultry
Shrimps and prawns	Most fish

Boiling meat from frozen can result in weight and flavour loss. Unthawed fish must be cooked at a lower temperature and for far longer than normal, which is likely to kill delicate flavours.

Roasting times for frozen meat on the bone

At gas 4, 350°F, 180°C

Joints under 1.8 kg/4 lb	
beef	30 minutes per 450 g/lb plus 30 minutes
lamb	35 minutes per 450 g/lb plus 35 minutes
Joints 1.8–2.7 kg/4–6 lb	
beef	35 minutes per 450 g/lb plus 35 minutes
lamb	40 minutes per 450 g/lb plus 40 minutes
pork	45 minutes per 450 g/lb plus 45 minutes
Joints over 2.7 kg/6 lb	As above or longer, needs testing

Bone is an excellent heat conductor, but roasting frozen meat takes longer. If using a meat thermometer to check that it is properly cooked do not let the point touch the bone.

Approximate cooking times for meat

Meats and Cuts	Roasting	Pot Roasting/Braising	Boiling
	minutes per 450 g/1 lb and temperatures		
BEEF Tender cuts rare:	15 + 15 over Hot	30–40 stove top	
medium:	20 Hot	40 in a warm oven	
Coarser cuts	20 Fairly hot		1 hour at a steady simmer
Boned/rolled	30 Fairly hot		
VEAL Thin cuts and cuts on bone	25 + 20 over Fairly hot		
Thick and boned and rolled cuts	35 Warm	40–50 in a warm oven	
LAMB Tender cuts	20 Fairly hot (+15 over for large cuts)	Total of 2½ hours in a warm oven	30
Smaller cuts for casseroles and stews		Total of 1½ hours in a warm oven	
PORK Small, thin cuts	30 + 20 over Moderate	60 stove top	
Thick cuts	35 + 25 over Moderate	60 in a warm oven	
Pickled cuts			Your butcher will advise